LUKA
MODRIĆ

LUKA MODRIĆ

MY AUTOBIOGRAPHY

with Robert Matteoni

Translation by Tomislav Kuzmanović

BLOOMSBURY SPORT

LONDON · OXFORD · NEW YORK · NEW DELHI · SYDNEY

BLOOMSBURY SPORT
Bloomsbury Publishing Plc
50 Bedford Square, London, WC1B 3DP, UK

BLOOMSBURY, BLOOMSBURY SPORT and the Diana logo are trademarks
of Bloomsbury Publishing Plc

First published in Great Britain 2020

First published in 2019 in Croatia as *Moja igra, autobiografija Luke Modrića*
by Hermes naklada, Zagreb

Original editor: Diana Matulić
Photo editor: Petra Purgar
Translation: Tomislav Kuzmanović

ISBN: HB: 978-1-4729-7794-6; Signed edition: 978-1-4729-8238-4; PB: 978-1-4729-7793-9;
eBook: 978-1-4729-7795-3; ePDF: 978-1-4729-7797-7

2 4 6 8 10 9 7 5 3 1

Typeset in Adobe Garamond Pro by Deanta Global Publishing Services, Chennai, India
Printed and bound in Great Britain by CPI Group (UK) Ltd. Croydon, CR0 4YY

To find out more about our authors and books visit www.bloomsbury.com
and sign up for our newsletters

CONTENTS

FOREWORD
BY SIR ALEX FERGUSON CBE

As we speak today about Luka Modrić, we are speaking about a wonderfully talented player who, in my opinion, is on a level with the great midfielders of the last 20 years, such as Xavi, Iniesta and Scholes. His award as the Best Player of the FIFA World Cup in 2018 was deservedly given to him; he was by far the Player of the Tournament.

When he joined Spurs in 2008 it was a surprise to us at Manchester United, as he was under our radar – although one of our scouts had flagged him up a year before. However, we had Keane, Scholes and Carrick. Once I had watched him against us, I never assessed him as too weak for the English Premier League. You cannot dismiss ability and that was the obvious talent Luka had. He developed very quickly and I made him my target in 2011, but Spurs wouldn't sell to us as we had already taken Carrick and Berbatov from them previously.

I named him as my player of the year in 2011, which was not a difficult decision. He signed for Real Madrid and the rest is history, as he matured into one of Real's all-time greats. The European match against them at Old Trafford in March, 2013, was my last attempt at winning the Holy Grail, but we were robbed by a disgraceful decision by the referee who sent off Nani at the moment when we were in complete control and winning 1-0. As soon as Nani was sent off, Mourinho sent on Modrić and the game changed – it was Luka's performance that killed us.

In the analysis of his career, especially looking at his background as a young boy, he is an exemplar to young players that talent outmatches brawn. When Paul Scholes joined Manchester United at 13 years of age, he was no taller than 5'3" and some wondered whether he was too small, myself included. But in no time, all our opinions changed because of his performances on the football field. In reality, the best way to assess players is the evidence you see on the pitch.

Luka Modrić is the shining example to all young players, irrespective of height, stature and strength. My deepest regards to a man who defeated all arguments about physique because he could play!

FOREWORD
BY ZVONIMIR BOBAN

Here is a special book about a humble genius from a small village near Zaton Obrovački in Croatia. When I was thinking about what to write in this foreword, the book's co-author and my long-time friend, Robert Matteoni, asked me to try to offer a different outlook on Luka – some deeper tactical reading.

I'm not sure if this is something I can deliver, but it doesn't matter, because the only thing that matters is that Luka Modrić happened and that he happened to all of us.

Luka and his football. So simple yet so special, so unique and different.

The ease and sophisticated geometry, the harmony, the dynamics, the calmness – this is too much to capture in one short foreword, regardless of how precise or well-written it may be.

And all the richness of Modrić's footballing intuitions, and his supposedly simple solutions, came out of the only source they could come from – the most revered number in football, No. 10. It's a paradox that at the top level of football, Luka has never really played as a traditional No. 10, but he was born a 10, he was made a 10 – and he has always been marked as a 10. No one can say that Luka is a No. 4, or a complete playmaker, or an 8. No one can say that he stopped being a 10. What can be said is that he is all of these at once. And all of this is found in one man, who has always played with an almost mystical dependability, regardless of whose shirt he has put on – his club's or his national team's. And who was everything – all he had to be.

Creating where it's the toughest, in those narrow ravines and rapids of the centre field, where everything happens and is felt differently – that's where the game is inspired and directed. There, around the centre circle, with a constant gauging and ability to recognise what only a few can see, Modrić has held on to his mantra and asked himself the most important question in football – a question to which he has always had an answer: *In these 90-odd minutes, in every second, whether the ball is in my possession or not, how can I be the best I can be for my team?*

It seems complicated, yet for him it's so simple. But on countless occasions he has had to find the answer to this question from within himself.

With self-sacrifice, with an ambition that long ago gave up on the 'I' to focus instead, a hundred times over, on 'we' – the only way that leads to greatness – Modrić has dealt with all of this with ease. Surprising ease. And all those adjustments, the incessant background chatter about taking the No. 10 from him, as well as from football, he quickly turned to his advantage, into his growth. When he needed to cancel out his self to build an even better Modrić, he did it quickly and convincingly, without ever doubting his path as a football player. That is his biggest victory. That is what makes him what he is today.

Of course, this requires exceptional character, great self-belief and fanatical dedication. I don't doubt that he inherited these values from his poverty-stricken childhood, spent in a harsh and barren environment, and the great support provided by his humble working-class family.

And so, from one day to another, from one training session to another, from one match to another, he built the stage for the greatest victories in football – collective as well as individual. All of them came his way – and all of them were deserved.

In the past couple of years, as we have watched him in his full maturity, Luka stands out as great No. 10. He shines – a complete football player.

When comparing him to the great midfielders of his era, many cannot single out his one elite characteristic. Indeed, Modrić isn't a playmaker like Xavi, he doesn't have the soft touch of Iniesta, or the great architecture of Pirlo – but then again, he has it all, in his way. In the ideal rhythm of delivering a pass, in his zigzagging miniatures, in the simple solutions that aren't just that because they determine what is going to happen next on the pitch, he built an entirely new figure – his own.

What none of those three other greats had, at least not as much as him, was Luka's ability to make all of his teammates better, at both ends of the pitch!

An inspiration to many, he has always remained true to himself. He insists on his vision of football – on putting the team before himself – and in that way, he has built his unique leadership as a player.

No, I didn't say he was a natural-born leader – I have never felt that in him – but through the way he plays and through the example he sets, he leads. Both his teammates and his squad and, most importantly, the fans of all the teams for whom he has played – be it at Dinamo Zagreb, Real Madrid or the Croatia national team, he has always managed to be Modrić. Two moments serve as powerful portrayals of this approach.

His, and our, 2018 World Cup offer powerful testament, giving us a bold image of a captain. A captain who is exhausted but who, in the last seconds of extra time, sprints through the thick Russian defence, all the way from the centre circle to the penalty box, to send a clear message – the message of giving yourself completely. The message that the right approach leads to victory. The message of value.

The second scene comes from the UEFA Champions League Final against Juventus when, after a dominant second half – with the last of his will and skill, he runs to the byline and makes a cross to Ronaldo and a decisive goal . . .

And this message is the true mark of the person Luka Modrić is.

When we speak of Luka as a person, fate caught him between Scylla and Charybdis and forced him to pay his dues by filling him with anxiety and forcing him to grow up quickly. His dues just had to be paid and he paid them, but this only made him stronger and better – as both a man and a player.

At the end of this letter to Luka, I return to my first words, because I believe they describe him best: a humble genius. It's a description that will resonate with all of us who love this, the most beautiful game in the world.

To have served as a role model for such a player is my great honour. For years my son, before going to sleep, put on Luka's shirt – a lasting memory that reflects my family's respect for this wonderful player and dear person. Respect for the great No. 10.

CHAPTER ONE

I stood on the podium, holding the trophy for the Best Player of the 2018 FIFA World Cup in my hands. When I was a child, and didn't yet know how hard it was to climb to the top, I dreamed that one day I would become the best in the world. And when it happened, and the Golden Ball trophy was in my hands, the only thing I felt was sorrow. It could've been the happiest moment of my career, but it wasn't. We had just lost the World Cup Final and, with the adrenaline still rushing through my veins, there was only one thought running through my mind: 'It's over'.

On the pitch, waiting for the official announcer to call me up to the stage, I tried not to look at the other trophy. But I couldn't stop myself. My eyes were simply drawn to it, to the trophy awarded to the World Champions. We really had thought we would be taking it back home to Croatia. At that moment, in rain-drenched Moscow, I felt such great disappointment. We came so close, and then, after all the struggle and sacrifice, it slipped through our hands. In that fraction of a second, I thought what it would've been like if they had called my name and handed me that trophy too – what it would've been like to lift it into the air with my teammates and cry out together with our fans: 'Let's go, Croatia!' What happiness . . .

The sound of my name from the PA system and the loud applause snapped me out of this dream. Everything that followed now seems purely automatic. It was like that from the moment when, back on the pitch, shortly after the referee had blown the last whistle and the French rejoiced, a FIFA official approached me. She led me behind the podium that had already been set up and told me I had been voted the Best

Player. She was kind, she congratulated me and gave me short instructions about the ceremony. I don't remember any of it because I just dragged myself around the pitch with my teammates, looking for a place where I could hide and cry. I looked over at the stands and all those people in chequered shirts, with their hats, scarves, flags and messages of support, who had come from all ends of the world and who had gone through who knows what to get to Russia, get a ticket and root for us. I thought about all those hundreds of thousands of people in Croatia who found themselves in city squares, in bars, apartments, wherever, who turned on their TV sets, feared and hoped for victory. At that moment I was overcome by a feeling that we had disappointed them – but this didn't last long. It was our fans at the stadium who did their best to ease our sadness. They showed us with their chants, with their songs and their gestures how proud they were. That only made it more difficult. I was devastated that we had failed to take the one final step to give them – and ourselves, of course – the incredible experience of celebrating winning the title of World Champions. (At that point, I couldn't have even dreamed what I would feel a day later, in Croatia, when more than a half a million came to the streets of Zagreb to greet us as if we were indeed World Champions.)

As I walked around the pitch, I tried to soak in as much of the atmosphere as I could, because I knew these were moments I would remember forever. At the same time, though, and haunted by all kinds of nightmarish thoughts, I felt a lump in my throat. Mario Mandžukić snapped me out of it. So big and tough, he's a real rascal who always holds a grudge and never forgets, but now he approached me and in a voice cracking with tears and pride, told me: 'Come on, I know it's tough, it's tough on me too, but let's not cry now. We gave it all we had, we did something big, we should be proud.'

Mario has been my brother-in-arms for the long 12 years in which we saw victories and defeats. He is proud and strong-willed, and he always holds his ground. I think we are similar that way, except that he is better at hiding his emotions. Vedran Ćorluka, one of my dearest companions and friends, soon came over and made more or less the same point. We cheered each other on because we all felt the same. They helped me not to break down. Instead, I shared the misery with my friends, my teammates, with the fans, and I managed to calm down just enough to follow the protocol.

When, accompanied by the loud cheers from my teammates, as well as strong applause from the French players, I finally climbed up to the podium, where Gianni Infantino, Vladimir Putin, Emmanuel Macron, Kolinda Grabar-Kitarović and other officials taking part in the ceremony had already been waiting, I focused as much as I could. It crossed my mind that the whole world was watching and that I shouldn't embarrass myself, my teammates, my country. This time, passing right by the World Cup trophy, I didn't even glance at it. It must've been my way of facing the truth that our beautiful story had come to an end, and of accepting the fact that moments of perfection are few and far between.

If you asked me now to recall everything that the presidents of FIFA, Russia, France and Croatia told me at that moment, believe me, I wouldn't know. I remember only fractions of those moments. I know they all showed compassion – as if they wanted to show that they sympathised with those who had to endure defeat in the World Cup Final. Infantino told me he was happy for me and sorry Croatia got defeated. Putin handed me the Best Player trophy, congratulated me in English and said bravo. Macron said we had played a fantastic tournament, or something along those lines. Our President, Kolinda Grabar-Kitarović, shared our grief at being defeated in the final, but also our pride that we had managed to reach the very top.

With great relief, I reached the place on the podium where I could be alone. At the moment that I was experiencing the highest personal honour of my career, I felt sad. The trophy in my hands, facing the photographers, I did what was expected, but I felt beaten. And then the cheers of support from my teammates echoed in the background, followed by the loud applause of the whole stadium. It was the first time that the reality of winning the award struck me, and I felt goosebumps. I waved at the crowd, and that's when the process of healing began. That's also when I slowly began to realise Croatia had achieved something incredible. I felt immense pride and I scanned the section of the stands where I assumed my wife, children, parents, sisters, friends were.

Kylian Mbappé, who had been voted the World Cup's Best Young Player, soon joined me on the podium. A tremendous striker, he is already capable, at now just 21, of changing the odds in a match of the highest level. Once he gains some experience, some routine, the sky will be his limit. 'Congratulations, I'm so glad for you!' he told me before I managed to commend him on winning the title and leaving a mark on the World Cup at such a young age. Mbappé seemed then like a humble young man who, despite all the glamour and pressure, stands firmly on the ground. If he keeps it up, this player, so young but already so dominant, will do wonders.

And yes, before I left the podium, by this moment a bit more aware of being voted the Best Player of the World Cup, the memory of my Grandpa Luka flashed through my mind. I was only six when the Chetniks killed him on his doorstep. He was a part of my life for just a short while, but that was long enough to instil in me a deep understanding of family love, dedication and loyalty.

CHAPTER TWO

Kvartirić, Croatia. A small stone house by the side of the road, the last one before the rocky slopes of the Velebit mountains. Six and a half kilometres from my parents' home in Zaton Obrovački. This house was the centre of my little world until 1991, when we had to run away. This is where my father's parents lived: Grandpa Luka and Grandma Jela. My grandfather was a road mender, who maintained the old state road that connected Dalmatia and Lika, the coast and the mountains of Croatia. My grandmother was a housekeeper, a hardworking and modest woman. The house they lived in was owned by the road maintenance company, but back then I knew it only as my grandparents' home. We called it the 'upper house'.

I never met my other grandfather, Petar, my mother's father. He died before I was born. His wife, Grandma Manda, still lives in Obrovac.

My parents worked at Trio Clothes Factory in Obrovac, four kilometres from our house. That's where they met. My mother Radojka worked as a seamstress and my father Stipe as a mechanic, maintaining the factory machines. When my mother returned to work after taking a year's maternity leave, they decided to enrol me in a nursery school in Obrovac. That didn't last long. Once, after arriving at work, my mother heard her co-worker, who had also left her child at the school, say that all the children were doing well except for this one kid who just wouldn't stop crying. She asked her what the child was wearing, and when her suspicions were confirmed, she decided, together with my dad, to take me out of the nursery school. They had thought about this before, not only because I was having a hard time adjusting, but also for health reasons. I was always sick, constantly having a runny nose, and once I caught bronchitis. As for my crying, it didn't subside, far from it: I cried and cried, so they realised they had no choice. Of course, back then I wasn't aware of what I was doing, but later I used to joke with my parents that I kept crying on purpose so that they would take pity on me and bring me home.

Instead of going to the nursery school, my parents now took me to my grandparents' house. It took us around 15 minutes to get there, and as I was happy to stay, my parents finally left for work without a knot in their stomachs. Especially when they realised how happy this turn of events made my grandpa Luka. I was his first grandson after two granddaughters, and my father always says he was in love with me. Grandpa Luka treated no one with so much softness and gentleness. Everyone was left speechless – particularly my dad, who knew how tough my grandpa was. When you are a child, you don't recognise it, but during those happy hours we spent together playing, talking to one another, I felt his kindness and his warmth; the patience with which he passed his knowledge on to me. I felt it in his kind-hearted reactions to my mischief, or when he took me to my bed and stayed there until I fell asleep. I couldn't wait to go back to him, to the stone house under the Velebit mountains, my eagerness expressing our special bond. Only today, after I've matured and gone through a lot, do I fully understand those emotions.

There are many memories from those first six years of my life, before the colossal and traumatic changes my family had to experience. To be fair, those memories come mostly as flashes, especially when some situation or place reminds me of that period – for example, when I go back to my homeland and visit my relatives who still live in the area; when I run into some people who were a part of my childhood; when I visit the family house my parents rebuilt. Finally, whenever I go back to the old stone house, up there in Kvartirić. Even though it was burned to the ground and destroyed so that only its walls still stand, I always feel this strong emotion that has marked me for life. An attachment to family and a feeling of safety in its surroundings. It hasn't changed to this day. No, the emotions are stronger than ever. I guess that's the way it is. As years go by, we turn to ourselves and those closest to us. We start a family, look forward to our children, raise them and watch them grow. I'm thankful to my parents because they instilled in me the feeling that family is the cornerstone of everything. They taught me that how I did in life depended on how close my family were. Today, I'm a father, and I live a completely different life from my parents. But when it comes to raising my children, I follow the sentiments they imparted to me from a very young age.

My father Stipe is a man of strong and clear convictions. At first glance, he may seem tough, but in reality, he's very emotional. A long time ago he told me that his reserve was shattered the first time he saw me. He greeted me with tears of joy in his eyes. This was the most special moment in his life. He was 24, and from then on, he could no longer hide his emotions and pretend to be a tough guy.

My mother Radojka, whom everyone calls Rada, is a strong woman. She is compassionate, but she also knows how to control her emotions. On countless occasions, she showed unconditional love for my sisters and me, but when things needed to be set straight, she was firm and persistent. From today's perspective, I think that the balance between firmness and sensitivity maintained by my parents is responsible for their harmonious life, and also for the harmony of our whole family.

I'm their first child. On 8 September, 1985, my mother went into labour at around 11 p.m. They were ready to rush her to the hospital. As is always the case, there was a certain amount of tension and a desperate anxiety for everything to turn out well. That's why my grandmother Jela, who had borne four children, came along to be by my mother's side. My dad quickly took them to Zadar Hospital. As the doctors weren't able to say how long the labour would last and when I would arrive into this world, they told him it would be best if he returned home and waited for the news. A man of discipline, he did as he was told. Most of my family was sure my mum would give birth to a girl.

She had five sisters and a brother, while my dad had two sisters and a twin brother – the odds were eight to three in favour of a girl. But, at ten minutes past two there I was! The labour went smoothly, without any complications. My father's brother Željko was the first to learn the happy news. We didn't have a phone in our house, and as he worked at a hotel, they called him so that he could pass on the news to my father. My dad quickly drove to the hospital in his white Zastava 850. The first time he took me into his arms – he always tells this story – he just couldn't stop the tears. Later on, when they celebrated, everything but the tears kept flowing and flowing. My father was beside himself with happiness.

Perhaps the best story about the day of my birth is the one about my grandma Jela. My father had found her at the hotel where she worked, and to celebrate the arrival of her first grandson she let her hair down a bit and drank a couple of shots. It was early in the day and after the initial euphoria, she was dizzy and then sick! They kept her at Zadar Hospital because she was dehydrated. We always laugh whenever we remember my grandmother's celebration – and her subsequent hangover!

My mother often describes the year of her maternity leave as one of the most beautiful periods of her life. Looking after me, the house, the rest of the family, she felt complete. As a newborn, I caused no problems. But at five months old, when she stopped breastfeeding me, things began to change. I became restless, I wouldn't eat and I refused to take the bottle. I would wake up in the middle of the night. A couple of years later, I was still a fussy eater. I didn't like meat, I avoided soup and salad, and I only wanted milk, cheese and bacon. These were plentiful at Grandpa Luka's house – produced by him. By his house, in Kvartirić, there was a pen, where he kept sheep and goats – up to 150 of them. There were also turkeys, hares, chickens – and a lot of work. Every member of the family helped, including me. At least, as much as I could at that young age. With my father or my grandfather, I took the sheep to pasture on the nearby slopes. But the real truth is that I was having a lot of fun. I was active and mischievous. One of my favourite things was to tug the goats' tails and laugh at their reactions. The animal world was very close to me. I had no fear whatsoever, not even when they warned us of wolves that used to roam this mountainous region. The only thing I was afraid of were snakes. When we took the cattle to pasture, my parents always warned me not to wander too far because there were dangerous snakes, horned vipers, hiding on the slopes and in the ravines. On one occasion, my father caught one of those snakes, put it in a large bottle and brought it to our house. From then on, I needed no warning – I stayed clear of snakes, even of that horned viper in the bottle, which we kept as a decoration. The fear of snakes has stuck with me to this day. Whenever I see one, I feel uneasy.

As a child, I took too much pleasure in games and discovering nature to be burdened by anything. While my grandfather or father kept an eye on the cattle, I played with my cousins Mirjana and Senka. On one occasion, Mirjana and I went with my grandpa Luka to cut some fresh twigs for the baby goats. He took us to the woods in his small red van, a Zastava 430, which interested me because it looked like an extended version of my father's white Zastava 850. My grandfather went to cut the twigs and Mirjana and I got into the van. We got lost in play; we pretended we were driving. I don't remember who, or how, but at one moment, one of us released the handbrake, having no idea where this could lead. The van was facing downwards, and it slowly moved down the slope. We were petrified – we didn't know how to stop the vehicle! Who knows what would've happened were it not for the stone fence right by the road?! No one was angry with us, neither our parents nor our grandfather. They were just relieved we were all right. The only consequences were a couple of dents and a few scratches, and a fear that stopped us from playing in a parked car ever again!

It wasn't the only time I frightened my parents. One afternoon, when I was about three years old, I was fussing about while my mother and grandmother picked beans. I guess I was bored, so I took one of the pods. I soon opened it and came up with the idea of sticking a bean in each nostril. I found it all very funny, but my mother noticed something was wrong. I could barely breathe. The beans had blocked my airways! She called my dad, and together they tried to take the beans out. They tried their best, but I just kept laughing. My dad finally managed to take one of the beans out with a pair of tweezers. The other one just wouldn't budge, though, so they had to take me to hospital. They were scared when at one moment I started to turn blue in the face and rolled my eyes. Luckily, it was nothing serious!

My mum always says I was a lively child but also polite and kind. For example, I was unusually quiet at children's birthday parties. Or when the adults played bocce – a ball game similar to boules – I loved to sit in her lap, watch them play and let her stroke my hair. Still, if something didn't suit me, I'd rip the flowers from her pots just to spite her. Also, I used to hide a lot, in both my grandparents' and my parents' houses. On one occasion, I hid and my mum got really scared because she couldn't find me. She called my name in a panic while I revelled in the fact that this time she couldn't find my hiding place. I snuck deep into a small closet and, to my mother's horror, just wouldn't answer her calls. When, all victorious, I finally came out, my loud laughter quickly faded. She was furious and, on that occasion, not very understanding.

I was particularly lively at my grandfather's house. My parents say I took my first steps there. I was just nine months old. I spent a lot of time at my grandpa's house, and somehow felt that it belonged to me more than my parents' larger and more comfortable house. On the upper floor, there was one bedroom, while on the ground floor there was the kitchen and another room. We also had a garage next to the house. My parents had to put a wooden railing on my small bed because I was a very restless sleeper and they were afraid I would topple down. There was no electricity at my grandfather's house; we had petroleum lamps. Later on, my father brought a generator. There was no water either, so we used the well. When we wanted to watch football on the TV, we had to go to the lower house.

Of course, like every child I had toys, I looked forward to presents, I played with other children my age, but I tell these stories because I want to paint a picture of what life was really like in the harsh surroundings of that small settlement on the slopes of Velebit. My everyday life was completely different from other children living in larger and more urban places. It was those early years, lived in harsh conditions but full of love and care, that shaped me as a person. But it's not like I just kept running around hills and ravines minding the grazing goats. I wasn't spending all of my time jumping from one rock to another, avoiding horned vipers. I wasn't only tugging the goats by their tails or chasing hares. Despite the fact I speak about the house without electricity and running water, up there by the road, I have to say that my parents' home was a comfortable place with all the usual, modern amenities. I had my room and a spacious yard full of greenery. My relatives lived in the neighbourhood, so there were plenty of kids to play and spend time with. We used to play hide and seek; we had our toy cars; we could run around the road freely because there wasn't much traffic.

But the thing that perhaps separated me from other children, as my parents later told me, was my great passion for one particular toy: the round one! They used to buy me toy cars; I received plenty of other gifts for birthdays, but none of them occupied my attention for long. Only the football! A photograph from my first birthday shows me sitting on it, and it's probably the only photo in which I'm not running around with it. When I was big enough so that my parents could let me play outside on my own, the ball became my best friend. I practised tricks with my relatives by the lower house on the dirt road. I used to bounce the ball off my grandfather's garage door. My father told me that by the time I was three or four they could see I had a special knack for it. An additional sign of my talent, he said, was that I was quick to learn new things – he only had to show me once how to receive and hit the ball and that was it. I kept repeating and improving the moves.

My dad also played football. He played for Rudar Obrovac, a team in the lower leagues. He played as a right-back, and was described by those who saw him play as a fast and energetic player who could run non-stop. Unfortunately, during one match, he tore his cruciate ligament, and that was the end of his career. His knee bothers him to this day. My grandpa Luka also played; they say he was good at futsal and had a special talent for basketball. Today, without false modesty, I can say I'm good at basketball, and I get by in, most other sports that include a ball. It must be something I inherited from him. Oh, Grandpa . . .

Grandpa Luka

Even before I was born, they knew what they would call me. My father Stipe was named after his grandfather so, following the old tradition, I got my name from my grandpa Luka. But the name, they tell me, was less important in securing my grandfather's affection than the fact that I was his first grandson.

He didn't just keep an eye on me until my parents came back from work; when I was little, he played with me all the time. As soon as I was big enough to walk around on my own, he took me with him wherever he went. Whether shovelling snow, stacking hay, taking the cattle to pasture, going to buy building materials, carrying out all kinds of repairs, as well as a whole line of other things that needed to be done around the house, my grandfather always treated me as his assistant. I loved it when we drove in his small van, or when we visited our relatives. I was very excited when he took me hunting for hares or partridges and he allowed me to hold his hunting rifle for a photo. He talked to me, teased me, taught me all kinds of things. With every day I spent with him, I learned so much. And I just couldn't wait for new adventures.

My grandpa was a tall and handsome man – his hair always tidy and slicked back. He radiated confidence and self-assurance. Today, we would call him a real tough guy. As a child, I didn't see him like that.

But the feeling of safety when close to him, the pleasure of spending time with him, that constant curiosity about what he was doing, these are the feelings that indicate how special he was to me. I simply adored him – even when he showed his authority as the head of the family and told me I had to cut my hair. My mum liked it when my hair was long, so I was used to it. But, when my grandpa thought it had grown too long, he wouldn't even ask my mother, let alone me; he simply took the scissors and cut it himself. Sometimes there were tears, not only mine but also my mother's, but to no avail. When my grandpa set his mind to something, that was it.

I was four when our happy family got a new member: my first sister, Jasmina, was born. It was yet another extraordinary experience. I don't remember whether I wanted a brother or a sister. I don't remember all the details of the family getting ready for the second child. I only know I was excited when she got home – when I first saw her, when I touched and kissed her. Jasmina became a part of my life, and as we were growing up, as we got to know each other, we formed a firm bond – brother and sister.

I didn't feel my life changed because now my sister was receiving her share of family attention and care. I was preoccupied with my own world and I took pleasure playing and enjoying the family gatherings. It didn't matter whether this was at our home, at the table, doing house chores, seeing relatives. What my parents later told me confirmed my impressions of those first six years of my life. As a child I had no fear – I was very active, cheerful and playful. But they always said I knew not to cross the line. When I was supposed to stop and listen to what they had to say, I stopped. When they told me to take it easy and calm down, I did. I'm convinced that the respect and warmth I felt in my family, as well as clearly set boundaries, instilled in me the traits that became, over time, an integral part of my character. My childhood under the Velebit mountains was at the same time beautiful and carefree, yet very educational. I quickly learned to be independent, to find my own way outside of my home. Back then there were no mobile phones, or computers, or tablets, or the internet. I spent my days in nature, taking pleasure in discovering its beauties, but I also learned to respect its laws. Everything was going so well, and it seemed it would only get better. Fate, however, had other plans . . .

I wasn't able to grasp what was going on, but I felt something began to change. As if everything around me that had been so good suddenly stopped working. My parents no longer went to Obrovac to work. When they talked to each other, they were quiet and serious. Even at my grandpa's house, I could feel it: the atmosphere wasn't the same anymore, even though he and my grandma, just like my parents, tried to keep things as they were. But that wouldn't last.

What I remember most about that horrible, dreadful day was my father's anxiety. My grandpa hadn't come home, so they went to look for him. I didn't know what had happened when they brought him to our house. The only thing I felt was grief. My father put his arm around my shoulder and took me to the coffin. He said: 'Son, go say goodbye to your grandpa.' I wasn't able to grasp that was the last time I would ever see him. My parents led me out of the room – they wanted to distance me from the tragedy.

The funeral took place in Obrovac. Grandpa Luka was a respected man, a real charmer. My father adored him, and I can only imagine how he must have felt. Years later, he told me about the horror of finding my grandpa's lifeless body covered in blood. It was on a meadow, just by the road, some five hundred yards from his house, where my grandpa had taken the goats to graze. It was December, 1991; the war had just flared up. My grandfather wasn't the kind of man who would be afraid of anything, but perhaps he wasn't fully aware of how serious the situation was. Grandma Jela later said she had seen some army vehicles on the road earlier that day. She hid in the house and locked the door. In the morning, my father, as if having a premonition, hurried to check on them. When he learned the goats had come back to the house without my grandfather, he knew something horrible had happened.

Grandpa Luka was mowed down by machine-gun fire. At close range. He was 66. My heart breaks every time I think of him dying, literally on his doorstep. What kind of people can coldly take the life of an innocent old man? This is the question I asked when I was almost 10. Our third-grade teacher told us to write a story about something that had left a mark on us, that made us sad or scared, and this was the first time it came out of me:

Even though I'm still little, I have experienced a lot of fear in my life. The fear of war and shelling is something I'm slowly putting behind me.

The event and the feeling of fear I will never forget took place four years ago when the Chetniks killed my grandfather. I loved him so much. Everyone cried, and I just couldn't understand that my dear grandpa was no more.

I used to ask if those who did this, and who made us run away from our home, can even be called people?

Since then, I have rarely spoken about my grandfather, especially in public. Our life was turned upside down by event after event; new traumas occupied our thoughts. My father went to war. Whenever we were together, he tried to make my sister and I feel safe, and he told us everything would be all right. Despite the tragedy and despite missing my father, which bothered me greatly, I never felt hatred in his words. He never even hinted at revenge. Looking back at it when I grew up a bit, when I fully understood what had happened during the war, I realised how dignified my father was in his pain. It's yet another sign of his kindness, but also of his responsibility towards his children. He has always told us that it doesn't matter where you come from, where you belong to, what you own or do not own; the only thing that matters is whether you are a good person or not. All those things were horrible and tragic. But, together with my mother, my father raised us to respect and love other people. To be a normal person who can tell the good from the bad. And I'm thankful to both of them because this greatly influenced the way I see the world. This was also shaped by the harsh conditions of exile, by the dread of shelling, and the fear for those closest to me; by the complicated years of facing the consequences of war and adjusting to the new reality – which overlapped with me reaching adolescence when wrong assumptions and a twisted outlook can take us in the wrong direction. My parents, though, knew how to keep me on the right path, and later, as my playing career developed, my determination to stay on this path only grew firmer.

I have no doubt that my father's approach to life has its roots in the spirit with which my grandfather raised him. Grandpa Luka had a great influence on me too, even though back then I was just a child and fate decreed that we would spend so few years together. I remember him often, and this is perhaps the first time I've spoken of him at some length. I miss him, and it would've made me immensely happy had we had a chance to share the joy of my success as a football player. I'm sure he would've been proud of it, just as he would've been proud of my family. He always said family should come first and he instilled those values into all of us, and that's why we're so close. Every time I go back home, I visit the places I visited with my grandpa. Memories come alive; I become emotional. I also bring my children, who live a completely different life, so they can get at least some sense of the surroundings and the time in which I grew up. My grandpa's house is now an abandoned ruin, overgrown with weeds. The sign saying '*Danger, Mines*' is an eerie reminder of the tragic events that took place there. The house belongs to the government, otherwise I would've done something with it. To honour my grandpa, my grandma, all of us, because it reminds us of an important part of our lives. At the site where on 18 December, 1991, they found my grandpa Luka, there is a small headstone. My father built it. Whenever I visit it, it reminds me of how full of life my grandpa was, and the things we did together come alive. And yes, I'm sure the first thing he would've done after congratulating me on my success would have been to take the scissors and say, 'Luka, I'm so proud of you, but you need a haircut. Come on, clean yourself up.'

Exile

After my grandpa's death, my father realised it was time to leave home right away and go somewhere safe. I was too little to understand what was going on, and my parents tried to make our life in exile as easy and as comfortable as possible. But I felt things were different, especially in comparison to the earlier carefree years in Zaton Obrovački. First, we went to Makarska, apparently to visit my uncle Željko, who worked there as a waiter. He was like my second father, not only because he and my father are identical twins, but also because he was always kind and protective of my sisters and I. He doesn't have children of his own, but he has always treated us as if we were his. We could rely on him for whatever we needed.

When you are a child, your parents are everything to you, and when they have a special relationship with other members of their family or friends, then those people become dear to you too. I felt the unconditional brotherly love between my father and my uncle. Even today, when I look at them, I see this incredible bond. They talk on the phone at least a dozen times a day; when one of them is away travelling or something, they call each other every 15 minutes or so – which is exactly how much older my uncle is than my father! My father is a bit quieter and faster to lose his temper, while Uncle Željko is more open and social, calmer and more composed, and just loves to tease or pull a prank on someone. I guess this difference in character is why the two of them get along so famously. I've never seen them argue.

In Makarska, we settled at a refugee camp called Children's Village. We stayed there for about four months and then, in April 1992, we moved to Zadar, where I was supposed to start school in the coming autumn. We were placed in the Hotel Kolovare. In the beginning, we had a room on the ground floor. My mother, father, sister and I had just one bed. The small space also had a toilet, while in the corner there was a small table on which our cooker stood. Then they moved us to the third floor, where we had two rooms – one for my sister Jasmina and me, while the other one was my parents' bedroom and our living room. This was our new reality. It may have appeared difficult, but I think we adjusted quickly. My family was used to a modest life even before we were exiled, so my parents didn't complain. Sure, it was hard on them because they were worried about me and my sister, and on top of everything, my father joined the army as a volunteer and had to go to the front. To ensure a better life for all of us, my mother found a job. Her workmate from the factory in Obrovac opened a clothes repair shop and asked her to join her. I think this did her good – not only because we had another income, but also because while she worked there, she could put her troubles aside, even if for a moment.

At the hotel, there were many children my age. We spent our days hanging about the playground in front of the building. We played football, dodgeball, hide and seek; we made new friends. Were it not for the frequent shelling, which made us run into the shelter, we children had quite a decent social life. The hotel was filled with people, who, just like us, had left their homes behind to save their lives, and there were many of our relatives. Among them, my father's elder sister Marija and her family. The shelling was frequent, some of it hit the hotel too, and during one of the attacks, Marija's husband Mile was wounded. The shell exploded near their room. Luckily, except for the fear and shrapnel, there were no serious consequences.

Perhaps it sounds odd, but I quickly got used to the sirens and running into the shelter. In the beginning, the shelling was frightening, but later I felt only unease. What did terrify me was the sound of missiles, that dreadful whistle followed by an explosion. We didn't always run to the same shelter – it depended on where the sirens caught us. Wherever we ran, there were always a lot of children, and we would soon organise a game of some kind. It made time pass faster. I felt safest when my family was together, but when my father was away at the front, we lived in fear. The fear was always somewhere in the background, but we learned to live with it and our life went on at an even pace. Until I started school . . .

The School Bell

Kruno Krstić Primary School in the Arbanasi neighbourhood of Zadar was about one kilometre away from our hotel. On the first day of school, my mother, naturally, walked me over, but the next day my parents allowed me to walk to school on my own. I liked this a lot, because along the way I could joke around with two friends I had made in the Hotel Kolovare, Marko Oštrić and Ante Crnjak. We were inseparable. Marko is from Pridraga, and we hit it off immediately the moment we met. We went to school together, we sat together, we trained together at Zadar. We became lifelong friends. We were best men at each other's weddings. Our families are close. Of all his qualities, I love him most because he has never changed. He has stayed a dear friend ever since my childhood and the war years. And he's still just like he was when we were six. To him, I have always been just Luka, not Luka Modrić, the football player. That's what I admire in him.

To be honest, I didn't do well in school – let's say I was an average pupil. I liked history and PE, and I always had excellent marks in those two subjects. But I didn't do very well in science and maths. One of the reasons was my last-minute studying. I was always running to training, every day and every evening, and then during the weekends we had matches. I would sit down and study only before parents' evenings and was happy with average marks. On the positive side, I was very tidy. This is one of the things that has stuck with me. I like it when everything is in its place, when my things are organised, and when at any given moment I know where everything is. When I get back home, I notice right away if something has been moved from its place or if the arrangement is different.

My parents were tolerant of my ups and downs in school. They told me to try and do my best, but, given our situation, I think they cared mostly that I made progress. What I liked best about school were my friends and classmates. We teased each other and came up with innocent pranks. My behaviour was generally good, though I did have my moments! It was all part of growing up. In a way, it made us feel like we were just children going to school and doing what children do, although the times were difficult and dangerous – we knew you could easily end up dead. Our teachers tried to make the situation manageable. As I loved PE, I particularly liked our PE teacher Albert Radovniković, but I also loved Mrs Maja Grbić, who was our form teacher and very understanding of the refugees such as myself. There were days when school was cancelled due to shelling. Going back to school meant the situation was calmer, but the fear we experienced couldn't be removed with an eraser. Our teachers needed to be patient and full of understanding.

I used every possible moment to play football. We would play on a concrete pitch behind the school, and when we came home we resumed the game in the hotel parking lot. Next to it, there was a patch of grass with a couple of trees on it. One tree served as one goalpost, a large stone as another. We played until we dropped. Sometimes, I'd stand between the posts and play as a goalkeeper, but I always preferred to dribble and shoot. That's when my father noticed I was good at it. When he wasn't at the front line, he'd take me to the pitch in nearby Arbanasi and show me how to control the ball; how to receive it and pass it on. I took great pleasure in it. Playing with my dad, the ball, the game – it was like those carefree days back home. But, unlike Zaton Obrovački and the open spaces around our house, in front of the Hotel Kolovare were numerous cars. Naturally, many times the ball ended up hitting a car. When the ball hit metal, there was a nasty clang. The glass on the surrounding windows was sometimes smashed too! On one occasion, the situation got a little bit more serious. As the ball hit the wheel of one of the parked cars, an older gentleman suddenly showed up. Steaming with rage, he took our ball and punctured it right in front of us! And then he told Marko and me to get lost. At first, I was shocked, but soon that turned to anger. I went back to our room and burst into tears because we had lost our leather ball, the only one we had. My father asked what had happened and when I told him, he immediately went outside. He found the man who had punctured our ball and asked for an explanation. The man worked at the hotel and my father found him with the screwdriver in his hand, the very same one he'd used to pierce our ball.

'First, put that screwdriver away, and second, I don't understand why you punctured the kids' ball?' my father told him firmly.

'The ball hit my car!' the man replied.

My father insisted this wasn't enough of a reason to be aggressive and was no way to treat children. He demanded he make amends. The man eventually apologised – and the next day he took us to the store and bought us a new ball. It was the first time I ever saw my father react like that! Of course, I was proud. And soon he made me happy again.

CHAPTER THREE

One day my dad came home and told me he had enrolled me in the Zadar Football Academy It was autumn 1992, not long after school had started, and I couldn't wait for the first training session. My friend Marko had also joined the academy, and my father took us there in his car. We were so excited! The training took place at the former army base we called Banine. The place was huge, and today it has been converted into a sports centre. In the beginning, we had no locker rooms, so we changed our clothes in the stands. I still remember my first football boots. They were bought by my father and made by Lotto, and were bright green. I thought they were the most beautiful thing in the world! My parents had to sacrifice a lot to provide everything we needed. My father was certain I would be good at football. Under different circumstances, maybe he would've been a successful football player himself, but he didn't get a chance. He told my mother that I had a special talent for the game and that he would make sure I got the opportunity to use it – the opportunity he never had.

My first coach was Željko Živković. After the initial session, he immediately put me into a group with older boys. I was physically weaker, but I wasn't afraid of anyone. I must have gained this confidence when I played football in the street, in parking lots, on concrete pitches, on the grass in front of the Hotel Kolovare. There, no one cared how old you were: you played with older boys and if you wanted to play, you had to learn to stand up for yourself. My shins were often sore from all the kicks. I flew down the hard, concrete pitch and got up all covered in blood. But I never cried or whined. I just picked myself up and carried on. Perhaps that was the reason the older boys accepted me and picked me to play for their team. I think the street gave me a level of toughness that would be of great importance later.

We trained three times a week. At first, my father took me there, but he was often busy and so later I would take my bicycle and go on my own. It was 20 minutes from the Hotel Kolovare to our training grounds. I know my parents worried in case the sirens went off and the shelling started as I was on my way to the training field, or when I was already there. If this happened, our coaches quickly took us into the club buildings, where we would take cover. Today, I'm a father, and when I look back at those days and remember how some other parents whose children also played football acted, I appreciate my father's approach even more. When he came to watch the training, he mostly spent time with Marko's father, a man of similar character, and he never meddled in the coach's job, nor did he ever put me or anyone else under pressure. There were many parents who did, of course. My father reacted only once, and this was to protect me from one such parent. He was one of those people who couldn't see past their own child and thought everything should be given to him. He kept shouting and making nasty comments all the time, and he must've said something to me. My father was on the other side of the field and he just lost it: he ran across the pitch and told him loud and clear to stop harassing the children. My dad can be very convincing when something rubs him up the wrong way! The harassment stopped.

I liked to train. Our coaches – Živković, then Matošević after him – taught us the basics, how to receive and pass the ball, and other elements of the game. Even when we had no training sessions, I still played football all the time. As always, we found some space in the parking lot in front of the hotel. We would just place two rocks on each side of the pitch and then play. Those were real battles! Mostly we played five-a-side, although sometimes there were more or fewer players in a team. When I played, the only thing on my mind was winning and being better than the others. It came with a price – all my trousers, t-shirts and especially trainers were all beaten up and torn. Back then, I didn't have a lot of clothes and I wasn't able to afford new trainers whenever I wanted. That's why I looked after the ones I had as much as I could. They weren't expensive, quite the opposite, but those simple white canvas trainers meant the world to me. So, whenever a hole appeared, I patched it as best as I could.

In 1995, after Operation Storm, which marked the decisive victory in the Croatian War of Independence, my father started his training to become an aircraft mechanic. As a member of the active-duty military personnel, he was employed at the Zemunik Airport, which also meant we moved to the Hotel Iž. This was a smaller and more modest hotel, a 15-minute walk from the Hotel Kolovare. My friend Marko Oštrić also left Kolovare and he and his family were placed in the Hotel Zagreb. But the most significant change was my new school. Having finished sixth grade, I transferred to Šime Budinić Primary School, which was closer to our accommodation. The school was nice and I liked it a lot, even though the teachers were a bit more strict. I soon adjusted, just as I did to our new housing at the Hotel Iž. We lived on the first floor. The space, not even 30 square metres (around 300 square feet), had one larger room that served as our living room, our dining room and my parents' bedroom. Next to the small bathroom was a tiny, improvised room with two beds where Jasmina and I slept. But soon there were three of us: my sister Diora was born in June, 1998.

I also remember the summer of 1998 fondly because of the fantastic success of the Croatia national team at the FIFA World Cup in France. I was almost 13 and old enough to understand that they accomplished something extraordinary when they finished third at the tournament, only being beaten in the semi-final. That wasn't the first championship I had watched. Even though I was only nine at the time, some of the details from the 1994 World Cup in the United States still lodged in my memory – especially Romário, whom I liked a lot thanks to his dribbling skills, or Bebeto's celebrations of his child's birth after every goal he scored. But I was most impressed by the anticipation and suspense during the penalty shoot-out in the final between Brazil and Italy. Back then, of course, I wasn't able to comprehend all the weight that pressed down on the players when they took the penalties to decide who would win the World Cup. Twenty years later, I now understand this only too well.

Back in 1998, whenever Croatia played, it was enough to watch people's reactions in the hotel, on the streets, in the squares, cafes and bars to know that something big was happening. I was impressed by the atmosphere; by the euphoria of the grown-ups as they watched our national team's sensational performances. Those emotions are held fast in my memory. Like every boy, I fantasised about experiencing all this as a player. I had long chosen the role and the number I would wear on my shirt when I grew up – the same as Zvonimir Boban, the team's captain: the No. 10. Boban was my idol. I followed his performances in the national team, as well as at AC Milan. I was growing up at the time when Milan dominated the footballing world – and when Boban was one of their best players. Someone from my homeland was an important part of that great team! It was only natural I became a fan of the *Rossoneri*. My parents got me a tracksuit with the AC Milan logo and I had stickers of my favourite player. I couldn't even have dreamed that one day my idol and role model would present me with an award for the best player of anything, let alone of the World Cup.

Staying in Zadar

During this period, one thing had a massive influence on everything that would subsequently happen in my life. It was time to rebuild after the war, and people were slowly returning to their homes. Everyone assumed that my parents would also go back home, to Zaton Obrovački. However, they reached a huge decision: we were staying in Zadar! Many of those going back tried to talk my parents into doing the same. The main reason we stayed was me – or rather, my parents' wish to make sure I received a proper education and the chance to be a football player. My father, as I have already said, was convinced I had the talent to become a great player. No one and nothing could tell him otherwise. Sure, it was important to get my mother's support, but when she agreed they decided they would do whatever it took to ensure I got the opportunity to do something big. Today, I understand just how bold that was and the sacrifices my parents had to make to get me where I am today.

From the very first training session, when I was only seven, playing football brought huge expense. Both of my parents were employed, and they were able to support the family, but they had to watch every penny. Yet my father always said: 'I didn't have a chance, but Luka will get one, no matter what it takes.' And that's how it was. They bought all the equipment I needed, they paid the club fees, they financed all my selection camps. Without my parents' support, and their firm belief that my talent deserved such sacrifice, I would never have been given a chance to prove myself. My uncle Željko also helped immensely – financially, morally, emotionally – almost as much as my parents. My father often said that without his support he would never have been able to cover all the expenses. But it wasn't only his financial contribution – he was there whenever and for whatever reason my family needed him.

I made quick progress in the junior categories. I was part of a gifted generation of players that achieved great results. Journalists wrote about us; they published photographs that now serve as a lasting memory. My mother is the main reason we have a good archive of photos and articles from those days. She followed the media, cut out articles from the newspapers, carefully arranged all the photos and saved everything. My father was responsible for the technical part. He recorded the games with his video camera and the recordings served a dual purpose: not only as a memento, but they also enabled him to show me how to correct a thing or two.

Whenever I flip through those photo albums or watch a video clip, I relive those moments. Not only the football, but the friendships. We spent time together, we travelled, we were literally growing up together. We often played in tournaments, both in Croatia and abroad. We enjoyed those travels because being a part of a club was not only a matter of playing and winning – we felt we were part of a group. There was a special bond between us. We were hungry for success, but we also looked forward to celebrating victories together. During those early days, everything was carefree and childish. You imagine you're a real player and a part of a great team. Later on, when you reach under-16 and especially under-18 level, you mature and realise that football is a very demanding sport. Not that the game loses its romance or that the team spirit is no longer there – all of this has to be a part of it, even at the highest level of professional football, otherwise there's no pleasure in it. But other factors of a footballer's career, as you make progress, become more prominent. By this, I mean the sacrifice you have to make compared to your peers, such as going to bed early while others go out and have fun with their friends, or the constant training and obligation not to lose your focus. Not only when it comes to practice and physical exertion, but also adopting the technical, tactical and competitive skills you are being taught. You need to make progress, and this will most certainly not happen if your mind is elsewhere and if you keep thinking about what your friends are doing, where they are, whether they are having fun, and where the girl you are attracted to is – the one you'd like to take out to see a film!

As a reminder of those youth days, I've got many team medals and individual trophies. The teams I played for did well, and so did I. There are many details – too many to list in this book – but one thing is lodged in my memory: our series of three consecutive wins at youth tournaments against Hajduk Split. For my generation, the players born in 1984/1985, this was a sensational feeling. We beat a great club that almost everyone in Dalmatia roots for and that practically every player hopes to play for one day. We did well at international tournaments too. At one such competition, in Bergamo, I won the trophy for the Best Player. The photo from the award ceremony was published in the newspapers; I was so proud. There were many spectators and I felt important. On top of everything, my best friend Marko Oštrić was the leading scorer.

The real story of this tournament was the little drama I went through the night before the final when I caught a fever. I went to bed, covered myself with a blanket and shivered like a leaf with cold. My temperature must have gone through the roof, yet no one measured it, because I didn't tell anyone I was sick! No one. Had our coach Domagoj Bašić learned I was ill, he wouldn't have let me play in the final. I dreaded such an outcome, and while I was lying there, tormented by the fever, the worry, and also the fatigue from the matches we had already played, I fell asleep. I woke up the next morning and didn't feel a thing. I wasn't cold, there was no pain, and I almost forgot what had happened the night before. I played in the final and scored a goal. A header, no less!

My Favourite Coach

During the 10 years I spent at the Zadar Youth Academy, I had several coaches. Željko Živković was first, and then came Davorin Matošević, Miodrag Paunović, Domagoj Bašić and Robert Botunac. Whether for a longer or shorter period, each of them played their part in my development. I'm thankful to all of them. Still, two people played by far the most important role in my growth – as a footballer and as a person. They are Tomislav and Domagoj Bašić, a father and son. Tomo Bašić was the legend of Zadar football and an expert – a man both notable and charismatic. At the time, he was the head of the Zadar Youth Academy, and he decided that his son Domagoj should coach the under-12 category where I played.

Domagoj was a talented player, whose career had ended early. From the first training session, he left a strong impression on me, and as the years went by his influence only grew. He was with us when we just entered puberty. At that age, you watch girls, you want to go out and have some fun, like the big boys. It's the age when you start thinking you are smarter than anyone! All kinds of big ideas come to your mind, and you think you always know best. Domagoj Basic was with us as we went through all of this. Today, I understand how important it is to have a coach in that period of your life who won't look at you only as a player. He also paid a lot of attention to our upbringing, directing and educating us. His training sessions were engaging, in part because he was a unique character. He didn't only say, 'Run, pass, cut in, take the shot.' He taught us, for example, how to deal with injustice. He would split us into two teams and then, as a referee, follow his own rules. He would make a call against someone on purpose and then watch as we reacted. Some of us were angry, others cried from misery at the injustice. Later, he explained that there were all kinds of things waiting for us in football, as well as in life. That there would be injustice, and that we needed to learn how to overcome such situations. He taught us to be responsible and to obey rules. He was adamant about it.

Domagoj Bašić was well-read. We were boys who had just reached puberty, and he asked us to read books too! In the beginning, this came as a surprise. We weren't thrilled, but the coach was strict about it. He would give us a book and a week to read it. After that, he would quiz us to see if we'd done what he asked. He'd gather the team in a circle and ask each player a question from this or that chapter. We could choose what we wanted to read; he had read all of the books a long time ago. And he was quick to tell if someone was bluffing. If someone failed to convince him they had read the book, he would send them home. I agreed to read *Robinson Crusoe*, *Heidi* and another one that I can't remember now. I read them all. He wanted to teach us that we had to do what we promised, regardless of whether we liked it or not! On this, he was consistent – and he sanctioned those who failed to obey him. When, for example, the Zadar Night took place – with thousands of tourists and locals gathering to celebrate the end of the summer with music and parties in almost every neighbourhood, he would warn us, 'I don't want to see you out after 1 a.m. If I catch you, you're not going to train here anymore!'

He did what he said and we adored him because behind that firm and unyielding attitude was a man extremely protective of us. He let no one attack us; he always defended and supported us. He filled us with a special kind of confidence. Besides his intellectual side, Domagoj also had style. Tall, handsome, always wearing his Ray-Bans, he radiated a unique energy. We also knew he had fought in the war.

Our training sessions most often took place in the evening, starting at 5 or 6 p.m. From time to time, we had a morning session, usually at

10 a.m. On one such occasion, we came to the training field but Domagoj didn't show up. We thought he was running late or something, but it was odd because he had never been late before. After two hours, someone from the club came and told us what had happened: our coach had passed away!

We were shocked. I can't remember if someone told us how he had died. We later learned that it was connected to some of his prior personal problems. But the cause of his death was not what mattered, what shocked me was the realisation that I would never again see the man who had not just been the coach I so respected, but also a person very dear to me. I'd already experienced what it meant to lose someone I cared about with the death of my grandfather Luka. But leaving my hometown had distanced me from the things and situations that reminded me of that tragedy. My parents also tried their best. Time did its work, and I gradually got used to the reality of not having a grandfather anymore. In the case of Domagoj, though, this was a man I loved as my coach and respected as a great authority.

During those delicate years of adolescence, such losses are painful – in part because you immediately become aware of the emptiness they create. I can't say that I grew up instantly, but this tragedy marked me and made me mature faster. Everything he taught us about responsibility, following the rules and carrying out your commitments, about dealing with injustice and periods when things aren't easy, became an even more important part of my outlook. There would be many difficult situations in my life when I went back to his words.

Robert Botunac arrived as our coach after Domagoj Bašić. He had a different approach, but my experience with him was good. Like Bašić, and other coaches, Botunac played me as an attacking midfielder, just behind the strikers. I was smaller than the rest of the players and physically weaker, but everyone noted how explosive I was. They said that I had a great technique and that my speed and agility compensated for what I lacked in size. I liked to dribble; sometimes I even went too far with tricks and fakes! It was about this time that I started passing the ball with the outside of my right foot. My confidence grew stronger when I realised I could outsmart and dominate players who were much stronger than me. That was confirmed at a big tournament in Vodice, where we played against the best teams from Croatia and I was voted the Best Player – even though Zadar didn't reach the final and we only came in third place.

Another story from this period also brings back fond memories. At the time, the media were focusing on – and younger players such as me were talking about – another attacking midfielder called Niko Kranjčar. The son of Dinamo Zagreb legend Cico Kranjčar, he was considered to be an exceptional talent who would soon play for Dinamo's first team. I watched him play, and it didn't take more than just a couple of touches to see he was a brilliant technician. It was a pleasure to watch him move and control the ball, and I soon had a chance to meet him in person. Dinamo came to Zadar to play a friendly, and their players stayed with our families. Coach Bašić made the arrangements and Niko ended up staying with my family, at the Hotel Kolovare. We spent two days together, hanging out, walking around Zadar, sightseeing, talking to each other. We had a great time. Back then we couldn't have dreamed that one day we would play alongside one another, for Croatia and for Tottenham Hotspur.

The Hajduk Disappointment

My time under coach Robert Botunac was also marked by my trial at Hajduk Split. Many articles and stories were written about it when I transferred to Dinamo, and later too, after I moved to Tottenham and then confirmed my value at Real Madrid. Dinamo and Hajduk are two Croatian powerhouses and their heated rivalry has been the cause of many quarrels. Therefore, every success in my career inevitably saw the media rehash the story about Hajduk coaches failing to recognise my talent. I've read different theories, which often reference such football greats as Josip Skoblar and Zvonimir Boban. Both of them had outstanding careers and the critics just couldn't wait to call out the coaches who had supposedly failed to predict this. In my case, however, there was a lot of misinformation. For example, the newspapers often said that Mario Grgurović came to the trial with me and that Hajduk selected him over me. The truth is that Grgurović already played for Hajduk and I arrived in Split later, together with my best friend Marko Oštrić.

My father always rooted for Hajduk. Just like the rest of my family. For us, Hajduk was an institution. For my father, just like every parent in Dalmatia whose child plays football, it would've been a dream come true if I had played for Hajduk. As a boy, I was a huge fan of The Whites from Split, and at no point in my career at Dinamo, Hajduk's great rival, did I either hide or deny this. It would have been silly and dishonest. Still, after all those great experiences wearing their famous blue shirt, it's only logical that Dinamo is the club that now has my heart. Just as it's natural to have great respect for Hajduk and everything this club means to all of its supporters and the people of Dalmatia.

With the help of uncle Željko, who contacted Hajduk's coaches through an intermediary, my father organised the trial. At the time, there were no training sessions in Zadar, so my father thought there was no need to inform anyone, not even Tomo Bašić, the director of the Zadar Youth Academy. Later, that would turn out to be a huge mistake. My father took us to the Poljud Stadium, where Marko and I stayed in the club's housing. The trials were conducted under the watchful eye of coach Mario Ćutuk and took place at the nearby training field. I had a feeling I performed well, and I expected their coaches and scouts to be satisfied. But before the two weeks agreed for the trial had passed, Marin Kovačić, the director of the Hajduk Youth Academy, came over to talk to me. I knew immediately this wouldn't end well. Kovačić was succinct: it was too early for me to join Hajduk.

I'll never forget that moment. The first great disappointment in my career. I just couldn't accept their decision, nor the cold manner in which it was delivered. It crossed my mind that maybe someone from Zadar had found out we had gone to the trial and intervened with Hajduk to tell them to reject us and send us home. I thought this because the same thing happened to Marko, who also seemed to be doing well during the trial. I rang my father and asked him to pick us up. He was unpleasantly surprised by such a turn of events. For him, I was always the best, wherever I played.

Later, when I had proved myself as a player both for my clubs and the national team, I no longer felt the bitterness that washes over you when you are a kid and someone says you are not good enough. It's understandable that at such a young age a player's talent can be misjudged – especially if the decision needs to be made quickly, among many children. I knew a lot of young players who were showing talent on the pitch; I was convinced they would become great players and live off football. In most cases, this wasn't so. As they were growing up, some of them lost the advantage of their physical potential. Others weren't persistent enough. Others still weren't lucky enough to get recognised and receive support when they needed it, so they became disappointed and gave up. For some, school was a priority, and they weren't dedicated to football and willing to sacrifice everything for it. No one can say with certainty that someone who stands out at 10, 12 or even 16 will be good enough to become a professional player. The opposite is also true: some players showed little promise in younger categories, but eventually stood out and had successful careers. There were those, like me, who hadn't yet developed physically and who were overlooked, yet they succeeded. Those pundits writing about an inability to recognise talent at Hajduk, or at any other club for that matter, always seem rather ignorant to me.

'Your son hasn't met the criteria, we're sorry. He's still too little,' the people at Hajduk told my father. It was hard for him to accept this, but he had to face reality. I wasn't disheartened. I got even more motivated to prove them wrong. On the pitch, I felt I could put in a solid performance, no matter who I played against. And that feeling is very important. I realised this later, when I played at the highest level, that each of us knows best what he can or cannot do. During training or a match, you know where you stand compared to others. If you can follow the pace, dribble past an opponent, take on a duel, deliver a quality pass, it means you have reached a desired level, and should look for new challenges and opportunities to make progress. Whenever I felt this, I knew I was ready for the next step in my career.

We soon came back to Zadar after my Hajduk heartbreak, but more problems and disappointments followed. Tomo Bašić found out that we had gone for a trial. It's an understatement to say he held it against my father. Up to this point, they had a great relationship and often spent time together.

'How could you do this without my knowledge?!' he asked, with reproach. It bothered him that my father hadn't informed, let alone consulted, him. Even so, Mr Tomo's response took my father by surprise – and hurt him. For me, it was the second shocking event in the space of just a few days.

'If he's not good enough for Hajduk, then he's not good enough for Zadar either! He's banned from training for the next three months!'

I couldn't believe what I was hearing when my father told me the news. It was hard to imagine I would have to spend so much time away from football, from my teammates and friends. I felt nauseous when I realised I wouldn't be able to play any matches for such a long time. *How could this be happening to me?* Just one day outside the club seemed to last a whole year!

From time to time, my dad would admit Mr Tomo had every right to be angry – but he just couldn't accept his drastic punishment. I know they had a bad fight and it took a while before they started talking again.

All of this drove me out of my mind. However, as my dad told me, there was no other option. We had to reorganise. Mr Tomo gave me a programme of stretching exercises, which was supposed to make me at least a little taller. I did those exercises a couple of times a day; they became an obsession. I kept hanging from fences. Whoever saw me must have thought I had gone crazy! The only thing on my mind was the ultimate goal: to grow taller.

When I wasn't stretching, I played football and basketball with my friends. When he came home from work, my dad would take me to a parking lot or a nearby concrete pitch to practise. We worked on my technique, on correcting my shooting and my positioning when receiving the ball. The summer slowly went by with me going to the seaside, swimming, hanging out with my friends, and doing stretching exercises non-stop. To my great surprise, by the end of the summer my wish had come true and I was taller! I'm not sure if the programme had much to do with it – it probably did, to an extent at least, but I think nature did her own work.

In the meantime, my dad and Mr Tomo made peace and started talking to each other again. One day, as they were having coffee, Tomo finally told him, 'Tell Luka he can start working with the team again.'

Back to the Ball

When my dad told me I could go back to the team, I was euphoric! Before the full three months were up, I had the chance to return to normal training. I was beside myself with happiness, though I also understood Mr Tomo's decision to distance me from the club. Both he and my dad regretted that the trial at Hajduk had taken place without his knowledge. He had always been nothing but positive. He had enormous experience and his advice always brought progress. Years later, when I had established myself as a professional, my father told me, 'Many beat their chests now, but Tomo Bašić was the one who recognised your talent and always said you would make it. For him, you were never little; he always had a clear vision of what would become of you.'

Mr Tomo was a real character – strict and demanding. When you're growing up, both as a player and a person, such authority provokes awe. But his advice was golden. As were his disciplinary measures. He would organise individual training sessions, tell us what to do, and, if he were not satisfied with our performance, he would send us away. Just like that. There was no fooling around with him. He was very knowledgeable, and it didn't take him long to recognise talent – to see who was a player and who was a fake. So, when he told me, 'Luka, you're the one!' I saw it as a confirmation that my time was coming. That I could do it.

Perhaps it sounds arrogant, but even before this I felt I had a lot to show on the pitch. Even when we were kids practising at Banine. There were many of us, so the coaches split us into groups. Mine was called the Hurricanes – named after a football cartoon popular at the time. The other group was called the Mistrals. They were our main rivals, but we also played against teams of older boys. No matter who was on the opposite side, I always managed to pull off whatever move I imagined. It could be said I was dominant once I had the ball at my feet; I seldom lost it. The older boys respected this, and they showed it when they selected players for their team.

Of course, there were many less gratifying moments. I used to get kicked a lot, especially when I dribbled. I entered a duel without fear, not worried if someone was stronger than me. The usual doubts, because of my height, followed me from the first training session, but I got used to it. After every good game I played, when they praised my performance, the inevitable *but* followed: 'The kid's a miracle, but he's too little!' Of course, there were players who were tall and strong, who stood out, who scored many goals, but as I grew older the advantage of physical strength evened out, and technical knowledge tipped the balance.

Now, after my experience at Hajduk, whenever someone expressed doubt in me, my motivation grew stronger. I had believed in myself ever since I was little, but perhaps it was experiencing that doubt that hardened my fighting spirit and self-confidence. It's also possible that it is something I inherited – my mother is very tough and self-assured, and my father is a fighter, persistent and never giving up.

Parallel to football, my education continued. After primary school, I enrolled in the School for Tourism and Hospitality, where I trained to wait tables. Had I not succeeded in football, I would likely have become a waiter! I liked the idea. During the first year, we had our practical training at the Marine Restaurant in Zadar, where they organised wedding dinners. Without false modesty, I can say that I was great at serving drinks. That was our main task. The only thing I didn't like was washing dishes! We trainees were good friends and we enjoyed ourselves whenever we were on a break or having dinner in the kitchen. But, after the first year of high school, it was time for a new challenge – and a decision that would affect the rest of my life.

***

In the immediate aftermath of his son's death, Mr Tomo kept away from the club. Our coach's funeral was too sad. For Domagoj's mother and father, and for his brother Silvio, it was a terrible blow. Mr Tomo seemed depressed, but he mustered enough strength to get involved with the club again and take care of a couple of the younger players like me. One day, he invited my father and I to come over and talk to him. He told us, 'Luka has great skill and the potential to become a great football player. He's outgrown Zadar. I think the moment has come to move forward. He needs to move to a higher level to develop further and take advantage of his potential.'

This happened maybe a year after the unsuccessful trial at Hajduk, so Mr Tomo's words meant a lot. I felt honoured because he wasn't the flattering kind and I knew he said what he truly meant.

'I'm ready, ready right now!' I blurted out after a moment of silence around the table.

My father had a similar reaction, but I recognised uncertainty in his eyes. A step forward, yes, but where and how? After we had burned ourselves at Hajduk, he was extra cautious.

Mr Tomo made it clear he wasn't opting for Hajduk. It was evident they weren't on good terms.

'I have a different idea,' he said.

The idea was Dinamo.

CHAPTER FOUR

What I cared about most was getting a step further in my development as a player. Mr Tomo was right. When you realise you aren't making progress in your current surroundings you have two options. One is to remain in the safety of this environment – and most often this means stagnation – and the other is to accept the challenge of a more trying setting, where you will need to improve if you want to play your part. As we all agreed that it was time to leave, Mr Tomo decided to get in touch with Zdravko Mamić. At the time, Mamić was serving as a member of the Dinamo board of directors and was also the owner of a management agency that took care of several young players and their careers. He had a reputation for being a very competent agent whose influence was on the rise. I knew all this from other people's stories and from the newspapers. Mr Tomo now persuaded him to give me a chance. After this, we needed to talk to the people at Zadar and convince them to allow me to sign for Dinamo. That caused some problems. The people at Zadar wanted me to sign a stipend contract to strengthen their position in any negotiations about possible future transfers. My father didn't want to sign anything. During the transfer window, he sent a written request to terminate my contract with Zadar. With this document in my hand, I was able to sign for a new club. It was agreed that Zadar would receive a solidarity fee for my training and education, which they later received after my transfers to Tottenham and then Real Madrid.

The summer of 2001 marked a big turning point in my career – and my life. While I was still in Zadar, enjoying the summer and hanging out with my friends, my parents went to Zagreb to sort out my status.

As I was a minor, just 15, they were the ones who signed the contract with the Mamić Sports Agency. They were met by Damir Jozić, one of the agency's employees, who was at their disposal the whole time. They also met Zdravko Mamić, who clearly left a good impression.

During the next seven years of my stay at Dinamo, including the two loans to Zrinjski Mostar and Inter Zaprešić, my father rarely communicated with Mamić. As I have already said, he didn't interfere in my career unless he had to, like signing the documents on my behalf because I was underage.

When I was little, he used to take me to training sessions, he showed me a thing or two when he had free time, bought my training equipment, took care of the expenses, and, together with my mother, he was my greatest support. He was caring, like every good parent. But, very early on, my parents allowed me to be independent. That's how I learned quickly to recognise a situation off the pitch, make a decision and take responsibility accordingly. There were situations my father thought weren't right for me. Going on my second loan to Inter Zaprešić was one of those moments – he shared his dissatisfaction, or hesitation, but as so many times before, the final decision was up to me. When I went to play for Zrinjski Mostar, who competed in a physically demanding league, I was still a junior. Many people said – you've already heard this many times – I was too frail, especially for such a challenging senior league. However, my father wasn't worried. He didn't try to talk me out of it. He saw my determination and told me, 'Son, if you think that's good for you, go and show them!' The only thing that mattered to him was that I was satisfied. He always said he needed nothing more.

My first contract with the Mamić Agency included paid accommodation, one meal a day and a monthly allowance of 500 Deutschmarks, 80 of which went towards my tuition. Moving to Zagreb also meant I had to change schools. I went to the School for Hospitality, which had the same programme as my old school in Zadar. It was an evening school, since most of my time was spent at team and individual training sessions, matches and travelling. My priority was football, and that's why I moved to the capital.

The excitement of moving to a big club and a big city simmered in me almost until it was time to leave. As the day of my departure drew near, I became more and more emotional. I was aware that life would turn upside down; at the same time, I gave a lot of thought to everything I had experienced. Leaving Zadar was difficult – I'd spent 10 unforgettable years in that city, and it's always been my town. Childhood, growing up, school, friends, first crushes and football were a part of it, along with shelling, fear and boyish disappointments. All of it kept running through my mind. At almost 16 years old, anxious because of the huge step I was about to take, I realised what I was leaving behind. The years in Zadar meant a lot to me, first and foremost because of the people around me: my dear parents, my lovely sisters and my best friend Marko Oštrić, as well as my other friends and my footballing father, Mr Tomo. They were staying behind; I was leaving. I would be alone in the big city, and I didn't know what was in store.

The night before leaving I wasn't restless. It was exciting to think about how things would turn out. I wasn't afraid. I knew this would define my career. I realised I would have to become independent – the situation demanded it. And I also knew that if I wanted to become a successful player, Zagreb was my big chance. I never once thought of staying at home.

In the morning, I was anxious but ready. I didn't carry a lot of luggage – all that I needed fitted into one sports bag. But just before leaving came a tough moment – saying goodbye to my family. My father was taking me to Zagreb to be with the under-17 national team and to play two matches against Slovenia. After that, I was supposed to stay in Zagreb and start training at Dinamo, so on that morning I said goodbye to Zadar. My childhood ended, and one way of life was simply no more. I was 15 years, 11 months old, but I knew from that day on I would have all the responsibilities of an adult. It was the only way to overcome all the obstacles on my path to the goals I had set for myself. It was the only way to deal with being away from my family and getting used to a new life in the big city.

When I was leaving, my mother was very composed. She is always calm, but I could tell she was trying hard not to show weakness and make my departure more difficult. I hugged her. You only have one mum! I didn't cry, but I felt a lump in my throat. My sister Jasmina was crying her eyes out. We are very close. Ever since she was little, she wanted to be with me. Even when I played football with the boys from my street, she would rather stay with me than play with other girls.

Getting in the car and closing the door was really tough. I turned around to wave at my mum, and I saw my dad crying at the wheel. As we drove away, the sight of my mother, my sisters and my town behind them simply crushed me. Tears started running down my face and I just kept quiet. As did my dad. It was the beginning of a new life. While the red Zastava 128 took us to Zagreb, I thought about everything I had gone through and what was yet to come. There had been difficult days in Zadar, filled with hardship and sorrow, but the moments filled with joy and happiness were countless. I grew up in a loving family, showered with affection. I learned to live a modest life and to be satisfied with what I had. I felt I had everything.

A lot has been written about my early life growing up in poverty, about the horrors of war, about my life as a refugee. It's true, we didn't have much. It's also true that for a long time shelling and fear were a part of my everyday existence. We did spend five or six years as refugees, in temporary housing shared with people who struggled with the same sad fate. But despite all of this, it would be wrong to say I had a bad life or that I struggled. My parents and all the other people around me who were part of those first 16 years of my life are the reason I have fond memories of those days.

If I were to tell just one story to draw a picture of this life, or even only a symbol, it would be the story of my shin guards. I wasn't a demanding child – quite the opposite. Like every boy who loves and plays football, I had my heroes. One of the first and the greatest was *El Fenómeno* – Ronaldo Luís Nazário de Lima, or more simply, Ronaldo. I loved the way he dribbled, the way he moved through the defence, the ease with which he scored. My dad knew how much I liked him, and he made sure to get me something with the great Brazilian's picture or number on it. He always did this. If he knew I wanted something, he would do whatever it took to make my wish come true. My mum supported him in this, and my uncle Željko helped whenever he could. That's why I never lacked anything – neither for football, nor school or my travels. I had my football boots, trainers, tracksuits – I even got a bicycle, bags, jerseys, balls and t-shirts. And that's also how I got a pair of plastic shin guards, the same as everyone else's. The only difference was that mine had a picture of Ronaldo on them! I was beside myself when my dad bought them. I looked after them as if they were all that I owned. The story that we were so poor my father had to make my shin guards out of wood is, like many stories about my childhood, just a myth.

In the Big City

When I arrived in Zagreb, I settled in a rented apartment in Ravnice. The place was close to the training grounds and the stadium, around 10 minutes away on foot. My roommate was Marko Čirjak, a great guy. I had met him back in Zadar, at a futsal tournament, which our team won. Čiro, as we called him, also played for the youth teams at Dinamo. Unfortunately, he didn't have a big career, even though he stood out back then as a midfielder. Today, he works as a sales representative and remains one of my closest friends.

This first apartment in Zagreb was quite small; we had just one room, a kitchen and a small balcony. Whoever had lived there before us hadn't cared much about the future tenants, as the apartment was full of rubbish! We had to clean it – and fast. Luckily, just like me, Čiro liked to keep the place tidy. We got to it and took the rubbish out. Then we relaxed a bit and had a long conversation. I was tired, so I quickly fell asleep and I think I didn't move until the morning. That was my first night in the big city.

It wasn't my first time here – I had visited Zagreb on several occasions when I played for Zadar. Even then, I had been impressed by the city, although we hadn't seen much of it. After the move, I spent most of my time between the apartment and the stadium. Our daily training sessions took place at the club, while we occasionally had individual sessions focusing on technique or fitness. These were organised by the agency, which also took care of our lunch – we ate together at Pod Mirnim Krovom, a restaurant not far away from the club – while for dinner we were on our own. My breakfast most often included a sandwich and chocolate milk.

Naturally, during those first couple of months, I sometimes felt homesick. I missed my family, the familiar atmosphere of Zadar, and I couldn't wait for the couple of days when I could catch a bus and go home. As always, my parents helped me through those moments. They often visited at weekends, to see me play and to check on me. My dad and I talked about my game. Those were friendly discussions. Back in Zadar, when I had just begun playing, there was a time when he just wouldn't stop criticising. On one occasion, he kept reproaching me and, when we got home, I burst into tears. Then my mum raised her voice and told him that since he wouldn't leave me alone, he was banned from going to my matches. She encouraged me, telling me to be patient, and was very tolerant towards me. My dad wasn't happy staying away, so he secretly went to the stadium and watched me play. I didn't even know he was in the stands.

When I played for Dinamo, I spent my summers in Zadar. The whole family would get together; it was just like before. Still, although my mum always seemed so tough when we said goodbye at the parking lot in front of the Hotel Iž, I think she had a hard time dealing with the separation. My dad is sensitive – even today, when we say goodbye he often looks away to hide the tears in his eyes. But he had this mantra that made it easier: 'I only care if Luka is happy!' He often says this when I ask for his advice. He says what he thinks and then adds, 'Son, I'm sure you'll make a good call. You always do.' He just loves football and seeing me play makes him happy. No matter what it looks like on the pitch, once the match is over, for him, I'm always the best.

'But have you seen something that could've been different?' I often ask him, 'Some wrong call or a decision I made?' No matter what I ask, I can't throw him off.

My mum's not so much into football. For her, this is a sport she watches because it's what her son does. She wanted me to go to college and get a good job. She insisted on my education, even when it became evident that I could make a serious career as a player. And she often complained.

When I moved to Zagreb, my parents kept calling me every day. 'God, Mum, stop calling him all the time, he's not a kid anymore! Luka knows how to look after himself,' my sister Jasmina used to say. But my mum just couldn't help it, even though she knew she was overreacting. She always had to ask, 'Are you eating? Are you getting enough food? How was practice? Are you tired?' She also told me every time to wear warm clothes so as not to catch a cold, or to use an extra blanket because nights inland were colder than at the seaside. Even today, when I'm 34 years old and have my own family and three children, my mum always asks the same questions and is just as worried as before.

Diora was too little to understand what was going on, but Jasmina, who was 13 at the time, knew everything. My parents had waited for the right moment to tell her I was leaving because they were worried about how it might affect her. It turned out better than they expected. She realised I was happy to be given such a chance, and that's what she cared about most. Even so, the actual moment of my departure was tough on her. She cried because she knew, just like I did, that a special part of our lives had come to a close. We are four years apart; we have always been very close and we went through a lot together. Of course, there were moments when I was about to go out and play with my friends and I wasn't exactly happy if my mother insisted, 'Luka, take Jasmina along. Can't you see she's crying? She just wants to play.' I used to think, *Why can't she play with other girls? What does she know about football?* But she always came with me. Jasmina and Diora are two of my favourite weaknesses.

Football Academy

At Dinamo, I instantly noticed the difference in the quality and intensity of training. It was highly professional, and conditions were unlike anything I had experienced so far. In fact, it took me a while to get used to the new schedule. My first coach at under-16 level was Miroslav Stipić, and later we got Stjepan 'Štef' Deverić.

Besides the training sessions, I soon realised what it meant to play for Dinamo. The difference was huge. At Zadar, the atmosphere was more relaxed and defeat wasn't taken as seriously. At Dinamo, alarm bells rang immediately. After the first couple of wins in the Croatian under-17 league, we lost against Cibalia, in Vinkovci. It was clear that the coaches were upset, and that I was one of the players whose performance wasn't satisfactory. So, for the next home match – which we played in Maksimir against Šibenik – I started as a substitute. As far as I understood, the problem was my reluctance to defend. At Zadar, I had more freedom and I mostly played in attack. That wouldn't do at Dinamo. As a midfielder, I was required to perform at both ends of the pitch. This meant playing a different kind of football, and it was clear that I wouldn't fare well unless I did what was asked of me. We were losing at half time and Hrvoje Braović, the director of the academy at the time, came to me and said, 'You're going on, and we expect you to change the scoreline and show us what you can do. With what you've shown so far, not even Zdravko Mamić can save you!'

I played as the central attacking midfielder in a 4-2-3-1 formation and had a good match. We won, and after that, my performances and my status changed for the better. I realised I had to run in both directions and contribute to the attack as well as the defence. I made progress, which Braović told me in front of all the players when we played in Kvarnerska Rivijera, a well-known youth tournament.

I became good friends with three of my teammates: Hrvoje Čale played as a left full-back, was a physically powerful player and had already appeared for the senior teams; Marko Cindrić played on the right and was as fast as a bullet – I was sure he would have a great career; and Vedran Ćorluka, who knew everything about the ball and played either as a centre-back or a defensive midfielder. Ćorluka and I later played alongside one another for the national team, as well as at Dinamo and Tottenham. Čale and I were together at Dinamo and briefly for the national team and we became great friends – so much so that I was best man at his wedding, he is my son Ivano's godfather and his wife Ilijana is my daughter Ema's godmother. We still spend our summer holidays together and our families are close. After my first season at Dinamo, I invited Cindrić to Zadar to spend the summer with my friends and I. He relaxed and had a great time, while I tried to be a little bit more active. I jogged, played football and basketball, went swimming. I didn't go out that much, though, as I wanted to get stronger and get ready. I knew what was waiting for me at Dinamo.

During the second season, I played for the under-17s and our coach was Dinamo legend Stjepan Deverić. By this time, I had become used to the life in Zagreb; I'd finally got the hang of it. Physically, I still hadn't reached the level of other players, but I felt I was getting stronger. This was evident during matches, because I played well. My performances put me among the best in my generation. The fact that I, just like many other players, had a contract with Mamić Sports Agency didn't help my status. Some other players came before me, most likely because they were physically stronger and because they played for the national team. They simply received better treatment. Čale almost made the first team, but it never bothered me if someone was making progress. I was happy for him. What's more, I was used to fighting for myself and I knew nothing would come easy. I always proved my worth on the pitch, and I was convinced that this sent the strongest message.

I first met Zdravko Mamić at Pod Mirnim Krovom, where I was having lunch with my roommate Marko Čirjak. Mamić approached me and asked how I was doing at Dinamo; if I was happy with my status. 'As long as I play, I'm happy,' I replied. This, together with a couple of words of greeting, was the extent of our communication.

Speaking of status, I do have to mention something that happened during that season. It indicates why I think Deverić had a huge influence on my development. He used to criticise me a lot during matches, and I mostly accepted that he was correcting me. But one time, I thought he went too far and I reacted. After yet another heated complaint, I stared at him, spreading my arms as if to say, *Come on, leave me alone.* It's an understatement to say he lost it: he let me have it! 'What's that, kid?! Who do you think you are?' It was embarrassing, but it had an effect. I never reacted like that again. Deverić was fair to me and we had a good relationship. I knew he respected me as a player. We worked together again during a very important time – my first senior year at Zrinjski.

Meanwhile, the senior people at Dinamo decided to assemble a secondary youth team – Dinamo II. This was done on the initiative of Ilija Lončarević, a man of great expertise who was the director of football at the time. The team was made up of the most talented under-16 and under-18 players. I played alongside these guys during the spring session together with Čale, Ćorluka, Lončarić, Šarić, Glavina, Kardum and Mikulić. Romeo Jozak was our coach, and we had a special training programme. This was a good thing because it prepared the players for senior football. But, in the summer of 2003, I suddenly got an opportunity to go on loan to Zrinjski Mostar, who competed in the Bosnian Premier League.

The vice president of Zrinjski was Zdenko Džidić, who had excellent relations with Dinamo and had arranged that his son Ivica, Davor Landeka and Leonardo Barnjak would go on loan to Zrinjski. Ivo and Davor were my friends from Dinamo, and they suggested I come along with them. Dinamo accepted the idea, as did my father, and I agreed!

I didn't know what to expect. The Bosnian league had a reputation for being brutal, especially on young and physically weaker players. They said I wouldn't be able to play because the sharp opponents would eat me for breakfast. But I wasn't afraid. I felt the time had come to make a new step forward – my step into senior football.

Things soon got complicated – not for the first time in my career! I had already arrived in Mostar when Dinamo called me and said, 'There's been a change of plans; you're urgently needed back in Zagreb!' On the one hand, I was glad, because this meant I would go back to the newly formed Dinamo II and play alongside my friends. But, half an hour later, while I was still thinking about what had happened, they rang again: 'You're staying in Mostar after all!' It turned out to be a happy turn of events, especially when it came to my development as a player.

After 11 years of learning, I finally stepped into senior football. The earlier move from Zadar to Zagreb had proved a wise decision. I had made progress as a player, trained with better players, the conditions were excellent and the coaches very knowledgeable. Dinamo Football Academy is the best football school in Croatia, and I believe it to be one of the best in this part of Europe. Many top players came out of it during my time. Those two years in Zagreb made me independent and dedicated to becoming a professional.

The First Loan – Zrinjski

Mostar agreed with me from day one. I felt it right away. I found an apartment near the stadium at Bijeli Brijeg. Sure, I had to climb three, maybe four hundred steps between the apartment and the stadium every day, but I didn't mind. I lived with Davor Landeka, another one of my teammates who became a dear friend, as did Ivica Džidić, who was of immense help because Mostar was his hometown.

During the first training sessions, I saw in the eyes of the club's staff, as well as of the people in the stands, the question that had followed me throughout my career: 'How is this little skinny boy going to play here?!' By now, I had become immune to this, so the worried glances didn't trouble me. It's true, however, that this was the first time I had to compete at a senior level, and a very aggressive one at that. But I was ready. Our pre-season training camp took place in Kupres. I played in a couple of matches and made it clear I wasn't exactly a child like some thought. I couldn't wait for the real matches. I chose to wear the No. 23 shirt. It was available, and it was the number worn by two athletes I was very fond of at the time. The first was Michael Jordan, a fantastic player who had retired from basketball a couple of months before. The other was David Beckham, who had signed for Real Madrid that summer and taken the same number. Beckham was one of the footballers I appreciated both as a player and an athlete in general. I was already imagining myself wearing the shirt and playing in my first senior game, but the coach soon brought me back to reality.

After the final training session before the start of the championship, the coach read the names of the players for the first game against Borac Banja Luka. I waited for him to call out 'Modrić', but he didn't. I was unpleasantly surprised, to say the least. I felt like crying, that's how miserable I was. I wondered why I had come here in the first place. Good thing I kept quiet, because the coach soon approached me and explained the situation. 'Luka, just so you know, you're not on the list because the club hasn't registered you yet.' I felt relieved – it wasn't my performance, but the documents. As I have already said, all kinds of complications have followed me throughout my career!

I played the next match against Široki Brijeg, but I don't have fond memories. It was a convincing 3–0 loss. However, the next game, the first in front of the home fans, is lodged in my memory. Our opponent was Čelik Zenica and I played well. Around the 50th minute, I got muscle cramps and had to be replaced. But the fans saw me off by giving me a standing ovation. It was the beginning of an amazing relationship between me and the Zrinjski supporters, which would remain until the end of the season and my stay in Mostar. The results weren't great because we had a young and inexperienced team, and five weeks into the season we got a new coach, Stjepan Deverić, who had been coaching me at Dinamo Under-18s. Zrinjski finished 11th out of 16 clubs. However, the foundations had been laid for the team that would win a historic first championship title the following season. This great success was achieved in the club's centenary year. By then, I wasn't their player anymore, but I rejoiced like I was there. Their tremendous treatment meant that I was indebted. I gave them my best, and they recognised it. I received a lot of praise for my performances; the papers said I was among the best players in the league. Still, my favourite recognition was the Filip Šunjić – Pipa Award, given by the Zrinjski Ultras to the best player of the season. It was important for one more reason – it was the first individual trophy I won in senior football.

From a footballing perspective, the Bosnian Premier League allowed me to gain experience. The coaches played me as a right midfielder, but after Deverić arrived, he saw me more as a right winger and gave me more freedom. That allowed me to show my attacking skills. What I had heard about the league proved to be true. The Bosnian league was very rough – away matches in particular. The worst was Trebinje, and only slightly less so Banja Luka and Zenica. The referees didn't even try to protect the players of the away team. My shins and legs took a lot of beating! To illustrate, my favourite shin guards – the ones with Ronaldo's picture – which I had been looking after for years, got ruined in Trebinje. Some guy did a two-footed tackle on me and pierced a hole in the plastic shin guard with his metal studs! Thankfully, Ronaldo protected me from a severe injury.

Luckily, I didn't get hurt that season. I learned to get out of a duel quickly, to lose the opponent the moment I received the ball, and to make a quick pass. I was agile and it helped a lot. I had no problems with the stamina, and the only thing troubling me was muscle cramps. Sixty minutes into almost every match, my calves would cramp up. I wasn't worried. I assigned this to my young age and the adjustment to the strains of senior football. I took a lot of potassium, did my stretching exercises regularly, practised well and continued to work on my muscle strength.

The matches were well attended, especially derbies against Široki Brijeg, Sarajevo and Željezničar. The atmosphere would sometimes be really impressive, but ethnic tensions were also felt. I always liked the passionate atmosphere on the pitch, as well as in the stands, but back in those days, the Bosnian and Herzegovinian League could be rather tricky.

I wasn't afraid, though. The days in Mostar and Zrinjski were wonderful – we had a great, close-knit team, the fans loved me and the people were friendly. I enjoyed it. The demanding league made me stronger, and the aggression that verged on roughness forced me to make my game simpler, quicker and more intuitive. The best indicator of how I felt was my wish, which I expressed to the people at Dinamo, to spend another year on loan at Zrinjski. I was aware I wouldn't be given too many chances at Dinamo, so staying in Mostar and playing in the Bosnian League seemed like the best solution. However, Dinamo had other plans.

The Second Loan – Inter Zaprešić

In mid-June, 2004 – at the Blue Saloon of the Maksim Stadium, among display cases filled with trophies – three other young players and I signed professional contracts with Dinamo. It was my first professional contract and I was incredibly happy. This five-year deal proved that I had achieved my goal of becoming a professional footballer. Now I wanted to win trophies.

During the summer transfer window, Dinamo loaned me to Inter Zaprešić together with Čale, Ćorluka, Marko Janjetović and Teo Kardum. Inter put together an excellent team, a mix of experienced and young players who had good chemistry. We owed much to Srećko Bogdan, our coach, who had once played for Dinamo and German side Karlsruher. But the beginning wasn't all that great. The coach was blowing hot and cold: I'd play in one match, then be benched in another – and things went on like this until the pre-season tournament in Slovenia. I played in the first match against Varteks and I wasn't good. For the next match, against Olimpija Ljubljana, I was supposed to start on the bench, but one player got injured, so the coach decided to put me in the first team. I played well and scored a goal, which meant I had practically secured my place in the starting line-up. But once again, I heard that unforgettable sentence – this time from one of the coaches, no less: 'How is he going to play . . . ?' At a tournament in Vinjani, I put in an excellent performance – scoring a goal in a 4-1 win against Zadar, my former club, in the final and being named as the Player of the Tournament. Just before the start of the league season, the coach told me, 'Luka, relax and don't worry about your status. You'll get 10 matches to prove your worth!'

Bogdan kept his word; he had a lot of faith in me. It means a lot to a young player – especially in terms of confidence – to feel he has his coach's backing. I played all 18 matches of the autumn season as a midfielder or attacking midfielder, mostly on the left side, and I scored four goals. My opening goal in the Croatian First League came against Varteks in the eighth game of the season, just nine days after my 19th birthday. I was happy because it gave us a 3-2 win, as we recovered from our first loss of the season a week before. We opened the championship in a fury, winning the first six matches of the season, and we were soon sitting at the top of the table. We were a hit, and kept first place until matchday 15, but in the following games before the winter break we ran out of steam and finished the first part of the season in fourth. Dinamo decided to bring me back from my loan during the season break, but, in the spring championship play-off, Inter battled Hajduk for the title until the last match. Unfortunately, they lost. I still regret that I wasn't able to participate in their title-chasing campaign.

The key reason for my return to Zagreb was the conflict between Dinamo and Niko Kranjčar. Niko was Dinamo's captain, and their biggest talent, and all the fans loved him. He was the subject of many heated debates, especially when, having fallen out with the club, he transferred to the ranks of Hajduk, Dinamo's biggest rival. As fate would have it, many unexpected things happened during that season. Niko immediately won the championship title with Hajduk, and Dinamo had their worst season in the history of the Croatian Football League. It was a humiliation. But they learned a lot from it. In the next 14 seasons, Dinamo won 13 championship titles! While The Blues grew steadily to become untouchable champions, Hajduk struggled, and has now not tasted league success in 15 years.

I was part of the Dinamo team during this saddest spring. Kranjčar's transfer left a void in attacking midfield, and the management decided I should fill it. On the one hand, I was sad to leave Inter Zaprešić – coach Bogdan has always said Inter would have won a historic first title with me on his team. I don't know what would have happened, but seeing how we played in the first part of the season, I'm sure it wasn't far from the truth. It would've been a fantastic success for a small team from the suburbs of Zagreb. On the other hand, I was happy I had returned to Maksimir. Dinamo is always Dinamo. However, during Dinamo's worst half-season, I played one of the poorest spells in my senior career.

I played just one out of four matches of the final round of the regular championship. We beat Kamen Ingrad to secure our place in the league, but a relegation play-off was perhaps the most painful period of my career. The management decided they needed a change at the helm, so now we were led by Zvjezdan Cvjetković, who replaced Ilija Lončarević. The atmosphere in the team was horrible; training sessions lacked structure. Matches were particularly excruciating because the fans made fun of us. And on top of everything else, I got injured. My foot was damaged and I was out for more than a month. I missed four matches, and in the following three games came on as a substitute. We played the last game of the season at Maksimir against Zadar. It was a suitable ending for a very difficult period: the match was abandoned in the 62nd minute, with Dinamo leading 7-0. Zadar had less than seven players on the field because of four red cards and injuries, and the rules said the game couldn't go on. It was the end of a season of great contrasts – a fantastic start and a dreadful end. But, as the 2004/2005 campaign saw its share of tears and joy, this period also brought the greatest happiness into my life: I met the woman of my dreams.

And Love Came Calling

Many picked up on one detail from the time I played at Inter Zaprešić – my short hair! Everyone knows I have always preferred to have long hair. At the time, though, I was serving my one year of mandatory military service, as part of the sports battalion, and had to have my hair cut. And that's when love came knocking on my door.

During my days in Zadar and Zagreb, I had a couple of crushes and short relationships, but my dedication to football and lack of interest in partying reduced my chances of meeting a girl who would make me think, *She's different from all the others!* I was still young and it didn't bother me much. I believed that it would happen sooner or later – and when it did, that I would feel it immediately. It happened sooner than I thought!

I first noticed this girl at Maxi Pub, on the south side of the Maksimir Stadium. Later, when I had returned from Mostar, I saw her a couple of times in passing. Čale and Ćorluka told me she worked at Mamić Sports Agency. As I seldom went there, I didn't remember her. Maybe we talked on the phone once or twice when they called me if they needed something? Who knows. In the summer of 2004, I realised I was intrigued. I was too shy to even think of introducing myself – I only knew her name was Vanja. I also learned she was five years older, though her looks didn't show it. She looked young, beautiful, and yes, I had an impression she was different from all the others. I just sensed it . . .

When the season at Inter Zaprešić started, I was preoccupied with football – training, matches, struggle, the slight euphoria on account of our string of victories. At the time, I needed to find a new apartment because I'd decided to live on my own. My agency was supposed to look into this. In August, I was selected to play for the under-21 national team that was now managed by Slaven Bilić, one of the people who would become an important factor in my career. I remember we gathered at Terme Tuhelj and the weather was sweltering. I felt sick that morning; I must've picked up stomach flu. While I was resting in my hotel room, the phone rang. It was Vanja. She was calling from the agency to arrange to see a couple of apartments they had selected for me. I was excited that she had called, but I didn't feel well. I asked her to call me back in the evening, around 8 p.m. She agreed. From that moment on, I just couldn't stop thinking about her. I knew this was my chance and I shouldn't miss it. Luckily, as the day wore on, my stomach problems eased.

I couldn't wait for 8 p.m., and I was very excited when she phoned. Of course, I hid it. She introduced herself, we exchanged a couple of comments and I told her I had seen her in passing. Then she said something about the apartments that were available for rent and that I should see them when I came back. Had this been the main topic, the conversation would've been short. So, I tried to ask more questions and open new subjects, just to keep her on the line a while longer. We talked about all kinds of things – about her job, about my teammates, about Dinamo and their season, about how I was doing at Inter Zaprešić, the youth team, how my life was in Zagreb. I felt she relaxed, and so it happened that our first direct contact lasted for over three hours! I can only imagine what it must've been like for Mario Grgurović, my roommate in Tuhelj, but I was thrilled – both with the way we communicated, as if we had known each other for a long time, and with Vanja herself. I liked her energy and her attitude. Finally, we agreed to meet when I came back to Zagreb. Of course, this was to find an apartment, but just the very idea of meeting her was . . . wow!

Deep inside, I hoped that the fact we had talked for three hours meant something. I sensed this could be serious.

We soon met, after a couple more phone calls, to see some apartments. Up close and in person, Vanja seemed as I had imagined her: beautiful and simple, funny and completely natural. She swept me off my feet — there is no better expression to describe it. We saw a couple of apartments and once again I picked a place at Ravnice, where I had stayed when I first arrived in Zagreb. More importantly, it was close to her apartment, just a couple of hundred yards away.

Back then, I didn't have a car or a driving licence, so of course I asked Vanja to help me move. She said, 'No problem' and showed up in front of my building at the arranged time in a big car. I came down with two bags in my hands. She asked if I needed help with the rest of my luggage.

'I don't have anything else, these two bags are everything I own,' I said, as if this was something completely normal. She was surprised.

'Are you really this modest? If I'd known this was it, I wouldn't have taken the big car. I thought you'd need it for your stuff.'

We laughed at this. I didn't care about material things — I lived in rented apartments and kept only what was necessary. I mostly ate outside, and as far as clothes were concerned I wasn't picky. I wasn't one of those who needed to have new clothes all the time. All I needed fitted into those two bags.

The drive to my new apartment took less than a minute. I invited her up to have a cup of coffee to thank her. Time simply flew by with her — and there was never enough of it. We met a couple more times for coffee. Sometimes I would stop by her place, as I lived nearby. We were friends who liked to spend time together and talk about life. Vanja told me she grew up in different, better circumstances than me, but even so, things were far from easy. Especially emotionally. She was born in Varaždin. Her mother, Vesna Juraić, had a complicated pregnancy and stayed at the local hospital for three months. Vanja grew up in Kutina, a town some 80 kilometres from Zagreb, where her father,

Milan Bosnić, played basketball and ran a restaurant. Her mother Vesna has a business degree. Vanja's grandfather on her mother's side, Milan Juraić, was a respected businessman and he was the head of Petrokemija Chemical Company. She grew up in a well-off family. She told me her family often travelled: they took summer and winter vacations, and even went to the Winter Olympics in Sarajevo back in 1984. When she was 11, this idyllic life ended abruptly. Her parents divorced and her mother decided to move to Zagreb and take Vanja with her. Her grandfather Milan and grandmother Dobrila already lived there. They had an apartment in Ravnice, where Vanja and her mum stayed until they found a place of their own. During the first six months, Vanja's mother commuted every day to Kutina, where she taught at a high school. Then she got a job in Zagreb and decided to rent her own place, also in Ravnice. She had a hard time making ends meet, but Vanja's grandparents helped. At first, Vanja felt the burden of the big change and couldn't stop thinking about what had happened, but she gradually understood that her family would never be together again, and she missed her father a lot.

That's It

Vanja's mother has two sisters, Jasna and Helena. Vanja has two cousins, Maks and Eva. Her aunts showered her with care and attention in an effort to fill the void left by her parents' divorce. Jasna is an architect and lives in Zagreb, while Helena is a designer and is the same age as Vanja, so they grew up together and are more like sisters.

At 12 years old, Vanja had to take on many responsibilities to help her mother. While other girls her age played and enjoyed their carefree childhood, she learned to cook, clean the apartment, and do the washing and ironing. In a couple of years, Vanja's mother saved up a little money and sold some of the family property to buy an apartment in Ravnice. By the time her mother got a job at Dinamo, Vanja was already in high school. Her mum worked at Dinamo for 14 years. As everyone in her family received a college education, it was only natural that Vanja would too. She chose a business school, and was a good student. One day, when she was 21, her mother surprised her: she had bought her a small apartment, two blocks from their home, and told her, 'Vanja, here are the keys, so now you have your own place. It's close to my apartment in case you need anything. But I want you to become independent and learn to look after yourself.'

This was a completely new situation, but Vanja knew her mother was doing this for her own good. She had no contact with her father, and she had to learn what it meant to live on her own and to stand on her own two feet. It made her tougher. She looked after herself, studied and in the meantime got a job. When one of the employees at Mamić Sports Agency went on maternity leave, Vanja replaced her. For two years she did administrative work for the players who had contracts with the agency and, of course, that is how we met.

Her story only added to my feelings for her. She was wonderful! The early years of her childhood were everything one could wish for, but when her family fell apart she needed to grow up quickly and take responsibility for herself. When I later got to know her mother, I realised what a wonderful woman she was too. It was more than clear why, despite all the financial and emotional troubles and obstacles that a single mother faces when raising a child, Vanja grew up to be such a down-to-earth person.

I was touched by her sadness when she talked about her father. When she was 13, she broke off all contact with him because she realised, painfully, he didn't love her back. The silence lasted for 10 long years. For me, it was difficult to understand such a relationship. Despite all the dreadful things that happened in my childhood, my family remained close and deeply connected. The emotional stories of our childhoods were completely different, but through our long conversations we quickly learned we had a similar view on many things; of what matters in life, and of what family means.

I was already very much in love when I first suggested we went out. It was 1 December, 2004, and it was our day. On that evening, at her apartment, we kissed for the first time. I can't say if I had ever felt so happy. I thought those butterflies in your stomach were just an empty phrase, but on that night, that's how I felt. I fell head over heels for her.

We were a couple! In the beginning, we agreed to keep our relationship a secret. We didn't want others to talk about it, and we didn't want it to end up in the media, as they were showing more and more interest in me. But it wasn't that simple. I had a hard time hiding my emotions from my friends Čale and Ćorluka. When the story broke, the two of them were the ones who were approached by many people asking about us. I was glowing with happiness; dating a girl who was sincere and sensitive, modest and gentle. She wasn't impressed by my professional contract with Dinamo. She didn't care that I owned almost nothing. She never once mentioned the fact that she had a business degree, while I had only an evening school diploma. I wanted to tell everyone I was happy to be in love with such a fantastic person. I wanted to share my happiness because she loved me for being Luka, and not someone who played for Dinamo. No one and nothing could tell me otherwise: that was it. Two months after we started dating, I knew I wanted to spend the rest of my life with her – and I told her that.

I was spending a lot of time at her place. We enjoyed each other's company, our conversations, watching films, alone and relaxed. One day, someone broke into my apartment – in the middle of the day they just walked in and stole my things. None of it was particularly important, except for a gold chain that was dear to me. However, I didn't feel comfortable anymore. About a month later, Vanja told me, 'Luka, you're spending more time here than at your place anyway, why don't you move in?'

She didn't have to ask me twice! I cancelled the contract on my apartment and moved in with her. Six months into our relationship, we were living together! From that day, when I was nothing more than a talented player, she entirely dedicated herself to our family and me. The strength of her character and the importance for me of this unique woman shows in everything that has followed. Had she not entered my life when I was just 19, I wouldn't have accomplished any of the things that today make us so proud and happy.

The Return of the Champion

After a dreadful spring with Dinamo, I needed to distance myself from everything. I had just gone through a turbulent season, filled with ups and downs, at two different clubs, and the only bright moment was the beginning of my new life with Vanja.

Dinamo went through a change too, as Josip Kuže was made the new head coach. A new squad was being assembled and I thought it was most important to win a place in the first team. By this point, before the pre-season, the papers were saying that the new Dinamo would be built around me. I also got my favourite No. 10 shirt. This symbolic act happened on 16 July, 2005, when Edin Mujčin played his final match and said his goodbye to Dinamo. We played the last pre-season match against Željezničar Sarajevo. Edin, an excellent player, came off in the 10th minute. When I replaced him, he gave me his No. 10 shirt and wished me all the best in my career.

We had a great start to the championship and by matchday 11, we had a four-point lead over our rivals. But then came October and a real debacle, as fourth-tier Naftaš Ivanić eliminated us from the Croatian Cup. This came as a huge shock, but it also reminded us we needed to stay humble. After that, we dominated the championship, played well and deservedly won the league. The fans came back to the stadium; there could be 20,000-30,000 people in the stands. After such a depressing spring, the atmosphere was now sensational. The terrible events of the previous season disappeared during these six months. It was wonderful to play football in front of great and supportive crowds.

There's nothing more a player could wish for. This is what gives you energy, what motivates you to jump over all obstacles, to sacrifice yourself in training every day. You do all this to make a match a special celebration of football. And that happens only when both the players and the crowd feel the same joy.

We had an excellent team and a great coach. Josip Kuže was a real character. A former player, a lawyer by education, he had a peculiar way of communicating. His comments were always hilarious! He was funny, but also wise when it came to creating a good working atmosphere. As a coach, he was studious and innovative – he didn't want us just to rely on our talent, even though the team had many individuals blessed with that. He insisted we repeat actions and movements until they became automatic. Kuže was a coach who knew how to lay out diverse attacking options. There aren't many like him. Under his command, I made a significant step forward, both in my game and my approach. During this successful season, I also made my debut for the senior national team. I remember our first training session after I came back from Basel, where we beat Argentina and Messi 3–2.

'Well done, Luka, bravo. But now you have to work even harder and invest even more energy. People are going to look at you differently now that you've played for the national team.'

I took Kuže's advice and worked hard because now more was at stake. I didn't lose my focus, despite that fantastic experience of playing for the national team. He made it clear – subtly and at the right moment – that higher expectations also meant more criticism. Kuže was true to himself. You could talk to him, express your position, tell him your wish.

And so, riding on the wave of a winning atmosphere, I asked him, on Čale's and Ćorluka's behalf: 'Boss, we'd like to go out. We're working and playing well, I think we deserve to relax. We're young, you know how it goes.'

He replied with a characteristic calm, 'Sure, boys, but make sure to be back by midnight.'

As often happens when you feel your parent, boss or some other authority is kind and open to you, you try to take advantage of it.

'Boss, how about a little longer? Young people don't go out before . . .'

I didn't have time to finish my sentence. With a raised voice, he cut me short: 'Are you negotiating with me? I said, by midnight!'

Kuže's message was clear: there's always a boundary you mustn't cross, regardless of how good the result, performance or relationship.

We made up for this when we celebrated the title. It was amazing, especially for younger players such as me. We played on 13 May, a special day for all Dinamo supporters, especially their most-committed fans or Ultras, the Bad Blue Boys. Back in 1990, on this date, there were riots before the match against Red Star Belgrade, and the game never took place. I was four and a half when this happened and, just like every young person, I didn't understand how important these events were. Not only for Dinamo and their supporters but for Croatia as a whole. For many people the day when the Bad Blue Boys bravely and proudly stood up against the rampaging Red Star fans symbolically marks the beginning of Serbian aggression against Croatia. Many Dinamo supporters gave their lives defending our country's independence during the war. Every year on 13 May people gather around the monument built in their honour at Maksimir to commemorate their sacrifice.

The day is also remembered by the then Dinamo captain, Zvonimir Boban. While trying to protect the supporters from the police, he took a beating but fought back and kicked a police officer. His teammate Vjekoslav Škrinjar was also clubbed. The Dinamo coach at the time also tried to protect the players and the fans on the pitch. It was Josip Kuže who, 16 years later, would lead us through one of the most successful seasons in recent Dinamo history. For me, 13 May, 2006, was one of the happiest moments during the three and a half seasons at Dinamo. On that day, everything was perfect!

After being humiliated in the previous championship campaign, we had won the title, and the season was concluded with the biggest

Croatian derby, against Hajduk Split. I loved the heated atmosphere of the derbies. We had played at Poljud in February, and I had scored a winning goal. In this final match of the season, I scored again, in the 11th minute, and celebrated the title for Dinamo. It was the highlight of an excellent season on a personal level too. Dinamo dominated the league with outstanding ease. We finished 11 points ahead of Rijeka and a remarkable 36 points ahead of Hajduk.

We celebrated together with 30,000-odd fans at our stadium. The open-top bus parade through the city was sensational – masses of people cheered us on as we made progress towards the main square. The place was on fire. We all needed it after the previous season's debacle. This was the first time I took part in such a celebration and the next day I wondered if I would ever experience something like that again. Little did I know this was just the beginning.

CHAPTER FIVE

2006 was a special year because it also marked the start of my career in the senior national team. It would take two books just to tell that story! Every match for Croatia is special. It's hard to put this vast collection of unique emotions and memories into a couple of chapters. So I will mention just the most special moments from this fantastic journey, culminating in the 2018 FIFA World Cup in Russia.

2006 was the year of the World Cup in Germany, and there had been a lot of media speculation about whether Zlatko Kranjčar should include me in the national squad. A friendly match against Argentina in Basel was scheduled for March. Before the team was announced, the better-informed reporters were sure that Kranjčar would name me. When the official call-up came to Dinamo, I was beside myself with happiness. My heart was threatening to explode! My dream was coming true. What I had been fantasising about ever since I had watched Croatia win the bronze medal in France back in 1998 was actually happening. Vanja was there to take part in my happiness. As she took me to the meeting place at the Hotel Sheraton, she saw my boyish excitement.

The players welcomed me as if I had always been part of the team. My dear friend Marijan Buljat, the team's joker Darijo Srna and the kind-hearted Marko Babić made the transition to the 'big boys' club' easy. I particularly appreciated Niko Kranjčar's support. Many people tried to create conflict between us, especially after he transferred to Hajduk and I returned to Dinamo, playing in a position similar to his. There was talk that Dinamo favoured him over me and that his leaving came as a godsend for my career. None of it was true. People said the same about the national squad. They said he played in the first team because his father was the manager and that I wasn't given enough space because of him. As time went by, our playing days for the national team and Tottenham clearly demonstrated that these stories were far from true. As far as I'm concerned, Niko Kranjčar was the best player at Dinamo before his transfer to Hajduk, and what earned him a place in the national team was his class. Ever since he stayed at our modest apartment at the Hotel Kolovare, we have had a good relationship and nothing but respect for each other.

In Basel, my excitement quickly mounted. At the team meeting before the pre-tournament World Cup warm-up match, the coach told me I would play in the starting line-up! Robert Kovač was injured, so they moved Igor Tudor to centre-back and I got my place in midfield. I couldn't wait to call my family. Two hours before the game, I rang Vanja, who was pleasantly shocked.

But then, surprise! There was a problem. The skin on my heel became inflamed. To avoid pain and minimise the pressure on the affected spot, I made a hole in my boot. I covered the injury with some white tape and debuted for the national team with a hole in my boot!

Argentina had some spectacular players: Messi, Riquelme, Tévez, Crespo. I wasn't afraid, though; it only made my adrenaline flow faster. I enjoyed the game. The coach told me to make myself available to other players as much as I could, to pass safely, and not to lose the ball. I went off a minute before the end of the match, and he congratulated me on a good performance. The winning 3-2 result only added to the special impression the evening left on me. Besides my debut, I remember the match because of Lionel Messi. He scored his first goal for Argentina, but his speed and fantastic control impressed me even more. He was agile, able to change direction suddenly, and it was obvious he would become a star player.

Just 100 days later, at the World Cup in Germany, I felt ready. We opened the tournament in Berlin against Brazil. It was so exciting to see

Ronaldo, Kaká, Ronaldinho, Roberto Carlos, Cafú, Dida and all the other stars up close. The atmosphere at the Olympic Stadium was phenomenal. Our supporters from all over the world, my whole family among them, cheered us on and hushed the Brazilian fans. I remember the moment the Croatian national anthem was played and all of our supporters sang along. I still get goosebumps. Unfortunately, Kaká scored and we lost 1–0. I didn't get a chance to play. In the end, I wanted to swap shirts with Ronaldo, but I only got his shirt later, in the dressing room. Ronaldo was my favourite player and I was glad to get his shirt – it was so cool. But then Stjepan Tomas asked me to give it to him because he had promised it to his brother Boris. I knew Boris from Zrinjski and I realised how much it meant to him, so I gave Stjepan the shirt while he gave me Kaká's.

For me, the World Cup is the pinnacle of every player's career. I was disappointed, though, because I didn't play much – almost 30 minutes altogether. I was on form, and I'm still convinced I should have played more. In the second group game against Japan, I was warming up in the terrible heat and overheated, though I got to come on for the last minutes. Disappointingly, we drew 0–0, which would cost us in our attempts to qualify for the knockout stage of the tournament. Now it was imperative that we beat the powerful Australian side in the last match. I remember the fans calling out my name at 2–2, demanding I get on the field. I did, in the 74th minute, but the result didn't change, and we were going home. I was disappointed by the outcome, but one great experience richer. I wasn't angry – I was thankful to Zlatko Kranjčar. He had included me in the national team and allowed me to play on football's greatest stage.

Ups and Downs at Dinamo

Before the 2005/2006 season and our championship run, I didn't have much contact with Zdravko Mamić, who had in the meantime become one of the most important people at Dinamo Zagreb. After my good performances for Kuže's team, I felt his attitude towards me change; he paid much more attention to me. He often came to watch our training sessions and once, when we were practising on the main field at Maksimir, before our match against Međimurje, he reproached me because of my poor heading abilities. Half-joking, he offered me a bet: 'Five grand you'll never score a header!'

I accepted the challenge. In the fourth minute against Međimurje, I scored for a 1–0 lead. A header, no less! My teammates knew of the bet, and when I scored they joined me in celebration, opening their fists and displaying five fingers to the box where Mamić was sitting. Soon after, when we were going on one of the away games, he came over to me on the bus and, his face all serious, gave me an envelope with €5,000. He told me, 'You'll get the same for every header you score by the end of the season.'

Unfortunately, I never scored another header that season!

My improved status at Dinamo Zagreb also secured me a better contract. When I had gone on loan to Inter Zaprešić, I had been making €12,000 a year. During the next three seasons at Dinamo, we won three championships, two cups and one super cup, and my contract was improved on three occasions. It was the club's way of showing they appreciated the progress I was making. For my part, by accepting a 10-year contract without a second thought, I also showed how content I was with Dinamo and their project.

During the second season, we wanted to continue our domination in the Croatian National League, but we were also ambitious to achieve a good result in European competition. In the summer of 2006, the UEFA Champions League qualifying round draw didn't go in our favour: we drew Arsenal. We put up a good fight, but they were stronger, and it was they who qualified for the Champions League. We sought to continue our European season in the UEFA Cup against Auxerre, but we lost both matches. Those were difficult moments because the early ending of the European campaign meant that the management lost faith in our coach Josip Kuže. The relationship had already been fractured by our elimination from the Croatian Cup to a low-tier opponent. We were not playing as well as in the past season. Our form was up and down; I don't know why, because in training and on the pitch we did the same as in the previous season. As so often happens, the coach was the first to take the heat. On matchday 13, an unexpected defeat to HNK Šibenik proved to be Kuže's last match on the Dinamo bench. The coach who had led us through a phenomenal season only a year before was now sacked. I felt bad for him because we had a great relationship. In almost 18 months of working together, he helped me take some significant steps in my career.

Kuže was replaced by Branko Ivanković, who soon stabilised the team and improved our form. We defended the league title in style, finishing 20 points ahead of Hajduk. We also won the cup and now we shifted our focus to Europe and the Champions League. Ivanković created a good atmosphere before our crucial qualifying match against Werder Bremen. He had great faith in the team's potential. We were full of confidence, and it showed in the first match in Bremen. We played well and even took the lead following Boško Balaban's goal, but, unfortunately, Werder won 2–1. We missed our chance to secure a big advantage in the first leg, but we were still convinced we could eliminate the Germans in the home leg and finally qualify for the Champions League. Their best player was Diego, a well-known Brazilian international, yet our coach Ivanković didn't hesitate to say I was a much better player. This provoked different reactions in the media, though Ivanković wasn't the first coach to make clear that he had great faith in my abilities. Even before, in the under-21 national team, the head coach, Slaven Bilić, had treated me as the team's leader. During the UEFA European Under-21 Championship qualifier against Sweden, two days before my 19th birthday, he called me over. When I approached him, he put his arm around my shoulder and briefly said, 'Luka, from now on, you're the captain!'

I was glad, of course I was, but I tried to remain calm. I knew Bilić rated me highly, which he showed by making a very generous comparison. These were the days when the great Andrés Iniesta was in the spotlight at Barcelona.

'Luka, look, Iniesta is a tremendous player. But you have to understand, you've got just as much potential as him. I'm sure you can play at the same level.'

Bilić and his assistant coach Aljoša Asanović were part of the Croatia team that won bronze at the 1998 FIFA World Cup in France. For us, they were legends – pure and simple. We absorbed their knowledge, listened to their advice and trusted them, because they were always ready to help us with whatever we needed. They had charisma and they filled our young squad with positive energy. One detail from the qualifier against Sweden paints the picture: we had some time off to go for a walk and Čale, Grgurović and I were strolling around the centre of this small town where we were staying when we ran into Bilić and his associates. He tossed in something along the lines of, 'What's up, you're out for a walk, huh?!' And when we laughed, he put his hand in his pocket and took out his wallet. He gave us each some pocket money. 'For shopping,' he said, patted our backs, and left. We were 19 years old, he was our idol and our boss, and he surprised us with this gesture. It wasn't the money, of course it wasn't; it was his approach. During the next eight years, I had an excellent relationship with Bilić and his team. His advice on many matters was golden.

Back at Dinamo, Branko Ivanković prepared us wonderfully for the return match against Werder. We were psyched. There were more than 35,000 supporters in the stands. Still, the visitors won 3–2 and our Champions League dreams were shattered. We didn't allow ourselves to sink like the previous season, though. After we drew Ajax in the UEFA Cup play-off, we put our heads together and gave everything we had to prove our worth. The odds were on the side of the Amsterdam greats – they had an excellent team with Stam, Huntelaar, Emanuelson, Suárez and Dennis Rommedahl, and they took the advantage from the first leg in Zagreb. They beat us 1–0 in front of 30,000 fans and everyone thought we were more or less done for. The return match was played in the Amsterdam Arena in front of 45,000 noisy fans. We soon hushed them and brought smiles to our supporters' faces. Thirty-four minutes into the match, after a foul on Mandžukić, I was selected to take the penalty kick. The ball ended in the net and the goal secured the lead, later taking us to extra time. We were confident we would win because we played well and displayed great courage – especially Mandžukić, who crushed every Ajax hope with two goals in the first six minutes of extra time. They were done for; there was no chance they would score three goals. What a phenomenal night, for all of us. For the first time, we felt we had enough talent to compete against top European clubs. Upon our return to Zagreb, at the airport we were given a heroes' welcome. There was music, singing – we were happy. No one expected Zdravko Mamić to put on a show by tearing up his shirt and stripping to his briefs! We knew he was exuberant in his celebrations, but this crossed the line of good taste. After such a great victory, he cast a shadow on both the team and the coach. All of the newspapers wrote only about this incident.

In the group stage, we played against four opponents in a single round-robin format, meeting two of them at home and two away. We drew against Basel and Rennes, and lost to Hamburg and Brann. Once again, after 37 years of waiting, Dinamo failed to achieve their goal to stay in the European competition until the spring.

The Blazing Renaissance

Croatia's sensational UEFA Euro 2008 qualification campaign took place in parallel with our triumphs at Dinamo. After the World Cup in Germany, the public demanded a change at the national team's helm and the introduction of younger players. Slaven Bilić, the former under-21 coach, was appointed the senior team head coach. For his very first match in Livorno against Italy, the reigning World Champions, he promoted several fresh faces. He played Eduardo da Silva and me in the starting line-up, while Ćorluka came on later in the match. We had a good game, a 2–0 victory; I scored a goal, as did Eduardo. Croatia opened the qualifications for Euro 2008 in style. We drew in Moscow against Russia, although we were closer to securing victory. In October, we secured a 7–0 win against Andorra. Then, four days later in Zagreb, we beat England for the first time in Croatia's history! The atmosphere at Maksimir Stadium was incredible. The stands were packed with 38,000 people. The England team were awe-inspiring: Lampard, Rooney, Terry, Ferdinand, Cole, Neville, Carrick, Crouch. Yet we were ready. Bilić, a great aficionado of English football, convinced us we could win. We played a 4-4-2 formation: Pletikosa in goal, Ćorluka, Robert Kovač, Šimić, Šimunić in the defence, Niko Kovač and I in the middle, Rapaić and Kranjčar on the wings, Petrić and Eduardo up front. I will never forget the match. We were taking the game to England, and it showed. The crowd carried us on. In the second half, our better performance was crowned by Eduardo's phenomenal goal. Eight minutes later, in the 69th minute, England scored an unfortunate own goal. Gary Neville wanted to return the ball to his goalkeeper Paul Robinson, but just as Robinson was about to whack it clear, the ball bobbled along the surface and rolled into the goal! The win was one of the greatest victories for the Croatia national team.

In the last match of the year, Eduardo scored a hat-trick while Srna added one more for a 4–3 win over Israel. This was a decisive push towards Euro 2008, but by then everything about the Blazing Ones, as we were now called, was euphoric. Bilić was the most popular person in the country, and the players noticed that the media were treating him as the future president! The whole country was in a trance. We brought the matches in the group to a routine and successful end. Paradoxically, our only defeat, in Macedonia, stamped our passports for the Euros. That was the second-to-last match of the qualifications, and at half time, as we were washing the mud from our jerseys because the pitch was a real bog, we learned that Russia had lost in Israel. We had qualified! We had a brief and noisy celebration in the dressing room, probably feeling relieved more than anything else. On the muddy pitch, in the cold weather, the more motivated Macedonians scored twice and took a deserved victory. In the end, everyone was happy – both them and us.

We flew from Skopje to London. Four days later, at the legendary Wembley, we were supposed to play for prestige and for pleasure. Back in Skopje, after the Macedonia defeat, I told Bilić: 'We managed to play here in this mud. Once we walk out onto the perfect turf of Wembley, we'll fly across the pitch and smash the English to pieces!'

For England, it was a decisive match: they needed one point to qualify for the Euros, ahead of Russia. We were confident and motivated to show ourselves in our true light at such a prestigious stadium, against the strong England team. Almost everyone believed that England would beat us, and absolutely everyone was convinced they wouldn't miss out on the one point needed to send them to the Euros. They had Gerrard for this match, and in the second half they also brought Beckham on; the two of them hadn't played in Zagreb. On our side, Srna came in instead of Rapaić, while Olić took the place of Petrić', who remained on the bench.

There were about 90,000 people at the stadium; the atmosphere was majestic. Wembley is a miracle – it's formidable and inspiring. In the north stand, just by the pitch, our fans cheered their hearts out. Fourteen minutes into the match, Kranjčar and Olić had given us a 2–0 lead, and England were shocked. We were flying. We dominated the first half, but at half time they came out with more determination. Beckham and Defoe, who would soon become my dear teammate at Tottenham, came on. The two of them brought the home side back to life. We gave away a penalty after a challenge on Defoe, which Lampard put away with confidence. In the 65th minute, Beckham crossed the ball to Crouch to score from a header and make it 2–2. To our two goals scored within seven minutes

England had replied with two goals within nine. There were 25 minutes to the final whistle. A draw would have meant both teams were going to Austria and Switzerland for the Finals, while the Russians stayed at home. In the 69th minute, Bilić brought on Petrić to replace Eduardo and eight minutes later, following Pranjić's brilliant solo run, Petrić took a shot from around 20 yards from goal, and fired the ball into the net! Croatia won, securing one of the greatest victories in our history. But the biggest winner was Russia, who now qualified for the European Championship. This game, I would learn later, was very important for my soon-to-be international transfer.

One thing stuck with me from that evening: the unique English spirit. They lost the game and failed to qualify, and I am sure they were devastated. However, they congratulated us, and took the burden of all the criticism and disappointment that soon rained down on them with dignity. There were other big teams and well-known players who never offered their hand in similar situations. The English approach to football is unique. After Euro 2008, I would take pleasure in it for the next four years. With one exception.

The 2010 FIFA World Cup qualifying draw offered England an opportunity for a rematch. And they were brutal. Under Fabio Capello, and the day after my 23rd birthday, they wiped the floor with us, 4–1 in the middle of Zagreb. It was Croatia's first competitive home loss in our history! They were even more merciless when we played in England: Lampard and Gerrard each scored two, while Rooney added one more for a devastating 5–1 win on my 24th birthday. I was unable to play because a day before the international break, when we gathered in Croatia to prepare for the matches against Belarus and England, I fractured my right fibula and was out for three months. It meant I couldn't play at Wembley. But I could see England were motivated to set the record straight. This time, fate turned her back on us. England won all of their matches in our qualifying group except for the second-to-last in Ukraine. That win, together with the routine victory against Andorra, meant that the Ukrainians were one point ahead of us and qualified for the play-off. For the first time in its short history, Croatia missed out on the World Cup.

The European Siren Song

During the 2006/2007 season, several players playing for Dinamo and the national team drew the attention of European clubs. I sensed I was on their radar too. There was all kinds of speculation in the press – among others that Bayern Munich had their eye on me – but that was just guesswork. I didn't think about it myself, because I wasn't keen on moving abroad. I was 21, but I was also experienced enough to know that patience is an essential element of steady development. I felt comfortable at Dinamo and after another successful season, I knew we had a new chance to do something in Europe. Dinamo announced they would put together an even stronger team, and the management claimed they wouldn't sell any of the important first-team players. The club honoured me by making me the captain and I started the 2006/2007 pre-season with the desire to make a good impression in Europe.

Qualifying for the Champions League and finally seeing the European spring were our goals, and I was convinced we would make all of that happen. However, things started to change during the pre-season camp in Kapfenberg. We learned that Eduardo had transferred to Arsenal. One of our most important players, and a goalscorer who had put in some brilliant performances for the club and the national team, Eduardo left us in the summer of 2007. It was a clear message that the stories about building a great team were just that – stories. That bothered me; I complained to the club's management. After Eduardo had left our Austrian base, Zdravko Mamić walked into my room. He told me, 'Luka, I've got a great offer from Shakhtar Donetsk. Do you want to go?'

'No!' I replied, and my tone made it clear that I wasn't interested in further discussions on the topic. The Shakhtar offer was substantial – I think they offered €20 million – but money wasn't the biggest factor when it came to my decision to transfer abroad. I respected Shakhtar, but when I thought about moving abroad, my wishes were different. The possibility ended here. My teammates heard that the club might transfer me too, but I told them I was staying.

Dinamo did sign new players: Mario Mandžukić transferred from Zagreb, and a month later Boško Balaban came back from Belgium. But just as we had made our peace with Eduardo's departure, we received another blow – Dinamo sold Vedran Ćorluka to Manchester City. This came as another shock because Charlie and I (Charlie was our nickname for Ćorluka) were practically inseparable. I felt bitter, because, on the one hand, Dinamo had publicly declared their high ambitions for the season – a factor in my wanting to stay and to postpone any talk about my international transfer – but on the other hand, they'd sold two top players in Eduardo and Ćorluka. Of course, I was happy for my former teammates – those were fantastic transfers – but I was also very disappointed because the team had lost two vital players. It was difficult to believe we could make a step forward in Europe. True, we did qualify for the UEFA Cup group stage in that great duel against Ajax, but that only added to the resentment because in the previous match against Werder Bremen we were without Eduardo and Ćorluka. We'll never know, but I'm sure we would have qualified for the Champions League, because we almost beat Werder without them.

Following this disappointment, my wish to leave grew. I received clear signals that there was great interest in me. Chelsea were the most persistent. Back when we had played the UEFA Cup match against Basel, the management told me that scouts from the London club had come to watch me. I later learnt it was their director of football, Frank Arnesen. I played well in that match – in fact, I think it was one of my best performances for Dinamo. During the winter break, which I spent in Zadar, I got word that Dinamo and Chelsea had reached an agreement. Zdravko Mamić flew to London, and I was sure I would move to

Stamford Bridge during the winter transfer window. I had already imagined myself playing alongside Drogba, Terry, Lampard, Shevchenko and the other Chelsea stars. While I stayed in Zadar with Vanja and waited for the call, I heard a rumour that negotiations had collapsed and the transfer had failed. Zdravko Mamić and his brother Zoran came to Zadar and delivered the 'happy' news. 'Luka, we decided we don't want to sell you yet.'

I was upset and didn't know what to do. I told my parents it was the end of the story, left their apartment and, in the parking lot in front of their building when I went through it once again with Vanja, I broke down. I couldn't stop the tears. Dinamo and Zdravko Mamić had sold other vital players giving the excuse that they couldn't turn down an offer from a big club. But, it seemed, they could keep me, even though this was also a big club and the biggest offer. I thought I had been treated unfairly. Until that point, I had great confidence in Zdravko Mamić, but after the failure of my transfer to Chelsea, I was angry. Our relations grew cold, and if I ran into him I just said, 'Hello' and that was it.

We went to the pre-season training camp in Turkey and I was not even surprised when they sold our centre-back Schildenfeld. I knew there was no point worrying over something I could do nothing about. In mid-January, coach Ivanković resigned following Mamić's harsh words in front of the players during the winter futsal championship. Even though Dinamo hadn't been defeated in the 2007 calendar, he had to step down. Zvonimir Soldo came from the Dinamo under-18s team to take over. Soldo had been part of that legendary bronze medal-winning team in the 1998 World Cup in France and used to play for Dinamo and Stuttgart. With the new coach at the helm, we repeated the previous season's result and won both the league and the cup for a second season in a row. The atmosphere at training and in the dressing room was splendid. Soldo proved himself a kind and dependable person, but the players were aware he wouldn't be able to take the negative atmosphere around the club for long. After we won the cup in Split against Hajduk, Soldo announced he was leaving. Another resignation, barely four months after Ivanković, even though the team had dominated and won all the trophies.

After the initial shock of not moving to Chelsea, I decided to reset. When something bad happens, you don't know what good it will bring. That's my motto, so I forgot about all of my problems and decided to focus on my performances for Dinamo and the national team. I knew a chance to move abroad would present itself sooner or later. I couldn't have imagined it would come so quickly.

CHAPTER SIX

Everything happened at lightning speed – sudden and exciting. It was Friday, 25 April, 2008, the evening before the match against Slaven Belupo. Sometime after 11 p.m., Zdravko Mamić called me on the phone to say Dinamo had reached an agreement with Tottenham and to ask if I accepted personal conditions – that is, if I was willing to move. I said, 'Yes' and realised my international career had just started. The excitement kept me awake long into the night. Vanja was with me and she knew all the details. I called my parents to share the news and they cried with happiness. We were very excited I was moving to England to play in a fantastic league. It was a huge step in my career. I had always liked Tottenham. I'm not sure what got me to start following them, but I knew a lot about them. I was excited that soon I would become a part of it all, and I tried to picture the atmosphere around Spurs.

Saturday morning was supposed to take its usual schedule, like on every other matchday. However, things soon turned hectic. It all began with me not having a proper suit! Until then, I had had no need, or wish, to own one. Now I needed to dress for the occasion. It wouldn't be right to go to London, take the medical exam and sign the contract in my jeans. As usual, Vanja was quick to react. The moment the first store opened at the shopping mall, we were there to choose a suit – which then needed to be tailored.

Daniel Levy, the chairman of Spurs, came to meet me. He seemed kind and relaxed. We were introduced, chatted a bit and later drove to the airport together. We flew to London on his private jet. Zoran Mamić, the then director of football at Dinamo, travelled with us. There wasn't much talk during the flight, which suited me. My English still wasn't good enough, and I was feeling the excitement of everything that had happened in the past 24 hours. The whole time I was thinking about what waited for me in London. It was a sweet expectation.

In London, I first took my medical, which was quick and showed no problems whatsoever. Then I signed the contract. The most impressive moment, however, was the arrival at White Hart Lane. Tottenham were playing a home match in the English Premier League against Middlesbrough. There were 36,000 people in the stands; the atmosphere was majestic. When I walked into the box, the greetings started coming from all sides. The spectators saw me come on the big screen and I heard them applaud. My first impression of Spurs' world was exhilarating. I felt pleased with the big challenge ahead of me and I looked forward to the opportunity to justify the fantastic treatment I was given on my first day at Tottenham. Later on, when I caught a moment to call Vanja, my parents and friends, I told everyone how impressive everything around Tottenham was.

But I needed to go back to Zagreb because I had four more games for Dinamo. The three league matches offered opponents who provided an ideal ending for my career in the Croatian Football League. First, we played against Inter Zaprešić, where I had started my senior career on loan from Dinamo, then we played the biggest Croatian derby against Hajduk in Split, before my farewell match was played in Zagreb against Rijeka, one of the big three of Croatian football. It was yet another very emotional moment. Around 20,000 fans came to the stadium to celebrate the title; the atmosphere was fantastic. Before the match, I received gifts from the club, and the supporters gave me a phenomenal farewell. The message on one of the banners on the east stand said: *'Luka, thanks!'* This simple, yet so touching, *thank you* was what I also wanted to say, both to the supporters and to Dinamo. The fans' ovation and their chants moved me to tears – especially when I was leaving the pitch with the score at 6–1 to Dinamo, waving goodbye to the supporters at beloved Maksimir. The game was still being played, with 80 minutes on the clock, yet the fans in the north and east stands, as well as those in the west, stood up and saw me off with huge applause. I was immensely proud. However, when I sat down on the bench to watch the rest of the match, I was overcome by sadness. Dinamo had given me everything, yet I was leaving. I put together a string of excellent performances that season, and not even the winter saga around the unsuccessful transfer could throw me off. In the spring, I was at the height of my popularity; I felt the fans' love and respect – all of which made me even sadder that we had failed to accomplish a good result in Europe in my three-and-a-half years at Dinamo. I think we could have.

After the match, while Vanja and I were having dinner at a restaurant, I sent a message to Zdravko Mamić: 'Thank you for everything. Had I left Dinamo in the winter, I would not have experienced this wonderful moment.'

I was touched by the farewell the fans prepared for me, and by the way the team reacted. We celebrated the title, which we all won together, yet they gave all of their attention to me. All of it made my departure even more difficult. I was very emotional and I remember telling Vanja, 'You know, I think one day I'll come back to Dinamo.'

I hadn't even left yet. We still had to play the return leg of the Croatian Cup final. We played against Hajduk at Poljud and since we'd won the first leg 3–0, the match was just a formality. Vanja took her car from Zagreb to Split but along the way she was involved in a car accident. Luckily, there were no consequences, other than she was late for the match. I played my last 88 minutes in the Dinamo shirt at Poljud and won the cup. After 148 matches, 37 goals and six trophies, I was ready for a new challenge.

UEFA Euro 2008 – the Euphoria and Drama

After my era at Dinamo came to an end and before the adventure at Tottenham began, I focused all of my attention on the European Championship, hosted by Austria and Switzerland. Like all members of the Croatia national team, I was extremely motivated to do something big. The tournament was being played on the 10th anniversary of Croatia's historic achievements at the 1998 FIFA World Cup in France. Most people believed the team was capable of repeating that triumphant campaign at the Euros. Slaven Bilić and his staff, some of whom had won the bronze in 1998, made us believe this. After we finished the qualification campaign in style, even the Croatian public, who had shown scepticism more often than confidence, seemed optimistic. And all this despite a gigantic problem at the beginning of the year.

At the hotel, where we waited for the afternoon league match against Varteks, we spent our time watching the English Premier League game between Birmingham and Arsenal involving Eduardo, our teammate from Dinamo and the national squad. Early into the match, unfortunately, he suffered a terrible injury when Martin Taylor, the Birmingham defender, brutally tackled him. The consequences were terrible; we could all see Eduardo's left foot broken at his ankle. A horrific sight. Poor Eduardo! Two weeks before, we had played against the Netherlands in Split. Eduardo had told me that Arsenal were treating him brilliantly and, like all of us, he was very excited about Euro 2008. Now, unfortunately, he wouldn't be there. Just as we had lost him a summer ago at Dinamo, undermining our efforts to secure a good result in Europe, now the national squad was robbed of this magnificent striker. In both cases, a question was left hanging in the air: What would've happened if we had someone of his class with us?

Eduardo scored 10 goals in our qualifying group. In the 16 matches under Bilić, he scored 12 times. As chance would have it, a year and a half later, I would be seriously injured in a Premier League match against the same team. A fractured fibula kept me off the pitch for over three months.

In February 2008, Croatia played the aforementioned warm-up match against the Netherlands in Split. We performed badly and the Dutch beat us 3–0. The defeat wasn't such a bad thing because the euphoria that had followed us in the media and the public eased up a little. We didn't feel the pressure because we knew we would be in great shape at the European Championship. Preparation matches are useful, but they are by no means a sure sign of what will happen at the competition. It is, however, true that Eduardo's absence disrupted us. We still had excellent strikers on our team, such as Petrić, Olić and Klasnić, but Eduardo was a different type of a player, more instinctive. Such players are tough to stop because they can create something out of nothing. Ivan Klasnić also had a good instinct – and his illness, a year and a half before the Euros, shocked us. Fate played some cruel tricks on our team. In 2007, Klasnić had serious health issues and had to undergo two kidney transplants. There wasn't much hope he would even be able to continue his career, yet he was brave, persistent and dedicated, and he recovered to play at Euro 2008. He even scored two goals.

Our outstanding performances at the Euros showed we had matured. We opened the tournament against Austria, the co-hosts, and won 1–0 after I scored a penalty to give us three important points. In the second group match, we swept the floor with Germany, the tournament favourites, with a convincing 2–1 win to show how powerful we were. It was our day; everything went in our favour. At the Wörthersee Stadium in Klagenfurt, we felt at home. Our supporters occupied more than half of the stands, and they were as loud as always. They created a fantastic atmosphere and we repaid them with a great victory to secure a place in the quarter-final. I was named the Man of the Match. We were extremely motivated and one moment in our dressing room at half time illustrates this best when our captain, Niko Kovač, and Vedran Ćorluka had a heated argument around failing to mark some players. Niko's brother Robert was the first to react and calm them down. For me, that was a sign they were motivated and focused, and that was confirmed by the result.

For the third group match, Bilić fielded a different team, who put in an excellent performance to beat Poland 1–0. The quarter-final against Turkey was played in Vienna, at the legendary Prater Stadium. There were many Turkish supporters, who are known to be the loudest fans in

Luka's first football, 1986.

Luka in front of his grandparents' house.

Luka (left), his mother Radojka and sister Jasmina. In the background is the red van that took him on his first driving 'adventure'.

Luka with grandma Jela in front of his grandparents' house in Kvartirić.

Playing with the animals. Left to right: cousin Mirjana, sister Jasmina and Luka.

Hunting with his grandpa. Luka was named after him.

Modrić Luka III d

Domaći rad 15.2.1995.

Pripovijedanje doživljaja

Iako sam još mali doživio sam puno strahova. Strah od rata i granatiranja već pomalo zaboravljam. Događaj i ljude koji nikad neću zaboraviti dogodio se prije četiri godine kada su četnici ubili moga djeda, kojega sam puno volio. Svi su plakali, a ja nikako nisam mogao shvatiti da moga dragog i dobrog djeda više nema. Pitao sam se mogu li biti ljudi oni koji su to učinili, i zbog kojih moramo bježati od ku

Luka's third-grade homework assignment, about the death of his grandfather.
A translation appears on page 15.

Luka attending his First Communion, 28 May, 1995.

In exile, Luka often played football in the parking lot in front of the Hotel Kolovare. Here he demonstrates his skills.

Luka poses with one of his first trophies, which was awarded to the best player at an international football tournament in Alzano, near Bergamo, 1997.

Luka (11 years old) and his future Croatia teammate Niko Kranjčar (12 years old), 1996.

Luka with his youngest sister Diora, 1998.

Luka with his grandma Manda, who still lives in her hometown of Obrovac.

Zadar Football Academy in 1994, with their coach Domagoj Bašić. Mario Grgurović (front row, far left), Luka Modrić (front row, fourth from the left); Marko Oštrić (front row, second from the right); Hrvoje Ćustić (back row, second from the right).

Luka's first loan from Dinamo Zagreb, playing for Zrinjski Mostar.

On the pitch, wearing the Inter Zaprešić shirt, Luka's second loan from Dinamo.

Slaven Bilić included Luka in the Croatia under-21 national team and named him the team's captain.

During his almost seven years at Dinamo, Luka won three domestic championships and two Croatian Cups.

Dinamo fans saying 'thank you' to their captain.

Luka with his football mentor Tomislav Bašić, during Dinamo's pre-season training camp in Kapfenberg, Austria, 2007.

Luka during his mandatory military service. He was part of the sports battalion and can be seen here with his uncle and father.

Luka playing against England at Wembley, in 2007. Croatia secured a 3-2 victory, which meant England failed to qualify for UEFA Euro 2008.

An embrace with Slaven Bilić, Croatia's UEFA Euro 2008 manager. The team reached the quarter-finals.

Luka with Niko Kovač, Croatia's captain and later coach.

Luka's wife Vanja. 'Had she not entered my life when I was 19, I wouldn't have accomplished any of the things that today make us so proud and happy.'

Luka and Vanja in front of their house in Chigwell following his transfer to Tottenham Hotspur.

'It was important Vanja felt accepted.' Christmas 2009, Chigwell. Left to right: father Stipe, uncle Željko, sister Jasmina, sister Diora, mother Radojka, Luka, Vanja and Vanja's mother Vesna.

Luka with Vedran Ćorluka, 'One of my dearest companions and friends.'

Luka with Darijo Srna, another close friend. Luka replaced him as captain of Croatia's national team.

In his first season with Tottenham Hotspur, Luka took on his former club Dinamo Zagreb in the UEFA Cup (6 November, 2008). His new club triumphed 4–0.

'Yes, I do!' Luka and Vanja's wedding photos.

Croatia under-21 friends and teammates: Hrvoje Ćustić, Ante Tomić, Luka Modrić, Ivica Vrdoljak and Karlo Primorac.

Friends for life: Luka and Marko Oštrić playing *tressette*, Luka's favourite card game.

Cruising the Adriatic:
Ilijana and Hrvoje
Čale, Jelena and
Marijan Buljat,
Luka and Vanja.

Luka and his friends
Marko Oštrić and
Marko Čirjak.

On vacation on
the Island of Mljet:
Marijan Buljat,
Hrvoje Čale, Luka
and Mateo Kovačić.

the world. Still, they weren't able to hush our part of the stands. The Croatian fans were sensational, and I once again had a feeling we were playing on home turf. The match was difficult and the high stakes took a toll on the players. The game went into extra time, yet I felt we had the upper hand. In the 90 minutes of normal time, we had shown as much: Olić hit the post, and we created some good chances. Still, during the first half of extra time, the Turks pressed before, in the second half, we regained the balance. It was a tight contest with both teams being careful not to concede.

In the last minute of extra time, we hit the Turks on the counter-attack. Klasnić passed the ball to me and I immediately distributed it to Srna on the flank. He tried to cross it, but the Turkish defender blocked him. The ball rolled towards the byline, and their goalkeeper, Rüştü Reçber, tried to prevent it from crossing the line for a corner kick. But I reached the ball before him and, as he sprinted back to his position, I crossed it with my left foot into the penalty box, where Klasnić came out of nowhere and headed the ball into the goal! The pitch and the stands with our supporters simply exploded. We all ran towards Klasnić and almost suffocated him. Bilić jumped up from the bench and ran towards us, beside himself with happiness. The last seconds of extra time and you score a winning goal – is there anything better?! The Turks were beaten. There were just a couple of seconds left in the game and everyone, including them, thought it was just a formality.

But the celebration threw us off, and we lost our focus. Bilić signalled to the assistant referee he wanted to make a substitution, probably so we could stop and pull ourselves together. Instead of controlling the game, holding the ball, we reacted naively and stupidly. As the last seconds counted down, Turkey hit a free-kick towards our penalty box. Several of our players jumped; I thought they would kick it back up the field and that would be it. It also seemed there was a foul on Šimunić, but there was no whistle. I watched in disbelief as the ball bounced to the Turkish player, who lashed at it with fury and scored past helpless Pletikosa!

Could this be happening?! I couldn't believe my eyes. Just moments away from securing a place in the semi-final, we had lost our hard-earned advantage. How could we be so unfortunate, so naïve?

I had a bad feeling before the penalty shoot-out. We seemed lost. The team that has been on their knees and then comes back into the game is always at a psychological advantage. We'd held the semi-final in our hands, but let it slip. This is a terrible pressure; it's hard to keep your composure, especially during the penalty shoot-out. And my theory proved true. I took the first penalty and missed the goal. Rakitić did the same. Only Srna managed to score, while the Turkish goalkeeper saved Petrić's decisive kick. In a matter of minutes, the situation had taken a drastic turn. Now Turkey gave themselves over to mad celebration and we, desperate and devastated, flopped down on the grass in the middle of the pitch. It's hard to describe our sadness – we cried like little children; we wept in the locker room for a full hour after the match. Bilić was devastated and speechless. No one said anything. They took us from the stadium to the hotel where we were supposed to have dinner, but the atmosphere was like a wake. A funeral. We kept glancing at one another in silence, our thoughts wandering. The next day the bus took us to Croatia – the mood was low. We stopped at a couple of rest stops to stretch our legs and we met groups of our fans who offered their support to ease our pain . . . the pain that was also theirs. The whole of Croatia was in tears.

We came so close to competing in the semi-final, but fate played a cruel trick on us. She allowed us to taste that magic moment, and then kicked it right out of our hands. We were young in Austria, full of enthusiasm, and in combination with the experienced players such as the brothers Kovač and Šimunić, we were firm and compact. I am convinced we were ready for the final – we played excellent football. I felt incredible. At 22, young and eager, full of confidence on account of the transfer to Spurs, I had the impression that no one could touch me. I felt strong and powerful, and I took pleasure in it.

The defeat would stay with us for years to come. Looking at it from today's perspective, I think this dramatic defeat had an immense influence on our confidence at the big tournaments that followed. But in the next decade, the next year with the number eight in it, 2018, would see us lift our frustrations and settle the score with fate.

Licking Wounds

After everything that had happened, I couldn't find peace, not even in Zadar, my hometown. Vanja and I rented a boat with some friends and went sailing, just to get away from all the bustle. I tried to make it all look normal. It was all in vain. You know the story about defeat being part of sport? True, losing *is* a part of sport, but it's so easy to say this, yet so hard to endure, like I had to back then. Half of the time, no matter what we did, my thoughts escaped to the Turkey match and the last moments of extra time. Those scenes troubled me, just like my missed penalty; they kept coming back, over and over again, persistently and obsessively, as if I hoped that thinking about it all the time would change something. Such are the days, weeks and months after traumatic losses. I wasn't consoled by being included in the Best Team of Euro 2008, the first recognition for me at a major international tournament. Personal recognition could never make me happy if my team weren't successful. Without a doubt, Euro 2008 is the greatest trauma of my playing career.

Still, the incredible setting of the Adriatic allowed me to slowly recover. I had to relax a bit, fill myself up with energy, my English story was to come. A new challenge, a new opportunity to prove my worth. Vanja and I talked about it all the time, but we also looked back at the first stage of my career and at our relationship. The topics we discussed were countless; we laughed and teased each other over some things, while others were serious.

Basically, from the first day of our relationship, Vanja had been my biggest support. She was always there, putting me and my obligations first, but she never saw this as something special or extraordinary, something that was only her sacrifice. For her, it was normal. Only one time did she make it clear I had stepped over the line. This was at the beginning of our relationship when I sometimes still acted like a careless teen without any commitments. The atmosphere at Dinamo was fantastic: we were a great group and we liked going out to dinner, spending time together and relaxing after the matches. For a while, Vanja was understanding, but as this became more or less a regular occurrence, she reacted. She calmly told me she thought this wasn't alright, both in terms of our relationship and my career.

Moving to London was our turning point. We were alone in another country, wholly dedicated to one another.

At the beginning of our relationship, some things bothered me too. One of the biggest was cigarettes. People who've met her after she quit say they can't imagine that Vanja ever smoked. I can – very much so. She smoked a lot, and it bothered me. Tobacco was never my choice. I tried a cigarette only once. I was maybe 12 or 13 and my friends and I found a pack of Marlboros. *What are we going to do?* we asked jokingly, because we were kids and kids do those kinds of things. We hid in the dark so no one could see us, opened the pack and I, trying to be a big-shot, lit a cigarette. I regretted it immediately. The stench, the nicotine, the smoke snuffed out any idea of ever taking a cigarette again.

I'm not much of a drinker either. With a meal, at celebrations or dinner parties I'll allow myself a drink or two – but I don't handle it well. One of the rare occasions my father got angry with me was connected with alcohol. It was after the goodbye dinner I had prepared for my childhood friends in Zadar. I had a few drinks, nothing major, but it was more than enough to make me dizzy. When I came home to the Hotel Iž, where we lived at the time, my father noticed my walk was different. My breath must have given me away. I defended myself by saying I wasn't drunk, but then, and in front of my worried mother, he made me stand on one foot to see who was right. Of course, I lost my balance.

The following day, feeling the nasty effects of my first hangover, I stood in shame as my dad gave me a good talking to: 'What were you thinking, son?! That's not how you'll get ahead in life, let alone in football. If you think you can keep that up in Zagreb, you had better stay here.' The hangover and his words of warning sunk deep in my mind. Of course, there was no fear it would ever become a habit. When the occasion calls for it, I can relax a bit, but tobacco and alcohol have never been my thing.

I asked Vanja to stop smoking on several occasions. It's unhealthy, and the smoke always bothered me, especially in closed spaces. It seemed my words weren't getting to her, as is the case with most smokers, so I stopped nagging; I knew it was useless. Some six months later, I was in Split with the national team. It was before the friendly with the Netherlands, as part of our preparations for Euro 2008. Vanja called me on the phone.

'How are you? What's new?' I said, the conversation taking its usual start.

'You know what, I stopped smoking! Some news, huh?!' she replied.

Regardless of how happy I was for her, I was a bit sceptical. But even if she didn't succeed immediately, at least she was trying. I saw it as an expression of her love for me. Vanja knew, like all smokers do, how unhealthy cigarettes are, but she was trying to get rid of this nasty habit for me. And eventually, she did! I have never heard her say she would like to light another cigarette, which shows how tough a character she is. When Vanja sets her mind to something, that's it.

It's a characteristic we both share. When I started going out with her, I knew Vanja was the one. My parents knew it even before they had met her. They noticed how much time I was spending on the phone when we weren't together. Just as they must've noticed the change in my behaviour.

My father met her first, almost by accident. He came to watch a Dinamo match and stopped by the Maxim Pub. Mate Režan, one of my friends from back in Zadar, was with him. He knew about Vanja and I, and when he saw her in the pub he introduced her to my father.

'Stipe, this is Vanja, Luka's girlfriend!'

Legend has it that my dad fell for his future daughter-in-law the first time he saw her. Back then, we were just dating, but he's always said he knew we were meant for each other. His first comment about Vanja gave it away: 'Son, Vanja is a miracle!'

My mum and sisters met the new woman in our family when we came to Zadar to attend the wedding of my teammate and our good family friend, Marijan Buljat and his wife Jelena.

'Vanja is so nice!' my mum said, while my sisters instantly became friends with her.

No one could tell me how to feel about Vanja, but I was glad my parents and sisters had a good relationship with her from day one. My parents would later show how happy they were with my choice: 'Luka, we couldn't have chosen better ourselves.'

It was important that Vanja felt accepted. And that she, a city girl used to somewhat different relationships, accepted the ways of my family. I know it sometimes seemed that we were all connected by an umbilical cord and it may have been strange for her. They often visited Zagreb, watched my matches, stayed at our place. When I got some time off, we would always go to Zadar. But even when we weren't in the same place, the phone line with my parents and sisters was open 24/7, just as with my uncle Željko. My grandma Manda, my aunts, Marija and Nevenka – Nevenka sadly passed away four years ago – and my dear childhood companions and cousins, Mirjana and Senka, as well as other relatives, make up my family and we are all very close. Vanja recognised all of these emotional relationships in my life and adjusted herself to them completely. It wasn't simple, but she did everything to make it so. She did this spontaneously; it never seemed she was doing this just for the sake of it. So perhaps it's not surprising that my family fell for her instantly.

Many details from back in those days clearly make the point of how close our family was. When I signed my first substantial contract with Dinamo, the first thing I did was buy my father a new car. He had been using a beaten-up Fiat Uno, and, as they often went to Zagreb or some other place to see me, I wanted their car to be safe, and more comfortable. I went to the car dealer and bought a new VW Passat. As I pondered how to deliver it to Zadar and surprise my dad, Vanja suggested, 'Luka, why don't you take the new car, and I'll drive behind you in yours? We'll take it to Zadar ourselves.'

So we picked up the car and drove to Zadar. We called my dad to come out in front of his building – he thought we needed help to bring something into the house. When we gave him the keys to the new car, he was shocked! Making your parents' lives easier, especially when you know they have always looked after you, is one of the best feelings in life. They sacrifice, they choose a modest life in order to make their children's lives better and they are happy when they see you have become successful. But when you can get something for them, especially when you know they need it, the feeling is wonderful. One material thing will never make up for what they have done for me, but it's a symbol that I will always look after them.

Another instance will perhaps paint an even better picture of my father. I had already established my name at Dinamo, yet they were still living at the army housing in the Hotel Iž. My sister Jasmina was studying in Rijeka, but my parents still lived in this small space with my younger sister Diora. After I had saved up some money, I bought my parents a spacious apartment in Zadar. It was a new building in a pleasant neighbourhood and Vanja decorated it. But, even though they were deeply moved by my gesture, they didn't move to the new apartment. My dad was simply not ready for all the good things that, in a short span, started happening after I became a professional player. He kept coming up with excuses why he didn't want to move to their new home. I think they would still be living in the Hotel Iž had I not insisted. They were used to a modest life and they kept their feet firmly on the ground. I think relations with people they care about is what matters to them most. They still have the same friends as before. They care for my grandma Manda, who lives alone in Obrovac. They look after our relatives. They are always at Vanja's and my disposal when we need someone to babysit. They finally moved to the new apartment after six months! They still live there.

Manda, my grandma on my mother's side, is the same – she just won't leave her hometown. She is in her 80s, yet she still lives alone in Obrovac. She's never even considered moving, and we did try to talk her into it. She recently had her hip replaced, which makes it difficult to move. On top of this, she lives on the fourth floor, in a building without an elevator. But, she says she doesn't mind; all is well. My parents visit her all the time, they buy her groceries and get her medication. We are taking care of everything she needs, especially when it comes to her health. But whenever I ask her if she needs or wants something, she always replies gently, 'I've got everything, Luka. Tell me, how are you doing, are the children well, are you taking care of Vanja?'

My grandma became a widow early. Grandpa Petar died before I was born. I spent more time with my grandparents on my father's side because their house was close to ours. But, every summer vacation, Vanja, the children and I visit my grandma in Obrovac or somehow talk her into coming over to Zadar. I have a house in Punta Skala near Zadar. It has three apartments so we can all stay there during the summer. There's also a small garden where my grandma likes to sit in the shade and talk. Her stories are always warm. Despite all the troubles she went through, she never complains. She is a composed, calm person, used to looking after others more than herself.

A New Life in London

By 7 July, 2008, after the European Championship, I had just cooled down a bit when my new club went on a pre-season training camp in Spain. As I'd played at the Euros, I was allowed a break, and had to report to Valencia only on the 18th. During that week, I was preoccupied with the beginning of my career at Spurs. Before I left, I invited all of my former Dinamo teammates to a farewell dinner. It was the symbolic end to my era in the Blues' shirt.

Vanja and I flew to London from Zagreb. Zdravko Mamić's son Mario came along with us. As I had to go to Valencia, Mario stayed with Vanja to help her settle during that first couple of days. We were staying at the Marriott Hotel, a 10-minute drive from the club's training ground – convenient for me, but difficult for Vanja. The hotel was in the middle of nowhere, next to the motorway. We spent two months there before moving to a house Vanja found for us in Chigwell.

Everyone in Valencia, starting with the Spurs manager Juande Ramos, made me feel welcome. The Spanish coach was extremely fair to me, although he had high expectations – it was he who had insisted on bringing me to Tottenham. He is a good man and a knowledgeable coach who just needed a bit more luck for things to work out.

Ramos introduced me to the new environment and the matches gradually, which was ideal, letting me adjust to a different rhythm and the considerably different demands of the game. To be honest, after the European Championship, all I did was rest. I needed to distance myself from football, first to deal with the disappointing defeat to Turkey and also to prepare for the new challenge in England. I arrived unprepared for what was expected from me. The intensity of training – three sessions a day – took me by surprise. There was a lot of running – along the golf course, along the beach – and in the evening we played different ball-related sports and games. I first made friends with the Ivory Coast midfielder Didier Zokora, who could just run and run. This great joker and prankster would soon become my next-door neighbour. The first consequence of the intense training sessions was that my knee tendon became inflamed. But as time went by, I adapted to the new regime and the new environment.

At the training ground in Chigwell, which was much more modest than the one Tottenham built four years later, I felt great. The dressing rooms and other facilities were in shipping containers, but I didn't mind.

What I was most enthusiastic about were the pitches, which were phenomenal! Four fields, each one better than the last. They were so inviting I couldn't wait to play. And there was something that caught me by surprise during the first couple of months in London: the weather. I expected rain and clouds, yet it was sunny and warm.

I soon developed a good rapport with my teammates, especially with Giovani dos Santos and Heurelho Gomes, our goalkeeper, and later with Aaron Lennon and Tom Huddlestone. However, I didn't even imagine that by the end of the summer transfer window Spurs would sign a tremendous new player. My great friend Vedran Ćorluka transferred from Manchester City. What a surprise this was – especially for me! It made everything easier.

In the beginning, I have to admit I had a lot of problems adjusting to driving on the left side of the road. The club provided me with a car, a BMW – the same one I had in Zagreb, but the steering wheel on the opposite side just didn't agree with me. Even though the training ground was a short 10-minute drive away from the hotel, on several occasions I hit the kerb. It was so annoying. Besides being worried I would wreak havoc on the road, I felt bad about the damage to the car. I told Vanja it would be best if she drove me until I got used to it. Many things demanded quick adjustment, so I decided to leave driving for later. Football was a priority.

I have to give credit to Vanja for being so understanding while I was getting used to living and playing in England. Driving was just one example. We were still dating when I started taking driving lessons in Zagreb. I soon learned to drive, but one thing I just couldn't get a hold of was parallel parking. Vanja was an experienced driver, so she took her small Peugeot 206 to a parking lot in Borongaj and taught me how to parallel park. It helped, and I passed my driving test with flying colours. I was finally able to get a car and be more independent; I could now go everywhere on my own. My first car was a VW Golf V. It was cool: silver, lively and comfortable. Unfortunately, I didn't enjoy it for long. After a couple of months, someone stole it. I felt terrible, as you get attached to your first car. After this, I used Vanja's car for a while. During the last season at Dinamo, I decided to treat myself to a BMW X5. When I transferred to Tottenham, I gave it to my father, who still uses it.

At the end of my first pre-season at Spurs, we played several matches. I will always remember my first appearance and contact with the fans at White Hart Lane. We were playing against Roma, and the place was packed. Back then, this still seemed remarkable because I had come from Croatia where there weren't many supporters in the stands – apart from special occasions. Soon, full stadiums, as there were and still are in England, would become something completely normal to me. The Tottenham fans met me with applause. I was impressed by the positive energy, the atmosphere, the supporters right by the field, and no riots or violence in the stands. Before the championship began, I felt a good energy and I had no doubt I would do well in the English Premier League. The training sessions with my teammates, who had been competing on this level for years, showed me that I wasn't falling behind – far from it. On the pitch, everything was going my way, so I thought I had what was needed. But then things took a wrong turn.

Ramos played me as a sort of winger and not a classic midfielder; our results were horrible. After the first three matches, in which we saw two defeats and a draw, we were sitting at the bottom of the table. Then followed the international break and I went to play for Croatia, but I didn't have the best of times there either. We beat Kazakhstan – I even scored a nice goal – but a few days later England taught us a lesson in the 2010 FIFA World Cup qualifiers when we lost 4–1.

The return to Tottenham was even worse. Eight weeks into the season, we had won just two points and were bottom of the league. After the sixth defeat in a row, the coach's position was under threat. That same week, we travelled to Udinese to play our first match in the UEFA Cup. We lost 2–0. Back in England, and before the game against Bolton, the atmosphere was delicate. In the evening, we were called to an urgent meeting in the conference room and the management explained that

Ramos had lost their confidence and that Harry Redknapp would be taking over as our new manager. The experienced coach would lead us in the match against Bolton the following day.

Redknapp chose a 4-4-1-1 formation and I played as an attacking midfielder, right behind striker Darren Bent. It was my best match so far. We won and got our breath back. The next match against Tottenham's local rivals Arsenal at Emirates Stadium was sensational. We scored first, but the Gunners fought back and took the lead, first at 3–1 and then at 4–2. We continued to battle, and in the 89th minute the score was 4–3, but in the fourth minute of injury time, following my shot that hit the post, Lennon equalised. His goal sent us into raptures, and Lennon almost suffocated because the whole team jumped all over him! On that day – I'm sure of this – we became a team. The winning series that followed attests to that: in the next home match, we beat Liverpool 2–1, the Russian Roman Pavlyuchenko scoring in injury time. We also took a 2–1 away victory against Manchester City, where I assisted Bent for the first goal.

Interestingly, Tottenham drew Dinamo in the UEFA Cup, which meant I would play against my former club. Dinamo arrived at White Hart Lane just five months after I had left Zagreb. It was strange to play against my former teammates, but I stayed professional. I provided an assist for the first of our four goals and left the pitch in the 75th minute to the applause of the home crowd.

And that's when I learned how wonderful a player's life can be in England. Especially after we replaced our bad results from the beginning of the season with a positive streak – against prestigious opponents at that. The fact that we didn't lose to Chelsea and Arsenal, or later on to Manchester United, and that we beat Liverpool and Manchester City was a clear sign our team possessed good quality, although losing points against clubs that were lower in the table meant we hadn't matured yet. The most important thing, however, was that we began to recover from all the traumas at the beginning of the season and, by the end of the year, we were 16th in the table. We did well in the League Cup and the UEFA

Cup, but, unfortunately, I would once again feel the burden of losing a decisive match on penalties. In the League Cup final, at a packed Wembley, Tottenham failed to defend the trophy they had won in 2008. After a tense game that finished 0–0, Manchester United performed better in the penalty shoot-out, winning 4–1. Only Ćorluka scored on our side. I never even thought of taking a penalty kick – the wounds from Vienna were still fresh.

Harry Redknapp is a special character. A charismatic manager who liked to create a positive atmosphere, he was very successful in motivating the players. One of the positives, especially for me, was that he genuinely admired Croatian players. He always spoke nicely of Slaven Bilić, Igor Štimac, Niko Kranjčar and Robert Prosinečki, whom he had coached at West Ham United and Portsmouth. It came as no surprise to me that, in a later stage of managing Tottenham, he had no fewer than four players from Croatia: Vedran Ćorluka, Niko Kranjčar, Stipe Pletikosa and I made up a quartet, giving our club the nickname CroTottenham.

Redknapp knew all the tricks of the trade. His training sessions were most often led by his assistants, but he kept an eye on everything. He always wanted his players to play in positions where they could give their best. With him in charge, my form quickly improved. He estimated that I could be most effective if he allowed me more freedom and creativity in attack. It worked well, so Redknapp told the players to give me the ball and asked me to deliver a through pass for the super-fast Lennon. Our performances continued to improve, and we finished the season in eighth position. Taking into consideration that ours had been the worst start in Tottenham history, this was a solid result. Credit for this, of course, goes to Harry, an old-school manager, and a very positive and kind person.

I had made good progress in my first season in the Premier League – I'd earned a good status at the club and the fans were happy with my performances. Naturally, though, they all expected I would be even better the next season.

One crucial moment during that first campaign happened at the time of our gravest crisis, just before the match against Bolton. While I was driving to the stadium, I got a text message: 'Call me when you can, and if you want to. Zvone.' That's the name everyone in Croatian football associates with Zvonimir Boban. *Can it really be him, my idol?* was the question running immediately through my mind. But then I thought maybe some of my friends were pulling a prank on me. Why would Boban want to get in touch with me? Still, I was intrigued by the message and I wanted to know who had sent it, so I dialled the number. The moment I heard the voice on the other end of the line, I knew it was him! It was one of those moments I will never forget, for as long as I live.

'Just stay calm and don't blame yourself for the poor results. It happened to me too when I transferred abroad. I needed some time to adjust. Relax, things will fall into place!' This is more or less what Zvone told me, and his words couldn't have come at a better time. Especially because they came from a man who had gone through everything that professional football can throw at you. We talked on the phone for about five minutes and I remember I was very excited – just like when I was a kid and I watched him conquer Europe with AC Milan, or when he led Croatia to its first World Cup medal. That conversation gave me the strength and the adrenaline I needed at a challenging moment of my career. From then on, everything became easier.

To Catch a Break

The summer after my first season in the English Premier League was much more relaxed than the one before. I was happy with how I'd adapted to the physically demanding English game. I had caught the league's rhythm, I had shown everyone I could compete at this level, and public reaction to my performances only added to my confidence. While vacationing on the Adriatic, Vanja and I looked back at our first year abroad. We'd had an excellent time in London, but without Vanja's support, this wouldn't have been possible. First and foremost, because during the early months she tried hard to make it easier for me to focus and prove myself at the club, even though she was having a difficult time. While I occupied myself with training, travelling and matches, she was mostly by herself. I knew from our days in Zagreb that she hated this. When I was away with Dinamo, she could call her friends, visit her mum or her grandparents; Zagreb was her home. London was a completely different world. I was even more worried when, two months after our arrival we moved from the hotel to the small and quaint town of Chigwell. The surrounding forests added to the charm of this quiet place, away from the bustle of London. Vanja decorated our two-storey house to her taste; I never meddled in it because she knew what she was doing! When I was at home, we had a wonderful time. After my training session, it would take me five minutes to get home and then we would have the rest of the day to ourselves. For the first time in the five years of our relationship, we could do whatever we wanted and whatever made us both happy. We got used to London, which we both liked. We would take the Tube and in about 40 minutes be in the city. When we took a car, it would take us about an hour and a half, depending on the traffic. After we had visited all the places we had planned for that day, and if I were free the next day, we'd stay at a hotel in London and then go back to Chigwell the following day.

That was the nicer part of the story. The darker part, when I was away, provoked smaller or bigger traumas. Vanja admitted she was having a hard time being left alone in the house. She would clean and cook, do house chores, to fill her time. She would go to a store or a restaurant to have lunch, which was pretty much all she could do in the small town.

When we learned there had been a number of burglaries in the area, we got worried. Staying alone in the house at night made her scared, and I worried about how she was dealing with it and if everything was alright. Soon, we realised that it made no sense, even though it was part of adjusting to life in England, so we made the decision that Vanja should spend the night at the Marriot whenever I was away.

The second season had a dream start. We signed a couple of new players, among them Niko Kranjčar from Portsmouth. Niko and I were finally playing for the same club, not only for the national team. Unfortunately, fate once again played a trick on us and prevented us from playing together. After four consecutive wins and great performances, I sustained a serious injury. This happened at White Hart Lane in a match against Birmingham. At the beginning of the second half, I got into a tackle with Lee Bowyer. He had a reputation for being a rough player, but our duel should have been harmless. I protected the ball but he wanted to kick it and fell on my leg. I felt a sharp pain in my right leg and I broke out in a cold sweat.

After the team doctors attended to me, I thought I could clench my teeth, endure the pain and continue to play. But the pain was too much to bear, and it was clear something serious had happened. The medical team decided to rush me to hospital – they suspected a fracture to my right fibula. The X-rays, unfortunately, showed they were right. When I was still on my way to the hospital, in the ambulance, Slaven Bilić called me on the phone. I cried because I realised I would be out for a long time. Bilić tried to encourage me, but I was too upset. Bowyer soon called and apologised. I never thought he did it on purpose – it just happened and I was unlucky. Fortunately, no surgery was necessary. I was given a protective boot to wear and then the recovery process began. I spent part of it in London and part of it in Croatia, where Stipe Pletikosa, my future teammate at Tottenham and my friend from the national team, was also recovering from a difficult injury.

In the 100 or so days I was out, Niko Kranjčar put in some great performances for the team. He scored some crucial goals and contributed to Tottenham's rise to the upper part of the table. We would play several matches together, but then in April, a serious injury kept him out until the end of the season.

**

Before the second season at Spurs, I brought up the topic of marriage with Vanja. We had been in a relationship for almost five years and had lived together for more than four. We decided we wanted to get married and live together as husband and wife. Even more importantly, we agreed we wanted to have a child! What's more, we both wanted to have at least three children. We had the same ideas about family, and talking about children only made us more excited. We planned to have a child soon, but then my injury and the long period out supercharged our plan. We wanted to become parents. As I was leaving for yet another recovery session at Spurs' training ground, Vanja asked me to meet her for lunch in London, at our favourite Italian restaurant. It never crossed my mind why she wanted us to go there. When I arrived, I looked around the seating area and saw her immediately. There was something odd about her – she seemed nervous. Just as I sat down, Vanja explained why she had insisted we met here: 'You're going to be a dad!'

It's hard to find words to describe that moment. Those who have experienced it know what joy this is. It was the most wonderful news in the world! And my wife wanted to give it to me in a special place. Typical Vanja. Despite all the morning sickness, which tormented her, she wanted to make this moment special for me, for us. And there you have it: at home, I'd never noticed something was going on. She hid it from me until she was sure she was pregnant. As we were having this most special lunch of our lives, we agreed on how to organise everything. We had already planned to get married after the end of the season. Vanja was explicit about wanting our doctors in Zagreb to oversee her pregnancy, and I agreed with her. It wasn't because she didn't trust the doctors in England, but because both of us wanted our children to be born in Croatia. Vanja also told me she wanted to move out of the big house into a single-level flat. As she would be spending most of the time alone with the baby, it would be easier to look after the baby if all of the rooms were on the same floor. So we rented an apartment. Our first house in Chigwell has many pleasant memories for us, but Vanja seemed happier and calmer when we moved into a spacious flat in a nice apartment building.

On 12 May, 2010, when Vanja was eight months pregnant, we had our civil wedding in Zagreb. It was an intimate ceremony – we invited only our family and closest friends – followed by dinner at a restaurant in Zagreb. We would have a big wedding, which we both wanted, together with a church ceremony a year later. I was thrilled. Besides my private life, the second season at Spurs brought me a lot of happiness. We finished fourth, which meant that Tottenham qualified for the UEFA Champions League for the first time. We reached our goal in style, beating Manchester City at their ground in a direct duel for fourth place, and we threw a serious party to celebrate! My injury marked the beginning of the season, but after I recovered I quickly caught up with my teammates and played well. The media praised my performances together with my team's success and I felt I had proved myself in the Premier League. I showed myself and others that I could be a decisive factor in a demanding league among top-quality players. No one mentioned my fragile physique, my lack of height or strength; positive reviews underlined my technical prowess and team spirit. The Premier League and its fierce rhythm made me a better player. My game became quicker and simpler.

The only blemish of the season was Croatia's unsuccessful campaign for the 2010 FIFA World Cup. It was the first time I failed to qualify for a major tournament with my national team. Instead of South Africa, I spent my summer vacation in Croatia. To be fair, it would be a completely different vacation from any before.

Fears for Vanja

On 8 May, 2010, just after the season's end, Vanja and I went back to Zagreb. The baby was due on 27 June. Vanja stayed in Zagreb to rest, and I had two more matches for the national team – friendlies against Austria in Klagenfurt and against Wales in Osijek. I was free from 24 May and I could now be there for Vanja to help her with whatever she needed. The weather in Zagreb was hot. I hoped we could travel to Zadar and cool down a bit by the sea, but the doctors told Vanja not to travel until she gave birth. Certain health issues required treatment. Nevertheless, she encouraged me to go to Zadar and spend a couple of days with my parents and sisters because we knew there wouldn't be time after the baby was born.

On the second night in Zadar, my father woke me up just after 5 a.m. Vanja had called, but I didn't hear the phone. My dad did!

'Son, wake up, Vanja has to go to the hospital, the baby is coming . . .'

I was up in a second, put on the first clothes I found and headed for Zagreb, 280 kilometres away. My parents followed me in their car. I stepped on it, the road was empty – I wanted to be there with her. When her waters broke, she was alone in the apartment. Her mother lives nearby and, when Vanja called her, she came over immediately and then brought all the things needed for the hospital. Later on, when we talked about what had happened that night, we laughed at the episode with the cab driver. When he came to pick them up and asked where they needed to go, they almost screamed, 'Take us to the hospital! She's having a baby!' The driver was shocked and, as he was worried by a pregnant woman in the car, he drove very slowly, 18 miles per hour.

'Please, step on it, it's not a problem!' Vanja encouraged him, wanting to get to the hospital as soon as possible.

When she called me, I was already near the hospital. Feeling the adrenaline rush, I cried, 'Vanja, please wait, if you can, I'll be there in a second.'

But she couldn't wait. I pulled up in front of the hospital just as she gave birth. It was 8.10 a.m. when our first child came into this world and forever changed our lives. The moment I first saw our son and took him into my arms was one of the happiest of my life. I hugged Vanja as hard as I could; I wanted those first moments of pure happiness to last forever. We promised each other that the next time she gave birth, we would be there together! And that's how it was. That was our first time, and we didn't know what to expect. We had known only that Vanja was due to give birth by caesarean section. We couldn't have anticipated that she would go into labour three weeks before she was due!

Vanja and the baby had to stay at the hospital for a few days. I was there the whole time. I even spent a couple of nights at the hospital. During those first four days, the nurses came to our room every morning and asked the same question: 'Do we have a name for the baby boy?'

We had a couple of options: Vanja was leaning towards Ivan, and then I suggested naming him Ivano. My little boy and my great love!

Two weeks later, finally, we were cleared to travel. I was looking forward to our first visit to Zadar. My parents and sisters were over the moon with happiness. Those were the days of joy; everything just came together. My childhood friends came to visit us and see the baby. And, of course, we often played cards: *briškula i trešeta*. I'm very good at it. The main rule is to stay focused and follow the game, remember which cards have already been played, and what trump cards the opponent may still have – that is, what card to play next and beat him. I hate losing, even in practice, and when it comes to cards, I tend to get very loud and quarrelsome.

One evening, on the terrace of our house in Punta Skala, preoccupied by the *briškula* I was playing with my friends, I didn't even notice that Vanja had come back home. It was about 11 in the evening. She went out on the balcony to hang the laundry when suddenly she felt sick. Somehow managing to come down, she complained about not feeling well. It seemed it was nothing serious, so I told her to lie down for a bit. My father walked her to our room. We soon heard a loud thud and then a commotion. I ran upstairs and saw Vanja's mother, who had just come out of her room. I was paralysed – utterly petrified – because Vanja couldn't breathe.

My best man Marko was quick to react, and we rushed her to hospital. Her mum held her in her arms as we drove because Vanja was half-conscious. As we were speeding towards the hospital, my father called his old friend, doctor Nakić. He told him what we'd managed to get from Vanja: that she had felt a pressure in her chest. The pain in her back was most likely due to the fall, but the pressure in her chest suggested she might be having a heart attack. When, after a crazy drive, I pulled up in front of the hospital, the medical team was already there ready to intervene. They examined her, and one of the doctors immediately suspected that a blood clot might have entered her lungs. They put her in the Intensive Care Unit and gave her treatment. Next, the doctors told us she needed to rest and sent us home. I was a bit less worried because she was in safe hands, but I still couldn't sleep a wink. We had an open phone line with the hospital, and I was reassured when they told me she was stable. The next day, when we went to visit her, we got a clearer picture of what had happened. The doctors concluded that the blood clot had been caused by her body's reaction to pregnancy. It was very serious, but, fortunately, it ended well. The fact that the next morning Vanja couldn't remember she had a son shows how serious the situation was. She was eventually released to home care, but I had to take her to the hospital to get shots every day for the next month, and she had to be closely monitored. She continued to receive anticoagulant therapy for the next year and a half. Unfortunately, that wasn't the end of it.

My First Champions League

At Dinamo, I never realised my biggest wish: to play in the UEFA Champions League. Europe's elite club competition, which allows you to test yourself against the best, is every player's dream. I came to Tottenham with this wish, even though qualifying for the Champions League is probably even more complicated in England. First and foremost, because the competition is extremely tough and seven or eight top clubs fight for the first four positions in the table. No other league is as competitive as the English Premier League. The Spurs tradition wasn't promising because they hadn't participated in the strongest club competition for almost half a century. But in the summer of 2010, my dream came true. In the two qualifying matches we beat Young Boys. Unfortunately, the first leg doesn't bring me fond memories – I injured a muscle, and we lost the game 3–2 away. I didn't play in the second leg, but my teammates put in an excellent performance and following their 4–0 victory we qualified for the Champions League with a 6–3 aggregate victory.

In the group stage, we drew Werder Bremen, who I knew well, Twente and Inter Milan, the reigning European champions. Despite this being our debut in the Champions League, we played very well and topped our group.

I particularly remember the match against Inter: I left the pitch 10 minutes into the game after our goalkeeper Gomes was shown a red card. In his place, Redknapp had to bring on Carlo Cudicini, our reserve goalkeeper, and for tactical reasons he decided to take me off and bring on some physically stronger players to compensate for our numerical disadvantage. We lost 4–3, but Gareth Bale shone in the match and everyone talked about his hat-trick. Injuries had, until then, plagued Gareth and he had a difficult path until he stabilised at Spurs. This match marked the beginning of his rise. Gareth and I were close at Spurs, and our friendship would only grow stronger. I scored my first goal in the Champions League in our home match against Werder, on our way to qualification.

In the round of 16, we drew AC Milan, the club I rooted for when I was a kid because Boban played there. This Milan team wasn't as strong as the 1990s team, but they had some tremendous players. One of my favourites was Zlatan Ibrahimović, whose football and spirit always delighted me. They also had Nesta, Seedorf, Thiago Silva, Gattuso and the virtuoso Pirlo. However, the weeks before our appearance at the legendary San Siro were not without problems. First, we lost 4–0 to Fulham in the FA Cup fourth round, and then the evening after the match turned into a real drama. Vanja made us dinner and then we watched some TV, but I went to bed early because I had a stomach ache. I thought I would fall asleep and the pain would go away – but it just wouldn't, and, around 6 a.m., I realised I couldn't endure it any more. I called our team doctor and he told me it might be appendicitis. They took me to the hospital and prepped me for surgery.

My spirit was broken, as always happens when health issues are involved, because they mean I won't be able to play. Besides, it was my first surgery, so I didn't even try to hide my fear. But it went well and was over quickly, and the new race against time began. The match against AC Milan was less than two weeks away, and I wanted to do whatever it took to be ready. I hoped our doctors would soon clear me for practice. Eight days after the surgery, I was already back at the training ground; three days later, I was on a plane to Milan with the rest of the team. Even though I was happy to be with the team, Redknapp surprised me at practice before the match: 'Luka, how about you start the match tomorrow?' Under any other circumstances, I would have jumped and said, 'Yes!', but so soon after the surgery, with only a couple of training sessions, it was a miracle I was even travelling with the team. Starting such a demanding game was too much, despite my wish to play. Redknapp accepted my opinion, but 15 minutes into the second half, he brought me on to replace Rafael van der Vaart. What's also lodged in my memory from that match is Gomes' performance. His saves kept us in the game and, in the end, helped us to secure a victory. Around the 80th minute, we made a quick counter-attack; I played a through ball for Aaron Lennon, who got into a one-on-one situation against his opponent, dribbled past him, and then crossed for Peter Crouch, who, in front of

75,000 fans in the stands, coolly scored for a superb 1–0 win. What a feeling! We had beaten Milan at the San Siro.

In the return match at White Hart Lane there were no goals, which was enough for us to advance into the quarter-final. There, we played against the great Real Madrid, and that's when I learned what it means to perform against the best. The atmosphere at Santiago Bernabéu was spectacular. At the warm-up, as we gazed up and down the giant stands of the footballing temple, Vedran Ćorluka told me, 'I have a feeling the fans are hanging above my head!'

Four minutes into the match it was 1–0 to Real. Fifteen minutes later we were down to 10 men because Crouch had received a second yellow. By the end of the match Real had easily beaten us 4–0. The return match was just a formality, but we wanted to show our fans we could compete against Real. We did well, and I remember our fans continued to support us even after the Brazilian Ronaldo scored, which proved to be enough for the Spaniards to win 1-0 on the night and 5-0 on aggregate. Finally that season, Tottenham had stepped into the big boys' club, which proved to be the only thing to console me after the disappointing fifth-place finish in the Premier League meant we didn't qualify for the Champions League the following season.

Stormy Seas and Marital Port

With the English Premier League season over I had a 10-day break before the final match of the season. We were playing the UEFA Euro 2012 qualifier against Georgia. It was the first competitive match in Split after a long 14 years of waiting. This itself made it different, as did our previous history in Split. Croatia had not come out victorious in any of the previous nine matches played at Poljud Stadium, three of which were competitive. The outrage in Split and Dalmatia because the national team seldom played qualifying matches at Poljud was justified. It burdened the atmosphere during the match, which was challenging in itself because it was June, the end of the season, so the team wasn't in good shape. Besides, the Georgians were a tough nut to crack. In Tbilisi, two-and-a-half months earlier, they had put up a real fight and eventually scored in injury time to make it 1–0, inflicting on us a first loss in our qualifying group. In this return match at Poljud, they once again played fanatically, and when they took an unexpected lead in the 17th minute things got even more complicated. Nevertheless, by the end of the match, with the support of our fans, we managed to break their resistance: first Mandžukić equalised in the 81st minute and then, in the 83rd, Nikola Kalinić scored to seal an important 2–1 victory.

I could finally focus on our wedding, with our church ceremony scheduled for 11 June. A year before, after the intimate ceremony at the town hall, we had celebrated our special day in the circle of our closest friends and family, but this time we had 170 guests. It was fantastic, and the party at the Westin Hotel lasted until 7 a.m. Mladen Grdović, my dear friend from Zadar, the acapella group Klapa Intrade and the famous Halid Bešlić put on an incredible show. I love their songs, and all of them contributed to a brilliant atmosphere. Grdović kept singing until well into the next morning, and when the people gathered for breakfast, around 10 a.m., he just went on!

I was finally ready for my summer vacation and some relaxation. But it didn't last long, as my agents – Vlado Lemić and Davor Ćurković – passed on Chelsea's wish to sign me. Before transferring to Tottenham, it had seemed I would move to Stamford Bridge. This new contact only added to the impression that Chelsea thought highly of me. They had brought in a new manager earlier that summer: André Villas-Boas replaced Carlo Ancelotti. These two coaches would soon become important figures in my career.

I was open to the idea of moving to Chelsea, but then things happened at lightning speed. First, Vanja and I took a private jet from Zadar to Cannes, where my management team were waiting. Then, a van with tinted-glass windows took us to Nice, some 30 kilometres away. There we were picked up by Roman Abramovich's security, who put us on a speedboat and took us to the Chelsea owner's yacht. It was all very exciting. Twenty or so people, who seemed to be part of the security detail, met us at the boat. It was quick and well organised; just as we made ourselves comfortable on one of the luxury decks, Abramovich showed up. He was accompanied by his wife Dasha and their son. I was fascinated by the discreet disappearance of all the security people just as he arrived. It was obvious they were well trained – their timing was perfect.

I had met Abramovich only once before. I was watching Chelsea play against Atlético Madrid at Stamford Bridge and was seated close to his box. This is where we met and exchanged a couple of words. During our meeting on the Côte d'Azur, he left an impression of a relaxed, somewhat mysterious person. He wasn't beating around the bush and said: 'We know you are a quality player. I'd like you to sign for Chelsea.'

I had come to his yacht to talk, so it was evident I wished the same. I had three successful seasons at Tottenham behind me. The club was now near the top of the Premier League, I had finally felt the pleasure of playing in the UEFA Champions League, and all the analysis showed I was one of the key players in the team's rise. My feeling was that it was time for a move – I wanted to fight for trophies and win titles, and I felt this wouldn't happen if I stayed at Tottenham. I wanted to move to a more ambitious club. Football is beautiful because everyone can play it and take pleasure in the game until they grow old, but a top career has a short span. At 26 years old, I thought I shouldn't pass on an opportunity that had opened up before me.

'Do you think Tottenham will resist your transfer? Are they going to put up a fight?' Abramovich asked.

'I think the negotiations are going to be tough,' I replied, because I knew the clubs were not on good terms.

We finished our drinks and after 20 minutes or so, Abramovich and his wife discreetly retreated to their quarters. As he said goodbye, he suggested we relax on the boat and have a swim, but we thanked him and left. Within 90 minutes, the duration of a football match, we were back on the coast of Nice. We walked around the town a bit and then took a plane back to Zagreb. Both Vanja and I were impressed by the lightning-quick meeting, but deep inside I knew Tottenham's chairman Daniel Levy wouldn't want to hear about it.

Before the start of the pre-season, English reporters called me and asked if it was true that I wanted to leave Spurs. I was honest, and probably naïve, when I said I thought it was time for a step forward in my career. That created a lot of fuss, which didn't quieten down until the end of the transfer window. Levy made a public statement saying that there was no chance of letting me leave and that I had a firm contract with Tottenham. I arrived in London before the pre-season training and went to talk to the chairman. There were no harsh words or insults as the media said, but the conversation was tense. He reprimanded me for publicly announcing I wanted to leave and repeated that Tottenham had no intention of selling me at any price.

A stressful period followed. The media analysed my status on a daily basis; Tottenham fans, understandably, mostly resented that I wanted to leave. On the other hand, Harry Redknapp showed understanding for my situation in his public appearances. It was far from easy at the time. Redknapp was an experienced manager and he had seen it all, so he was aware of the opportunities open to me at a more ambitious club. He also knew he needed me, and, like any manager, he wanted to have a strong team. He did everything he could to please me and make me stay. During our pre-season tour in South Africa, he even made me captain. But my head just wasn't there, so I handed in an official transfer request. However, nothing happened.

On Saturday, 6 August, we played the first home game of the new season, a friendly against Athletic Bilbao, who came to White Hart Lane for our final test before the start of the competitive campaign.

There had been a lot of speculation about the fans' reactions at White Hart Lane after the story about the transfer to Chelsea leaked. I began on the bench and was quite nervous. When Redknapp brought me on, the fans gave me a fantastic reception and a hero's welcome! It was touching, especially because those days were filled with anxiety and concern. Personally, I saw the fans' reaction as an expression of their understanding of my desire to move to a more ambitious club, as well as their hope and encouragement that I would stay with Spurs. Their treatment during the previous three seasons had been nothing but positive. I had given my best for Tottenham, and they recognised it. Their rapport now and this warm reception, after everything that had been going on that summer, gave me immense pleasure.

There were still three weeks until the end of the transfer window. Chelsea kept coming back with improved offers; Levy continued to reject them. All of this aggravated me, and Redknapp realised I was in no state to play. I wasn't in the team for the two matches against Hearts, when we qualified for the group stage of the UEFA Europa League, or for the Premier League opening match at Old Trafford, where Manchester United beat us 3–0. The next week we played a home game against Manchester City, and Redknapp asked me to play. We had a couple of injured players and hadn't opened the season as well as was expected. A couple of hours before the match, I told him I wasn't focused and that I would rather not play. Redknapp insisted and, as he had always treated me well, I agreed. But my fears were confirmed – I wasn't fit to play. We lost 5–1, and I was replaced 60 minutes into the match. It was one of my worst performances for Spurs.

Three days after that match, the transfer window closed and, while I was with the Croatia national team, I realised my move to Chelsea wouldn't happen. Two UEFA Euro 2012 qualifiers followed, against Malta and Israel, and after two turbulent months I felt I needed to distance myself from the club. I watched the first away match against Malta from the bench. I was saving myself for the match against Israel four days later in Zagreb. It was a very complicated match for the team – as well as for me, because I was just searching for the right form. Israel took the lead at the most awkward time, a minute before the end of the first half. But, at the beginning of the second half, in the 47th minute, I equalised with a strike from more than 30 yards out. It was one of the most beautiful goals I have ever scored and, best of all, it initiated our superb comeback. In the next nine minutes the now fit Eduardo scored two goals, the first courtesy of my assist, for a 3–1 win. This match and my performance put me on the road to finding my form.

I returned to London with a clear idea in my mind: forget what had happened because the story was over and get down to work – dedicate myself to the training, reach the necessary level, and be at the manager's and the team's disposal. Redknapp had an even better idea. He played me in the first team in the very next game, and, by the end of the 2011/2012 Premier League season, I had played 90 minutes in all the matches, except against West Bromwich Albion when I came down with a virus. I think I had a great season. After our match against Wolverhampton Wanderers, we had a streak of 10 wins and just one draw and reached second place. We put in some wonderful performances, with only a defeat against Stoke City stopping us momentarily, so that by the end of February we had 16 wins, five draws and only two losses in 23 matches. At the close of the season, we lost our momentum somewhat and, following a couple of poor performances against bottom-of-the-table clubs Norwich and QPR, we fell to fourth place. We were a point behind third-place Arsenal. However, we repeated the previous season's result and ended among the Champions League places.

Unfortunately, a new campaign in the elite competition was taken from us because Chelsea, who ended up sixth in the Premier League, unexpectedly won the Champions League. As the defending champions, they qualified directly for the next season's group stage, while Tottenham competed in the Europa League instead.

I had a couple of meetings with the chairman Daniel Levy during that season. In January, he even came to my home and tried to talk me into extending my contract with Tottenham. It would've been my second extension. Among other things, Levy then told me he'd let me leave for an offer from a big club such as Real Madrid. At that time, I still wasn't giving much thought to the continuation of my career, so I told him I wouldn't sign anything. My main focus was to play well for Tottenham and to prepare for Euro 2012 in Poland and Ukraine.

This is a good place to say something about the Tottenham chairman. Despite all the turbulence in the summer of 2011 and what followed later, I always had a good relationship with Daniel Levy. First and foremost, he was the one who brought me to Tottenham – for a record fee in the club's history. That only showed how highly both he and the club thought of me. They gave me a big chance. My status at White Hart Lane was excellent, and I think I earned it with my behaviour, performances and by always giving my best for Spurs. Generally speaking, Daniel Levy is an excellent chairman who fights for Spurs' interests. The club's recent results only attest to this. However, I resented him because on a couple of occasions he had promised to let me move to a bigger club and then broke his promise. For me, one's promise and one's word are more important than anything. Anyone who knows anything about my relationship with the clubs I have played for knows money has never been my priority – otherwise, I would have chosen some other destinations and be better off financially. In professional football, money is the consequence of what you show on the pitch. To prove your worth on a daily basis, you need to be completely focused, ready and, more than anything, motivated and challenged. If you no longer feel this, it is time to move on. In my career, there were several such moments when big decisions and changes needed to be made. They are never simple, but they are unavoidable. Staying in your comfort zone is easier, but you soon learn the results are then limited. That's not in the club's or the player's best interest.

CHAPTER SIX

The move to Tottenham was one such decisive moment in my career. I had key-player status and was very popular, yet I left Dinamo to fight and prove myself in the most physically demanding league in the world. Many pundits were sceptical of how I would manage in the brutal pace of the Premier League – that is, they were worried whether I would be able to demonstrate my technical skill when competing against such tough and strong opponents. I wasn't afraid, nor worried. On the contrary, all the doubts that followed me from the beginning of my career always served as a strong motivation. From the parking lot in front of the refugee hotel, in schoolyards, on football pitches of youth leagues, I always showed I could take my game to the older, physically stronger players and that always gave me confidence and faith in myself. As I grew older and made progress, my conviction only grew stronger. All this time, and even now at the zenith of my career, many have tried to find different ways to disprove this. But I never lost faith. I patiently endured all the criticism that came at a time of crisis. I never wavered, I only found new motivation in it. With time, my performances would prove them wrong.

The four years at Tottenham, in the Premier League and in European club competitions, were no different. And famously so. The Premier League was a decisive point in my career. I would either become a star player or someone who showed promise but was then consigned to anonymity. Many occasions proved that I had made a step toward the highest level. It wasn't just the interest and offers from bigger clubs – the persistence Tottenham showed in wanting to keep me on their team proved this too. Nevertheless, one detail told me that the time had come to make a new big decision. The media speculated that Manchester United were interested in signing me; they supposedly saw me as an ideal replacement for the legendary Paul Scholes. Such stories, although unconfirmed, were very pleasing to hear. Even back when I was a teenager, Scholes was one of my favourite players. I watched him as he played for United together with Giggs, Beckham and other stars.

In the footballing world, rumours and gossip are part of a daily ritual, and they intensify as the transfer period comes near. So, I didn't pay much attention to the one about Manchester United either. But I did read Sir Alex Ferguson's words on the occasion of the award for the Player of the Year for 2010/11. The great Scott Parker from West Ham United, who would sign for Tottenham in the summer transfer window, won the Football Writers' vote, while my teammate Gareth Bale claimed the PFA award.

'For me, the best player of the Premier League is Luka Modrić,' said Ferguson.

It wasn't just another opinion that was nice to hear – it was an opinion expressed by a legendary manager, a charismatic expert, who had become such because he was always careful to praise. Ferguson's words were confirmation I had succeeded in what I had been fantasising about when I came to England: I had proven myself as a player.

I didn't know where I would go from Tottenham. I didn't know if and when Daniel Levy would agree to sell me. But I was convinced it was time to move on, to a new and bigger challenge.

I had an excellent relationship with my teammates at Spurs. I was also fortunate to become part of Tottenham when a great team came together. We were also a great group of friends. That, of course, was still somewhat different from Croatia. In England, players do not meet after training, they do not often go out together or visit each other's homes. Everyone had their schedule and habits. But, in training, during the matches, when we travelled together, we got along well. Vanja and I loved those relaxing moments in the family box at White Hart Lane after the game. Players' wives and children or girlfriends would get there and socialise. We also took pleasure, each in our own way, in the fantastic atmosphere in the stands. Vanja often told me how she felt watching the game at our stadium. My feeling down on the pitch was similar. The culture, the experience of the match, the respect for the players, all of these things make English football one of a kind. For English people, football is a religion, and for the players, especially for those coming from abroad, this is a magical feeling.

I also got to know the meaning of a Christmas party in England! I remember the first time I went out with my teammates – we went out, to play bowling, at 3 p.m. I thought we would have a couple of drinks and maybe some food and be done by the evening. That's why I didn't tell Vanja when I would be back. But with the bowling and the dinner and drinks not actually starting until 10 p.m., the party dragged on. Vanja got worried because I didn't get home until early the next morning. From then on, we knew what English team building meant!

The boys knew me well; they knew how I thought. In England, people are very respectful and do not pry into another person's business. That's why my teammates never discussed my potential transfer, but after four wonderful years, during which we felt at home in England, Vanja and I knew this life had to come to an end.

CHAPTER SEVEN

While I was enjoying a good run at Tottenham in the autumn of 2011, Croatia was going through a new crisis. In October, we lost the UEFA Euro 2012 qualifier in Athens to our direct rival, Greece. One point would have been enough before the match because we were assuming victory in the last game against Latvia in Rijeka. However, Greece completely outplayed us at the Georgios Karaiskakis Stadium in Piraeus. It was one of the worst matches Croatia has ever played. Although my own form at club level had shown considerable progress, my performance in Greece was poor, to say the least. The Greeks ended the night celebrating direct qualification for the prestigious tournament in Poland and Ukraine, while dark clouds were once again gathering around the Croatia national team. There were reasons to be worried. We had not participated at the previous FIFA World Cup, so Croatian football would have taken a serious blow if we had also failed to qualify for the European Championship. For the first time since Croatia had gained independence, the national team faced the danger of failing to qualify for two international competitions in a row.

On the flight back from Athens concerns were voiced, especially by some from the Croatian Football Federation. While the players and the coaching staff mostly kept quiet, preoccupied with their thoughts and disappointed by our performances and results, the Federation was making arrangements and plans on how to move on, and with whom. More than anything, they were dissatisfied with Slaven Bilić. But, while the manager can be attacked and asked to step down, this doesn't work with the players. Ever since I had become part of the national squad, I noticed that some of the people travelling with us, and not only from the Federation, influenced morale within the national team. I didn't particularly like the fact that the players and the coaches mixed with Federation officials, let alone with others, and I know most players thought the same. The team has its rhythm, its moods, its routines and needs – especially after an important match is lost, such as the one in Greece.

To reach the European Championship we had to play the match against Latvia and then a crucial play-off game – the first such game since I had become been part of the national team. We stayed at our training camp in Rovinj and the atmosphere was miserable. The question of whether Bilić would remain as manager hung in the air. The press wrote about it at some length and, understandably, Slaven seemed concerned. I can't remember if I ever saw him in such a state during the eight years he was in charge of the youth and senior national teams. He invited Vedran Ćorluka and me to his room: 'I want an honest answer, do I still have the team's support?' We said 'Yes' – players didn't want Bilić to leave and we were determined to show this in the very next match against Latvia and to secure a victory that would lift the spirits around the national team. I think that conversation was important to Bilić and it helped put an end to the strange agony caused by the defeat against the Greeks. The Croatian Football Federation didn't sack Bilić, and he led us in the dead-rubber match against Latvia.

Despite the bitter taste from Athens, the Kantrida Stadium in Rijeka, Croatia's third largest city, offered a positive atmosphere. The stands were packed, and, except for a few jeers, the fans gave us their support. They were rewarded: Eduardo and Mandžukić's second-half goals led us to a 2–0 victory and removed at least some of the pressure.

In order to qualify for Euro 2012 we now had to win a play-off, and in what seemed like a touch of fate we found out that our opponents would be Turkey! We were motivated to wash away the bitter taste of our devastating defeat at Euro 2008 and to qualify for the next tournament.

Now that we'd learned we would be playing against the Turks, we were psyched to the max. We had an opportunity to get revenge for our traumatic defeat at the last Euros. The truth is, however, that a wish is seldom enough. Turkey had a strong team and an excellent coach in Guus Hiddink. Also, when they played at home, they were strong. As hosts, they had beaten all the teams in their group, except for Germany, who had gone through qualifying unbeaten.

A month after the disaster in Greece we set off, aware that expectations were low that we could be successful. The general assumption was that the Turks were the favourites, and we could feel it when we arrived in Istanbul.

Our coach, Bilić, was focused on every detail. He had some doubts about who to play as left-back and striker, and he shared his thoughts with a group of the most experienced players. He wanted to hear our opinions, and I think this is a wise approach, especially when the situation demands it. Bilić's idea was to attack right from the start, press the Turkish last line and prevent them from developing their game. The aggression of Ivica Olić combined with Mandžukić was ideal for such a choice. That's what Bilić decided, although it wasn't easy to leave our leading striker Eduardo on the bench. The manager's other surprise was the choice of Ćorluka at left-back and of Gordon Schildenfeld as his central defender. Gathering the players he had selected for the first team at his hotel room, he explained every detail of his plan and encouraged us.

In the fiery atmosphere of the Türk Telekom Arena in Istanbul, the noisy home supporters went quiet in the second minute when Olić scored an all-important goal for us. It also helped instil in us the belief and conviction that Bilić's tactics were working. We put in an excellent performance and did exactly what Bilić asked. Mandžukić and Olić stifled their defenders, preventing them from being able to develop their game, which made the Turks nervous.

Our manager's bold approach and our determination to show we were worthy of playing at Euro 2012 led us to a great victory. Mandžukić and Ćorluka, who had played a fantastic match, added two more goals for a 3–0 win. It was a real triumph – exactly what we needed to get back to normal. The return match in Zagreb ended in a draw, but after our win in Istanbul it was most important we brought the game to a routine conclusion, without stress. We had set the record straight and qualified for Euro 2012 at Turkey's expense. Of course, the wounds left after the disappointing penalty shootout in Vienna four years earlier will never heal. But at least we managed to lift ourselves for this play-off.

***

For me, as far as club matters were concerned, the year of the Euros started well. Tottenham successfully sailed through the season, and big and ambitious clubs continued to show an interest in signing me. Officials from Paris Saint-Germain got in touch and in January, Leonardo, the former Brazil star of PSG as well as of AC Milan, called me on the phone. I had watched him play at the 1994 FIFA World Cup in the United States. 'We think highly of you and we would like you to join PSG,' he said briefly. It was a pleasant conversation. I told him I didn't know what would happen until the summer transfer window, but I was honoured by his club's attention. I was interested because PSG had great plans and had already signed some top players. It was a big and tempting challenge. After a while, I met Carlo Ancelotti. In January, the Italian had taken over the role of manager of the French club and he made it clear he wanted me in the team he was putting together for the next season. We met at his house and had a good talk. It's always like that with Carlo, and the time we subsequently spent together at Real Madrid only confirmed my first impressions and showed what a wonderful person he is, as well as a fantastic, trophy-winning coach.

***

In late February, in advance of Euro 2012, Croatia hosted a friendly against Sweden. One of the reasons I was looking forward to the match was Zlatan Ibrahimović. The first time I saw him on the pitch, he became one of my favourite players. His technical prowess, as well as his sensational, acrobatic moves, showed his outstanding class. I always liked his relentless competitiveness and fierce attitude. In our region, where his parents come from, we often say that such characters are not all there. Ibra has character, he speaks his mind, and I will always choose such people over pretence and fakeness.

In Zagreb, the scoreboard showed 3–1 for Sweden – but Ibra beat us practically on his own. After the match, we shared our impressions. I had a couple of duels with Ibra, just as I would later run into him when our clubs met, and I learnt first-hand he's as tough as a rock. You think you can take the ball from him, yet he positions himself in such a way that you can't get near him. His posture and supreme technique are out of this world. What a great player! The transfer window the next summer would make it possible that we could have ended up playing for the same team, PSG, but in the end it didn't happen. In the past, there had been a lot of talk in Croatia that our football federation should try to persuade Ibrahimović to play for our national team, considering that his mother is Croatian. Unfortunately, he chose Sweden. Who knows what would've happened if we'd also had Ibrahimović within our ranks . . . ?

Later in the year I joined Croatia's pre-Euros camp in Rovinj. Although the weather was humid, we trained well. There was a games room at the hotel, so we relaxed playing table tennis, billiards or computer games.

One day, Mario Mamić, my representative, called me on the phone. 'Are you sitting down?' he asked. This first question told me he had something important to say, something that would make my knees buckle. It did! 'Real Madrid called. Their manager wants you for the next season!'

I was shocked and didn't know what to say. My first thought was: *It's a dream come true!* Real Madrid is an institution; the best football club in the world. Soon, I received a call from my other representative, Vlado Lemić, who had all the details. He confirmed my hopes: José Mourinho, at that point at the top of his career and probably the first name among world-class managers, wanted me to play for Real Madrid. *Could it be any better?!* My thoughts were running wild. I saw myself in Los Blancos' shirt, playing alongside star players at the packed Bernabéu, winning trophies. However, many obstacles needed to be overcome before I could finally put on their shirt.

In a footballer's career, from the beginning and basically right to the end, there is something special about being approached by a club that wants to bring you into their ranks. When you are younger and you experience this for the first time, it takes your breath away. You do get used to this over time, but even so, every such call fills you with pleasure. And, although I was 27 and had already gone through a lot in my career, I was extremely excited.

It was wonderful to enjoy the idea that I might join Real Madrid, but it soon became a burden. No one outside a very small circle – Real, my agents and me – was allowed to know about the agreement. It was difficult, I wanted to share my happiness with the whole world. I did tell Vanja. She is my love and the mother of our children, but also my friend and my support. I have shared everything with her from the first day we met and she is the first person I go to for advice. When I told her about Real, she was as excited as I was. We were both fully aware of what this meant for my career.

When I learned about Los Blancos' interest, I didn't want to hear about any other offer. I only saw myself playing for Real Madrid!

As part of our Euros preparations, Croatia played in Pula against Estonia and in Oslo against Norway. I didn't play because I had some minor injuries. Bilić didn't want to risk anything in advance of the European Championship and it was obvious the club season had taken its toll. I needed to get some rest and not take any chances before the tournament.

I still travelled with the national team and upon our return from Oslo we got three days off before we were scheduled to go to Poland – and then on to the tournament. I spent the break in Zagreb. I love tennis, and I challenged my great friend Čale to a match. We were playing in the neighbourhood of Ravnice and during a short break between the games I checked my phone, thinking I might have a received a message from Vanja.

'Hello Luka, I'd like to call you after practice. Best, José Mourinho.'

It was *the* moment. The fantastic story about Real had just become reality. I could no longer focus on tennis. We quickly finished the match. But my excitement was soon replaced by anxiety. I went home – all sweaty, my trainers red from the dusty tennis court – sat at the table and waited. Vanja noticed I was restless and told me: 'Go take a shower, I'll wait by the phone. If he calls, I'll come to get you.'

I didn't listen to her. I spent an hour or maybe two waiting for the phone to ring. Finally, it did.

'I want you on our team for the next season. I like the way you play, and I have faith in you. I'm certain you'll prosper at Real Madrid.'

Mourinho won me over immediately. I don't think José needs me to speak of his greatness, but I saw right away that he had a unique way of treating his players. He explained what position he saw me in: 'You're a midfielder and I see you as a No. 8. Not as a 10, not as a 6, but an 8!'

In all the excitement, I replied, 'Thank you, coach! I'm honoured to hear you want me at Real Madrid. I'll do my best to prove worthy of your confidence.'

'OK. Let's stay in touch. Best of luck at the Euros!'

I was as happy as a child. Mourinho's call meant the big transfer was under way. At that point, I couldn't have imagined what it would take to bring Tottenham chairman Daniel Levy to an agreement. After this first call, Mourinho would often text me, before and after my matches.

***

Unfortunately, the draw for the Euros was not kind to us – we got two tournament favourites, Spain and Italy, as well as Republic of Ireland.

The Spaniards were defending the title they had won in Austria and Switzerland in 2008 where, after a penalty shoot-out, they had eliminated Italy in the quarter-final. What's more, they were arriving in Poland as the reigning World Cup holders, having triumphed in South Africa. By contrast, Italy were just recovering from the fiasco of the 2010 FIFA World Cup and arrived at Euro 2012 full of determination.

In our first match in the group stages we beat the Republic of Ireland 3–1, with Mandžukić scoring a brace and Nikica Jelavić netting the other.

Meanwhile, Spain and Italy drew 1–1, which meant we simply needed to get a good result from the second match against Italy to progress. Much of the success enjoyed by the *Azzurri* rested on their outstanding midfielder, Andrea Pirlo. Several pre-match pundits had drawn a comparison between Pirlo and I, which was pleasing to hear because he was a top-class midfielder. Bilić told us to limit his time on the ball. But no matter how well we did this, Pirlo still punished us by scoring a fantastic goal, lifting a free-kick over the wall in the 39th minute. We didn't give up, though, and in the second half we played better: Mandžukić scoring in the 72nd minute. Before the match he said he'd dreamed of scoring past Gianluigi Buffon – and it came true. (The legendary goalkeeper was one of his childhood idols, and Mandžukić would later sign for Juventus and play alongside Buffon.)

My club future now lay in Spain, but if Croatia were to qualify for the knockout stages we needed to overcome *La Roja*, a team that had an immense depth of talent, from Casillas and Ramos to Alonso, Xavi, Iniesta, Torres and others. They were a team in their prime.

We put in an excellent performance against the World and European Champions, and showed we could compete against the very strongest teams. However, Navas' goal in the 88th minute led them to victory – though before that, they hadn't created a single chance. If the match had gone our way, that would not have been undeserved: yes, we wasted a couple of big chances, but I'm convinced the referee failed to give us one, possibly even two, penalties in our favour. Unfortunately, back then VAR didn't exist!

If we leave the final result and the inevitable sadness to one side, I enjoyed playing in that match. I felt I had the strength and the skill to do whatever I wanted. Bilić gave me more freedom in the game, and, in my opinion, that was one of my best performances in a Croatia shirt.

It was also my first encounter with players from Real Madrid and Barcelona, notably the players who had made Real the most successful national side in Spanish history. I swapped shirts with Andrés Iniesta, whom I had always liked as a player, and I also exchanged a couple of words with all the Spanish players. Sergio Ramos approached me, hugged me and said, 'See you in Madrid!' It was a sign that the Real Madrid players were talking about my arrival. 'I hope so,' I replied.

Navas' goal and our 1–0 defeat meant that our dream to qualify for the knockout stage didn't come true. The tournament's final revealed just how complicated our task had been – with our group stage opponents, Spain and Italy, playing in it. The former had eliminated France and Portugal, while the latter sent England and Germany home. In the end, Spain were crowned the champions with a convincing, yet somewhat unexpected, 4–0 victory, thus securing a fantastic series of three consecutive trophies: the FIFA World Cup and two European Championships!

On account of the fierce opposition, but also our good performances, Croatia's fans remained realistic and accepted the disappointing end of the road without resentment. They cheered us on in every match we played in Poznan and Gdansk. Elimination saddened us, the fans as well as the players – especially since we'd come so close to qualifying from the group stage – but we had given our best and played good football, and that was what mattered.

I was required to take a doping test after the Spain match, so I was fairly late to join the rest of the team at our hotel and the sombre mood was understandable. Bilić didn't have much to say after our elimination, but we could all sense this was his last campaign at the helm. I was sad he was leaving because we had an outstanding relationship. We had spent two years together at the youth team and six at the senior team at a time when he made a name for himself as a manager, just as I did as a player. Bilić has been one of the most important people in my career and, as far as I'm concerned, nothing can break that bond.

Another Summer of Unease

Upon my return from UEFA Euro 2012, I was looking forward to a holiday. I had around 30 days to regenerate and I planned to use them to prepare for a new stage in my career, the biggest and the most important yet. I never thought for a moment that matters could end up being as complicated as they were the summer before when Chelsea had made their offer. However, the reality proved even worse.

I was spending time in Zadar, which had become our tradition, and Vanja and I now invited some friends to join us for a cruise around the Adriatic. During the week, I decided to call the new Tottenham manager. As fate would have it, the summer before André Villas-Boas had been at Chelsea hoping to bring me to Stamford Bridge. Now, just a year later, he had taken over as Tottenham manager and was adamant that he wanted to keep me at White Hart Lane. This time, however, I was determined to leave. I was certain Daniel Levy would keep his promise. I contacted Villas-Boas to tell him as much because I had seen he was telling the papers I would stay at Tottenham.

'Coach, don't count on me. The chairman promised he'd let me go if Real Madrid sent an offer.' That was more or less what I told him, and he replied, 'I understand. We'll talk more when you arrive.'

That told me the transfer wouldn't be as smooth as I expected. I went to London for the first day of pre-season training and decided to see Villas-Boas right away. It was a difficult talk right from the start. It was clear that a new summer ordeal was about to begin and that would create problems. I was enraged, and when the next day the manager told me I had to go on an American tour with the rest of the team, we argued. In a stern voice, he told me I had to behave like a professional and that this wouldn't end as I imagined. He talked about other people having a bad influence on me. I retorted that I wasn't going to the United States under any circumstances and then brought the argument to an end: 'For me, my word is my bond. And that's why I'm going home!'

I wasn't joking, and the next day, when the rest of the team were on their way to the United States, I went home to Zadar. It caused tensions and I was worried to see it become a huge scandal. Throughout my career, I had always been nothing but professional. But now, this seemed to be the only way to make Levy keep his promise. Whenever I reminded him, 'Chairman, what about your promise?', he would reply, 'We'll talk.' Then he would always find an excuse to avoid the topic.

When I came back to Zadar, my representatives called to convey Real's position; they advised me to return to London to calm the situation down so that the negotiations could continue. I was very nervous, but I understood that the best option was to go back to Chigwell, train and wait for the outcome. Four days later, I was once again at Spurs Lodge, where I impatiently waited for the news. There was a certain symbolism in that because Tottenham would soon move from the 16-year-old training ground to a new, luxurious Enfield Training Centre. However, Levy's secretary reminded me I was in for more uncertainty. When she saw I had returned, she came to see me and handed me an envelope. In it was my plane ticket for Los Angeles, where Spurs were preparing for the new season. I took the ticket and later threw it away.

Every day I went to the ground and trained. It was gruelling. I had spent four wonderful seasons at Tottenham, the fans loved me, the public respected me, and all of this made those final days of my career with Spurs even more difficult. Meanwhile, even when the first team had come back from the United States, I still trained alone. My pre-season 'training' was anything but a structured preparation for the new campaign. On one of those difficult days, José Ángel Sánchez, Real Madrid's managing director, called me on the phone. Florentino Pérez, the Real Madrid president, was with him. They offered me their support, which meant a lot at that moment and allowed me to keep my faith that things would eventually fall into place. They told me they were standing beside me and waiting, and asked me to be patient. They had talked to Levy, and said negotiations were under way.

Those negotiations were tough. My representatives kept me informed about everything. As did José Mourinho. Levy was driving them crazy: it seemed that every time they reached an agreement, he asked for something else. I was under a lot of stress. So were Vanja and the rest of my family. When I went back to London, I told Vanja to stay in Zadar with Ivano and enjoy the summer. After a while, she joined me because it seemed that negotiations had come to an end. Twice my representatives called me to say, 'Finally, we've agreed on everything, you're flying to Madrid.' And when, all happy, I would head for the airport, new information would arrive: 'We have to put it off, there's a new development.'

The second time that happened, I was on the edge. Falling apart. Tortured by the lack of progress, I remember asking Vanja, 'How can Levy be so unfair?'

Vanja and I concluded that the torture would continue for a while, so we agreed it would be best if she went back to Zadar and stayed with Ivano. It made no sense to wait and waste her time in London. By the end of the transfer window and the final resolution, my parents came to stay with me.

During this long period of negotiating, going back and forth, there were several times I got scared that Real might withdraw. The very idea made me nervous. Mourinho played a vital role; he was determined to bring me to Real, insisting on the transfer even when the Real officials lost their patience with Levy. As they told me, Mourinho himself called the

Tottenham chairman and tried to persuade him to accept the offer, 'otherwise Real could back out it.' Taking everything into consideration, that wouldn't have been a good outcome for Tottenham. Having a disappointed player on the team – one who has been deprived of perhaps his last chance to play at the top level – would mean not just the danger of missing out on a significant transfer fee. Even if they forced me to stay at Tottenham because I had a valid contract, as had happened the year before, this time they faced the risk of me being a player completely out of shape.

After one of those solitary training sessions, at the pitch hidden behind the club facilities, I went to take a shower. When I came out of the dressing room, I ran into Levy. He seldom went to the training ground. This time he couldn't avoid me. He was typically dry and cold during this short conversation that began with a question: 'How are you? Nervous?'

'I'm begging you to keep your promise. I'd like to play in the Super Cup against Barcelona. Don't take that away from me.'

Then he told me, 'I'll let you leave on Monday.'

I hoped this could be it, but I didn't dare feel relieved. Too many things had already happened and, with just five days before the end of the transfer window, there wasn't much cause to be hopeful.

However, on that Sunday evening, 26 August, my managers informed me that everything had been agreed and that I was flying to Madrid in the morning! Vanja and Ivano, who had flown in from Zadar with Mario Mamić and Predrag Mijatović, were already there.

Finally, the day came. On Monday morning, after a good night's sleep, I flew to Madrid with my parents. I felt a whole lot lighter. During that pleasant flight, I thought about what my first day at Real would look like. The moment was special – my thoughts flew from one story from my past to another, to all those steps I had to take to make my footballing dreams come true.

I was met at the airport by the Real officials. Reporters from Real Madrid club TV recorded every moment of my special Monday. I felt like the most important person in the world. It was impressive, and all the torment of the last couple of months was wiped away. I felt obliged to call Levy and, despite everything, express my thanks.

'Thank you, Mr Chairman, for letting me go. It's a great opportunity for me. I'm sorry it had to end this way, but I'm thankful for the past four years. I wish you and the club the best of luck in the future.'

Levy is a man who rarely shows his emotions or gives away much. He was strictly professional: 'Thank you for everything you did for Tottenham and best of luck at the new club.'

The medical went without any problems. Then we went to Santiago Bernabéu. First, I went to Florentino Pérez's office to sign the contract, then they took my photo in front of the impressive collection of trophies Real had won. When I climbed up the stairs, many employees came out of their offices to greet me. I was so excited! As I entered the club's home, I became aware of what an institution Real Madrid is and what a unique atmosphere rules over this footballing temple. After the press conference, I went down to the pitch to be presented to the fans. Walking into the dressing room of this cult club was particularly impressive – the shirt number 19 lay ready in front of a locker with my name on it. I had the option to choose number 5, 16 or 19. My favourite, 10, belonged to Mesut Özil; Denis Cheryshev wore my next choice, number 23; and Xabi Alonso was number 14. Nineteen can be read as a one and a nine, which added make the magic number I had always wanted to wear. I quickly changed and, when the club officials called me, I walked out of the tunnel onto the pitch where I would have to prove myself worthy of the Real shirt. My heart was pounding like crazy. I generally don't care too much about formalities, but Real had protocols that had to be respected. Stepping out onto the pitch of Santiago Bernabéu with Vanja and Ivano, my mother and father, and hearing the loud cheer of my new supporters, made that Monday one of the most memorable and most important days of my life.

There was a full schedule, and the proceedings dragged on. I didn't want to miss the first training session at Valdebebas. I wanted to meet my new teammates as soon as possible. I wanted to meet my new coach – it would be the first time we had met in person. I needed football, I needed it fast! I wanted to be a part of the team, to feel the training and the game. When I arrived at the training ground, Iker Casillas, Real's captain, was the first to welcome me. He told me to make myself at home. Some of the players had already gone out on the field. The Brazlian Kaká was still in the dressing room and he welcomed me to the club. Cristiano Ronaldo shook hands with me and greeted me as if we were old friends: 'You're here, finally!'

Other players came to meet me, and then they told me I should go see the coach at his office. Mourinho welcomed me and immediately got to the point: he briefly explained what kind of a club Real was, and what the obligations and expectations were for every player. He told me what he expected from me and told me he was there for me. I thanked him for everything, and that was it. After all the worrying about the transfer – and some luck that finally made it happen – I needed to get down to work.

The first training session showed me the kind of pressure that was part of everyday life at Real. Mourinho gathered the team in the dressing room. It was a crisis meeting because Real had suffered a bad start to the season. In the first two games in La Liga, Real drew against Valencia, then lost to Getafe. Between these two matches, we were defeated 3–2 in the first leg of the Spanish Super Cup against Barcelona at Camp Nou. I didn't speak Spanish, so I didn't understand what he was saying, but his tone and body language made it clear he was angry.

The Real Deal

The excitement of my first day in the Real shirt didn't end with the first training session at Valdebebas. I went to La Moraleja, a neighbourhood where a lot of Real players live. Predrag 'Peđa' Mijatović, one of the great players from recent Real history, had also made a home there. I still remember the winning goal he scored in the 1998 UEFA Champions League Final against Juventus in Amsterdam. He had also served as the managing director at Real before Pérez returned to the club – and it was he who had recommended me to José Mourinho. We became close friends. His advice – coming from his vast experience and his detailed knowledge of Real's system – was of immense help. He and his wife Aneta helped Vanja and I to settle in Madrid. They were there for us whenever we needed help, and that was very important.

When I pulled up in front of Mijatović's villa, I couldn't in all honesty have imagined how this day would end.

'Empty your pockets!' my representative Davor Ćurković told me. Puzzled, I took everything out of my pockets. Davor and Zoran Lemić grabbed my legs and arms, and threw me in the swimming pool! My father, who else, jumped in right after me. Everyone else cheered – my wife and son, my mother, Vanja's mother, Peđa, my managers Davor Ćurković and the brothers Lemić.

It was a fantastic party to mark the end of the first day at Real.

The next day no longer belonged only to me – I had to enter Real's working schedule. I trained with the team, and Mourinho included me for the Spanish Super Cup rematch against Barcelona. This would be my first *El Clásico*, my first trophy battle in the Real shirt.

'I'll give you 20 minutes at the end of the match, and then you'll be in the first team against Granada in La Liga.'

That was the manager's plan and when we retreated to our pre-match camp, I felt excellent. All of the players helped make my first days at Real as easy as possible. With time, they would all become my friends, as was the case in every other club where I played. We were waiting for my first *El Clásico* at a hotel because the players' accommodation facilities were still being built at Valdebebas. A year later, every first-team player would have his own, ultra-modern five-star room. As for conditions, Real's camp is top-class. The pitches are phenomenal – like carpets.

Real's camp is a perfect combination of functionality and beauty – spacious and a proper reflection of the club's reputation.

Before my first derby in the Real shirt, I felt the adrenaline flowing. The atmosphere around the stadium was electrifying. The streets around Bernabéu were packed; it took our white bus 15 or 20 minutes to reach the entrance into the dressing rooms. The fans surrounded the bus, singing and chanting, jumping up to see us and show how much they supported us. I sat next to Xabi Alonso on the bus, who explained that this was one of the traditions at Real. It was very impressive and, perhaps more importantly, it gave us a strong motivation.

The atmosphere in the dressing room was typical of football matches: focus, pre-match preparations, excitement, encouragement. Everyone had their place, according to shirt numbers. To one side, Raul with the number 18, to the other, Gonzalo with number 20. Higuaín scored the first goal in the 11th minute. The noise at Bernabéu was deafening; I got goosebumps. The celebrations and the noise are always spectacular, especially when Real plays against Barcelona. It was surreal just to be there. I had watched the first match on TV in London, still stressing about the transfer. In the return match, I was one of the players – an actor in *El Clásico*. I was immensely proud. The only thing missing was to get out on the pitch. I just couldn't wait for Mourinho to bring me on. When I got up from the bench and ran into the warm-up area, I first heard a murmur from the crowd, then loud cheers and applause. I was burning on the inside. Seconds trickled away and I realised I wouldn't play the planned 20 minutes. The score was 2–1, Ronaldo scored Real's second before Lionel Messi pulled one back and the match was still open. In the 79th minute, Mourinho first took off Ángel Di María and replaced him with José Callejón, and then, three minutes later, Karim Benzema came on for Higuaín. I was fast losing hope of making my debut, but then someone called me from the bench. Adrenaline rushed through my body as Mourinho told me, 'You're replacing Özil and playing attacking midfielder. When Messi has the ball half-right, always move towards the middle. Alonso and you have to close him there. When we're on the attack, take the ball and distribute it!'

In my first *El Clásico*, I played the last seven minutes of regular time, altogether around 10 minutes with injury time, which was enough to leave a positive impression – and win my first trophy with Real (thanks to away goals). All of my dreams had come true. My heart was full! I even had a chance – although I couldn't quite convert it – to score my first goal. When that happened, as well as when I quickly dribbled my way out a sticky situation, I heard that murmur of the crowd followed by applause. Down on the pitch, after the final whistle, I was beside myself with happiness. When we climbed up to the box to receive the trophy, Pepe and Ronaldo passed it on to me. I lifted it into the air, rejoicing like a little child. I was in seventh heaven! Afterwards, I received a message from Mourinho: 'You were excellent! Congrats on your first title, there are many to come. The crowd saw what kind of a player you are and I'm sure they'll enjoy your future performances.'

The start at Real was perfect, but the continuation would be a bit more dramatic.

***

Before the international break, we played against Granada in La Liga. I was included in the starting line-up, just as Mourinho had promised. Once again, the stands were packed, and we took a comfortable 3–0 victory. I played as attacking midfielder for 57 minutes, and I did well. After the exciting summer with very little training, my lack of fitness and rhythm made my start difficult.

Brimming with happiness, that summer I had also played my first match for Croatia as a Real player. (The previous international gathering had taken place when I had been training on my own in London.) The game was scheduled for 15 August in Split, and the opponent was Switzerland. It was Igor Štimac's debut as Croatia's manager. Štimac had played for the celebrated 'Bronze Generation' and had also been Slaven Bilić's teammate, both at Hajduk and for the national team. His coaching staff included three more members of the team that had won third place in France: I knew Krunoslav Jurčić back from the time he had managed Dinamo; Igor Tudor was my teammate in the national squad; and Alen Bokšić was one of the greatest attackers in Croatian history.

Switzerland swept us off the pitch and took a deserved 4–2 victory. I got on 23 minutes before the end, and I managed to show only how unprepared and ineffective I was.

I had a decent relationship with Štimac. In the beginning, though, I found it strange that he was chosen to lead the national team because until recently he had been at war with the most influential people at the Croatian Football Federation, particularly Zdravko Mamić. The public were also surprised by the alliance and didn't approve, and this negativity would burden much of Štimac's era. Many observers suggested that the players should say something about the relations within the Croatian Football Federation and the national team, but that was simply impossible. In the final analysis, it wouldn't make sense. The player's job is to play and not to be in charge of the Federation's politics or to appoint and sack managers. The main problem was that the negative atmosphere and antagonism towards the Croatian Football Federation turned into animosity towards the team. The only thing we could do under such circumstances was to focus on our performances on the pitch and distance ourselves from all the problems off it.

In the autumn part of the World Cup qualification campaign for Brazil 2014, we found a good rhythm. The two matches in September brought us a victory over Macedonia and a 1–1 draw with Belgium, our main contender for first place in the group. October brought two more important wins – against Macedonia in Skopje and Wales in Osijek. We put in some good performances, particularly in Osijek, where the atmosphere was outstanding – as is always the case when the national team plays in Slavonia, the easternmost part of Croatia. Unfortunately, such an atmosphere was becoming a rarity, and the lack of unity started to plague the national team.

Limited Game Time

When I moved to Real Madrid, I thought the Spanish league was more technical and physically less demanding than the English Premier League. I soon learned I was wrong. In terms of tactics and technique, Spanish football was at a very high level. But I was surprised by the level of aggression, especially at away matches. Every opponent in La Liga, if you aren't giving 100 per cent, can cause big problems. Every team is technically and tactically well-versed and fast-paced. In England, the atmosphere in the stands is a bit less hostile; the fans support their team and don't bother about the opponent so much. Spain has a different mentality, and the supporters show more temper. There are venues, such as Sevilla or some smaller stadiums, where the crowd literally stands just above your head and creates enormous pressure. Such away matches can be tricky.

Getting to know the reality of Spanish football and the adjustments to life at Real proved problematic. But this was something I'd expected, assuming it might be even more difficult. The main problem was the fact that I had missed the pre-season training. After the euphoria and the high levels of adrenaline that initially kept me going, the spin of everyday life at Real and its competitive rhythm began to take their toll. I started to worry. But Mourinho is an experienced coach, and that's why he watched over me and limited my game time. I didn't like this because, like every footballer, I wanted to play. For example, I had a hard time when I didn't get even a minute in the second *El Clásico* of that season at Camp Nou. And that was four days after the away match against Ajax in the UEFA Champions League, which we won 4–1. I thought Mourinho was saving me for Barça. But that's why Mou is a great coach: he prepares you gradually to reach your peak. The series of matches that followed allowed me to catch my breath and gather my strength for the difficult period ahead. I scored my first goal in a Real shirt – with my left foot! – against Real Zaragoza in a 4–0 victory. Nevertheless, I fluctuated wildly during the whole autumn season. I played a lot in the Champions League, but in Dortmund, against Borussia – when we lost 2–1 – I gave one of my worst performances ever.

The media follow Real every step of the way; the pressure is enormous. Before my transfer from London, the newspapers had provided detailed reports on every stage of the negotiations. After my good start in the Real shirt, there was a lot of expectation, even euphoria. But that soon changed. After a series of hot and cold performances, the pressure was on. The pundits discussed where I should play: as an offensive or defensive midfielder, or as a classic box-to-box player? Such debates usually signal that your performances aren't convincing. I was sure my position wasn't the problem – I just wasn't ready. I had demonstrated that I could play all of the midfield positions, but I felt best at the position Mourinho had in mind when he brought me to Real – a No. 8! This is where my ability to make a quick transformation from defence into attack, take possession of the ball and dictate the rhythm of the play, could come to the fore. At the same time, playing at No. 8 meant that I could join the attack, reach the opponent's box and create an opportunity to score from a distance. Fortunately, Mourinho thought the same. He would occasionally play me as an attacking midfielder, but my natural position was in the centre of the pitch, the place where the game is made.

I always dealt well with the criticism. It didn't bother me because I knew what was at stake. It all depends on how you play. I learned from the Croatian media, which had taken it from the Spanish newspapers, that there was a poll voting me the worst new La Liga signing. This was at a time when I still didn't speak Spanish. Such things will get to some players, and not others, but I have always thought the performance on the pitch is up to the player. And I felt I could reach the level necessary to play for Real Madrid. I learned this in training, as well as in matches.

I never doubted myself. And that's what mattered the most. The only thing I couldn't do was hurry the time I needed to become ready. I had to be patient.

Meanwhile, I trained hard. I also tried to learn Spanish – I even watched Mexican soap operas! Communication is critical. At Tottenham, when I had just arrived, I was relatively quiet. We had learned the basics in school, but in England I realised how little English I knew, especially when I heard all the accents. But I didn't avoid conversation. You make progress on a daily basis and you soon feel you can talk to the people around you. You understand what someone tells you, you can read everything, and it's easier to become a part of the group. I knew it would be the same in Spain. I also think learning the language is a sign of respect for the country. In the beginning I used English, both with the coaching staff and a lot of my teammates. Kaká, Ronaldo, Alonso and Álvaro Arbeloa spoke good English. By the time of my second season at Real, I had a good command of *Castellano*.

Early in 2013 we enjoyed a series of good results in the Copa del Rey – first we eliminated Celta, then Valencia and finally Barcelona over two matches, which meant we would play against Atlético Madrid in the final in May. I wasn't too happy with my playing time in those matches – I felt better and better, but Mourinho had other plans. I first lost my patience during an away game against Deportivo. In the next 10 or so days, I saw little action.

Against Manchester United at Santiago Bernabéu, Mourinho played me for the final 15 minutes. Four days later I didn't even get to play against Rayo Vallecano because of a yellow card suspension. I had finally been selected for the first team for that match in La Coruña, and was certain I was playing well, when I glanced at the fourth official and I couldn't believe it when I saw my number on the substitutes' board. I had just been on the attack and could have been awarded a penalty. But it no longer mattered. I went off the pitch at 0–0; Real eventually secured a 2–1 victory. I was angry after the match and talked with Rui Faria,

Mourinho's right-hand man. It was the closest thing to talking with Mourinho because I'm sure Faria told him everything. We were on the training pitch at Valdebebas and I spoke my mind.

'I feel great, but I need the coach's support. I need to play continuously because that's the only way to show my worth.' This pretty much summed up my position.

Faria listened carefully and then calmed me down. 'Mourinho is delighted with your work and your progress. In the first leg against Barcelona in the Copa del Rey, you came on in the second half and contributed to a better game and a draw. Everything is all right. Just be patient and you'll get your chance.'

I'm not sure if this conversation had much effect on my status, but I felt better, despite the fact that Mourinho decided to keep me on the bench during the return match against Barcelona at Camp Nou. We won, which was important for morale. Even better, we now began a series of solid matches in which there were more opportunities for me to play. Just as the coach had promised.

The Turning Point

Sir Alex Ferguson: one of the best football coaches of all time; one of the most charismatic people in football. When I played in England, Sir Alex inspired awe, and I was so proud when he named me as his player of the season. He later wrote in his autobiography that he wanted to bring me to Manchester United, but didn't want to get into another round of draining negotiations with Daniel Levy; they had fought hard to bring Michael Carrick and Dimitar Berbatov from Tottenham. I was truly appreciative when Sir Alex described me as 'an example of a player in the modern game who would never dive and stays on his feet.'

I had received signals that United thought highly of me, and when I was at Tottenham, I met Tomislav Erceg, a football agent from Croatia. In his company was a man who wanted to communicate what the people at Old Trafford were thinking – most likely wanting to test my mood about a possible transfer. Manchester United is one of the clubs that has fascinated me ever since I was little, on account of its tradition, its stories and its importance. For these reasons above all, as well as for its tremendous atmosphere, I liked playing at Old Trafford. True, when I played there for Tottenham, I lost every match. But we played good football.

My first match against Manchester United in the Real shirt ended up in a 1–1 draw. We were satisfied with the result because United had created more chances. The rematch was complicated right from the start: three days before the match, we had played in an important *El Clásico* in Madrid. The coach included me in the starting line-up and I remained on the pitch for the full 90 minutes, getting excellent marks for my performance, and we won 2–1. An assist to Sergio Ramos' winning goal in the 82nd minute added to my already good mood. I took the corner kick, then Ramos jumped high into the air and headed the ball home.

We travelled to Manchester with the mission of making our way into the UEFA Champions League quarter-final. Despite my solid performance in *El Clásico*, I knew I would start on the bench.

In the first half, we had a hard time at Old Trafford. Manchester United were pressing us, and it was a miracle we were 0–0 at half time. Mourinho sent a couple of players to warm up. I expected to come on early in the second half, as the injured Ángel Di María stayed in the dressing room, but Mourinho chose Kaká as his replacement. The second half opened with a bad start when, in the 48th minute, Ramos scored an own goal. We were holding on and then, in the 56th minute, United's Portuguese winger Nani was sent off by the referee for a violent foul. Mourinho immediately called me up from the warm-up area. 'You're replacing Arbeloa and playing in front of Alonso and Khedira. Get the ball to Özil, Kaká, Ronaldo and Higuaín.'

I was eager to play. I knew the setting and I felt at home. The first three or four quick and successful passes showed this clearly. We pressed them hard and circled around Manchester United's penalty box, like in handball. I felt I could do whatever I wanted with the ball, and, seven minutes after I had come on, I made some room for myself and kicked the ball with everything I had from more than 20 yards out. The ball had a wicked curve and it bounced off the post and into the net! What a feeling, scoring in such a match, at such a moment! I knew the goal would change my status at Real; in fact, everything that happened during the 31 minutes I spent on the field would do so. Just three minutes after I had scored, I initiated a move for the second goal. I passed the ball to Higuaín, who played a one-two with Özil and crossed to the far post. One of the former Manchester United greats, now wearing our shirt, was there to put it into the net. Ronaldo scored from a tough position, with a goal that secured a place in the Champions League quarter-final for us, although he didn't celebrate out of respect for his former club and their supporters. They gave him a hero's welcome – an old English football tradition.

After the match, I was so happy. Mourinho acknowledged my good performance with a brief, yet loud, 'Bravo!' while we were still on the bus.

Following the fantastic evening at Old Trafford everything in my life changed. After the match, I did indeed become a true Real Madrid player. I had put in good performances even before this match, but after those 30-odd minutes that brought focused play, goals, a change of score and our advance into the quarter-final, my status was no longer an issue – least of all for Mourinho. For him, as well as for me, that game at Manchester United was the true confirmation of my worth.

Eleven days after Old Trafford, we played against Mallorca at Santiago Bernabéu. The visitors took the lead twice in the first half but then, in the span of just five minutes, from the 52nd to the 57th, we scored three goals and turned the tide in our favour. I scored for a 3–2 lead two minutes after Ronaldo had levelled, which sent the crowd into raptures. I was super excited. It is one of my favourite goals: the ball bounced off to a point some 25 yards from goal before I sprinted towards it and smashed it with a powerful right-footed shot. It crashed into the back of the net, and the crowd responded by making so much noise I thought the stands would topple! Then, while my thrilled teammates were congratulating me, I heard a loud chant, '*Luka Modrić*' and a standing ovation from the whole Bernabéu. It was absolutely fantastic, and the final confirmation that the Real fans loved me. The feeling has not changed to this day.

I later watched the match on the TV and saw Mourinho's reaction after I scored. I could tell he was glad. His gesture meant something along the lines of, '*See, haven't I told you . . . ?*' In one of the last matches of the season, against Málaga, we claimed a 6–2 victory. I made an assist to Raúl Albiol for the first goal, and then scored my third goal of the season to give us a 5–2 lead. Two minutes later, in the 65th minute, Mourinho substituted me. I walked off the pitch to a standing ovation, and, before I took my seat on the bench, the coach called me over. He whispered in my ear, 'See, remember when they said you were the worst signing, yet you can play like this.' The pleasure was mine – and thanks to him.

This was the beginning of a winning streak, but it was enough only for the second place in La Liga, 15 points behind Barcelona. In the Champions League, we eliminated Galatasaray after Manchester United, but, unfortunately, buckled against Borussia Dortmund in the semi-finals. In the first semi-final match, the Germans swept us away 4–1, Robert Lewandowski scoring four goals. Despite the unfavourable result, we believed we could still cancel out Borussia's advantage. That's when I learnt what *remontada* meant: our fans were sure of a comeback and they carried us from the moment we arrived at the stadium until the end of the match. We came so close. We put in a fanatic performance, missed a number of chances, and then in the 82nd and 88th minutes scored two goals. In the following minutes, and injury time, we searched for the third goal that would complete the *remontada* and knock Borussia out. We had a couple of chances, but Jürgen Klopp and his team made it into the final.

After our elimination, morale at Real was low. The only trophy we could still win was the Copa del Rey. In the final, we played at home against Atlético Madrid. We had a fantastic start when Ronaldo headed home in the 14th minute following a corner kick – but Atlético equalised in the 35th minute. Both sides fought bitterly to the very end and the match went into extra time. I was substituted, and, in the 99th minute, Atlético's Miranda scored for a 2–1 victory. Our last chance to win a trophy was gone.

Mother Courage

I've taken a lot of space to describe my first season at Real because I think its course determined my overall career in Madrid. If I were to grade it from one to 10, I would give it a seven. Perhaps that score could be higher on a personal level, because I had earned my place at Real Madrid – proving myself on the most prestigious stage, where there's no room for hesitation or chance. The second part of the season was better, but that was expected. Every player needs some time to adjust, which was particularly true for me because I entered Real's daily grind without pre-season training. That's why I was more than satisfied with how the season ended. My coach and teammates helped a lot. Xabi Alonso was extremely helpful, as were Arbeloa, Khedira, Özil, Ramos, Pepe and Ronaldo. From day one, Cristiano was a great support. I got to know him much better than when we had been opponents back in England. I knew he was a top-class striker, and now I could see why. He is an absolute phenomenon when it comes to his dedication to practice and preparation. I was also impressed by Kaká. Some tried to imply we were each other's competition, but from the day we met, he told me he was at my disposal for whatever I needed. After all, we played together a lot.

What mattered to me the most was the fans' respect and attachment. The supporters at Bernabéu are very demanding. They are used to the very best; mediocrity cannot be accepted, and a relaxed approach even less so. Deserving their support, let alone becoming their favourite, is tantamount to winning a trophy.

The first year in Madrid was sensational on a private level too. After spending the first two months in the Sheraton Hotel, Vanja, Ivano and

I rented a house in La Moraleja. It belonged to Júlio Baptista, a former Real player. Vanja and I always give a lot of attention to picking our home. We spend a lot of time within our four walls, with our children, families and friends. I remember, when we were leaving our London flat, we stopped at the door and glanced back once more at the place where we had spent a beautiful part of our life.

When we were packing our belongings to move to Madrid, we did it ourselves. Vanja was pregnant – during her second pregnancy, we went through all the difficulties about transfer negotiations, moving homes and adapting to life at Real and in Madrid, as well as the criticism and frustration. To explain how complicated it was, I need to go back.

I'm not sure Vanja would want me to tell this and make it public – she dreads the idea of someone pitying her. Yes, she has health issues, but so does everyone else. What's more, she thinks we lead a wonderful life. And it's true. We feel privileged. But the fact that we are well off, that I play for the biggest football club in the world, that I'm known around the world, doesn't change the most important thing – we are just ordinary people, like everyone else. We have our good and bad days, difficult and happy moments, our worries and pleasures. We are strong, but also vulnerable. And the fact that today we can enjoy life with three amazing children by our side is for the largest part Vanja's doing. I want people to know what a brave woman she is. To tell my stories about my footballing career, I've expended many words on injuries, my sadness when kept away from the field, my despair after defeats. But when I remember all the difficulties Vanja has gone through, and how determined she was when dealing with them, all of my problems fade away.

About a year passed after Ivano was born. Vanja would occasionally have headaches and feel numbness on the left side of her face. She thought it would pass and didn't pay much attention to it. But in 2011, one day I came home to our London apartment and saw she was worried. She said she thought she had lost hearing in her left ear. She had tried washing it out but to no avail. She had an MRI and the doctors diagnosed her with schwannoma, a benign tumour in her inner ear. Naturally, we were scared, but the doctors calmed us down by saying it was something that could easily be treated. We went to get a second opinion from a Croatian doctor who is a great authority in the field, Josip Paladino. The unanimous conclusion was that the best treatment was Gamma Knife radiosurgery. But it had to wait.

In the meantime, Vanja got pregnant again. We moved to Madrid, and as she had suffered a pulmonary embolism after giving birth to Ivano, we were extra cautious while she carried our second child. She was under constant supervision and had to receive anticoagulant therapy.

Once again, we wanted her to give birth in Zagreb. Her due date was 25 April, 2013. Just the day before I was in Dortmund with Real, and we lost 4–1. Mourinho gave me a day off and, immediately after the match, I took a plane to Zagreb. The birth of our daughter was the second most beautiful and memorable moment in our lives. Everything went well. This time we chose the name quickly – we both liked short names, and on this occasion, it was Vanja who decided – her name would be Ema! This was another day filled with so much happiness. After a handsome boy, now we had a beautiful baby girl, and, on top of everything, Vanja was doing well. So much so that I could return to Madrid. The next day I was already training with the rest of the team. Vanja and I were in touch all the time. Video calls allowed us to be together, even if only virtually. I could see Ema every day, until they travelled to Madrid. From the day of Ema's birth, Vanja took care of everything. Her mother and my parents occasionally came to visit her and helped around the house or babysat Ivano. However, with two children, Vanja's health issues and my frequent absences, we decided to hire a housekeeper.

At the beginning of 2014, Vanja decided to go to London for her surgery. Her mother and her cousin went with her; I wasn't able to accompany her because it was a very intensive period at the club. I was worried and it was hard to focus on football. Still, I kept my fears a secret from everyone at the club, even from Vanja. I knew she was going through a lot, and that she was trying to hide her anxiety and fear about the surgery from me. I had to be strong, both for her and for our two babies. It was something we had to go through ourselves. We stayed positive – as was the outcome.

When she returned from London, she had to change her routine. I helped out whenever I could and, after six months, she had her first examination after the surgery. We were hopeful and, thankfully, the symptoms had retreated, a good sign. The doctors said the growth was reducing. Today it is four times smaller than when it was discovered. Vanja has regular check-ups and feels great.

Within a few years, everyone in our family was doing well. Our lives were complete: Ivano and Ema were growing while my career was going through a very successful period. Then Vanja said something that, I'm convinced, had been on her mind for a long time. Feeling well and having experienced no problems after giving birth to Ema, she said: 'Luka, I'd like to have another child!'

I didn't want to hear it. True, Vanja had always said she wanted three children – I too hoped for three or four children and a big happy family. But circumstances were now different. Vanja had risked her life twice, and I didn't want her to do so again. She consulted her doctors in London and asked if the tumour could grow as a response to pregnancy. They told her the odds were 50–50. She asked for a second opinion from the doctors in Zagreb about the risk of developing new blood clots; they told her she would have to receive therapy, yet there was a risk involved and it was up to her. In the end, the doctors told us what we already knew – everything would probably be fine, but it might not be. Vanja was resolute. I realised this when she told me, 'You know what, you do your best on the pitch and I'll do my best for the family!'

On 2 October, 2017, Sofia was born! I had to drive to the Petrova Hospital from Rijeka – where Croatia were preparing for the World Cup qualifying match against Finland – to be there when she came into this world. The delivery went without as much as a hiccup and Vanja and our second princess were doing great. That lifted the burden from my shoulders and gave me another boost of energy.

However, a year later, in Madrid, we went through another shock: Vanja was at home when suddenly her arm went numb and started to turn blue. All the symptoms told her it was another blood clot. She managed to remain calm and immediately called the doctor, who was our neighbour and who sometimes came over to our house. She confirmed Vanja's suspicions and took her to the hospital. The scans revealed that the thrombus had travelled to her neck. The doctors later concluded that it had formed again because Vanja had stopped taking her anticoagulant medicine.

The doctors ran every possible test. Eventually, they decided she would have to take preventive medicine for the rest of her life. Today, whenever she travels by plane or needs to have an IV drip – basically whenever she finds herself in a stressful situation that could potentially cause blood clotting – she needs to give herself a shot. She is so practised that she gives me shots. When I had an arthroscopy, I had to take anticoagulants. I had to stay at home, and it was Vanja who gave me shots. She did it like a seasoned pro. After a while, I told her, 'I want to try it myself!' It was a bit tense, but I managed. And that's when I realised what she has to go through on a daily basis. She had never shown she was having a hard time.

Her determination not to give up on her wish for three children despite all the risks showed her strength. Much later, she confessed what her doctor had told her after Sofia's birth: 'Vanja, such courage is rare. I would never have decided to have a third child if I were you. You're really something!'

Her maternal instinct was stronger than anything. All those crises and difficult situations caused me a lot of stress, but I had no right to be weak when she was so brave and strong. That's why today we are a family that is happy and blessed.

CHAPTER SEVEN

The Uncompromising Mourinho

The first season at Real was behind us. We had come to know Madrid and its daily rhythms. It's a fantastic city, full of parks and green oases, and the climate is wonderful. In the eight years we have lived here, there have been maybe two days of snow and temperatures below zero. The weather is mostly pleasant. The worst discomfort comes when the dark clouds gather above Bernabéu or Valdebebas.

After our defeat in the final of the Copa del Rey, the atmosphere at the club became difficult. We had won only the Spanish Super Cup and lost on all other fronts. For Real, that was a disaster. The dressing room talked a lot about what would happen next, but I tried to stay out of the speculation. However, I had a feeling that José Mourinho would leave. His relationship with some of the players wasn't great. For example, in a home match against Manchester City, he left Sergio Ramos on the bench; the player held it against him. Mourinho also had a number of disagreements with Iker Casillas, the Real Madrid captain, and then benched him. When he decides something, Mourinho sticks to it. He is open and always says what he thinks to your face. Some can deal with it, some are irritated by it. Today, players are sensitive to criticism. It turns out that, when someone tells them something they don't want to hear, they get offended, like true prima donnas.

It's not that I love it when the coach criticises me, but I don't mind if he openly tells me when something is wrong with my game. That's the only way to correct it and change. There were a few such cases with Mourinho. We were playing against Deportivo, I think, and at half time he was visibly upset. He reproached me, 'Luka, what's up with that? You're playing like Zidane, and he's 50 years old!' I understood what he wanted. My technique was all right, but I had no rhythm, I wasn't speeding up the game. Mourinho insisted on aggression, on constant running with or without the ball, on high intensity. I thought the comparison with Zidane was funny. And effective, because I winced. However, at half time, there was also a heated exchange between the

147

coach and Mesut Özil. Mourinho left him on the bench and brought on Kaká. Before the team came out for the second half, Ramos, who was friends with Özil, put Özil's shirt under his own as a sign of support. When the media learned about this, it caused a lot of talk about the conflict between the coach and some of the players. The situation was touchy, to say the least.

On one occasion I was startled by the ferocity of Mourinho's reaction towards Cristiano Ronaldo. We were playing a cup match and had a 2–0 lead. The opponent's full-back attacked along our left-hand side. Ronaldo didn't follow and Mourinho yelled at him, demanding that he run after the player. After the attack, Mourinho continued to criticise and they got into a conflict. In the dressing room at half time, Ronaldo was desperate, almost on the verge of tears. He complained, 'I always give my best, yet he keeps criticising me.'

Soon, Mourinho walked into the dressing room. He stood in the middle of the room, angrily reproaching Ronaldo for his lack of responsibility. The argument escalated, it got embarrassing and tense, and the players had to intervene to calm the situation down. In truth, that was nothing out of the ordinary – such things are very common in football and their relationship was soon back to normal. But that's Mourinho: headstrong and in your face – no matter who's on the other side. And as is often the case in football, when there are no results, the coach is the first to take the heat. Even if he's the expert who, just a year before, won the league with a record number of points. Before his arrival, Real were unable to get past the round of 16 in the UEFA Champions League. But with Mourinho at the helm, they reached the semi-final on three occasions (losing, unfortunately, to Barcelona, Bayern and Borussia).

The dressing room responded in a typical fashion to his departure – some were pleased Mourinho had left, others weren't. I wasn't. I respected him, for two reasons: first, he is a quality manager and a special person; and second, he was the one who insisted on bringing me to Real.

After the final match, we all said goodbye. He said that the club had terminated his contract by mutual consent.

'I wish you all the best in the rest of your career. Take care!' Mourinho told me before we took our picture together. I wanted to keep it as a lasting memory.

***

My parallel football life wearing Croatia's shirt was going through a series of ups and downs. In the spring of 2013, two matches in March brought us great joy. First, we beat Serbia in Zagreb in front of a packed crowd. Our rivalry against the Serbs is wrought by complicated relations between the two countries and the heavy burden of a recent armed conflict. Our footballing competitiveness is particularly strong, and was especially so at that time, when Serbia had very strong individuals in their team. Our two main men up front, Mario Mandžukić and Ivica Olić, led us to a 2–0 victory. Four days later, after a fierce battle, we managed to beat Wales in Swansea. Gareth Bale gave his side a lead from a penalty, and Dejan Lovren equalised with a long-range shot in the 77th minute. Three minutes before the end of regular time, Eduardo secured a valuable victory for our side. At the time, there was much talk about Bale's transfer to Madrid in the summer. I often talked to Gareth on the phone, and he said he would love to move to Real but expected problems with Daniel Levy. Real president Florentino Pérez asked me what Bale thought and told me to encourage him to come to Madrid. Everyone was for it – Real, Bale, even the media who heaped praise on Gareth. Eventually, it happened. I was glad because Gareth is a top-quality player. Also, we are very similar in character – reserved and preferring to spend time at home with our families.

In Swansea, I earned a yellow card suspension for Croatia's June match against Scotland in Zagreb. Unfortunately, we lost thanks to a Robert Snodgrass goal, which obstructed our path to the 2014 FIFA

World Cup in Brazil. True, in September, Mandžukić's goal led us to a draw against Serbia in a tricky clash in Belgrade. But a month later in Zagreb, Romelu Lukaku's two goals to secure victory for Belgium meant we failed to qualify directly. Four days later, when we travelled to Glasgow for the final match in our qualifying group, it was clear we would have to go through another play-off. The point we secured in Belgrade proved key to keeping our position ahead of Serbia.

We played a dreadful match at Hampden Park, and we looked like a deflated balloon. You can lose, but the way we fell against Scotland was just disgraceful. The score was 2–0, and there was no one to blame but ourselves: the players and the manager. We knew there would be consequences and we heard that Igor Štimac had offered his resignation right after the match. The officials accepted it and the following day named Niko Kovač, who had been in charge of the under-21 team, as temporary manager. Even then, I was convinced we would qualify for the World Cup. But the chronic loss of form in the second part of the qualifications was something I just couldn't explain. Except for the UEFA Euro 2008 campaign, when we put in some convincing and confident performances during the whole cycle, every other qualifying stage always opened with a good start followed by an inexplicable fall. Was it complacency? Injuries? The classic Croatian 'take it easy' story? Something else? I don't know, it remains a mystery.

We knew Niko Kovač well. Until 2008, he had been for many of us on the national team our captain and our leader. We expected he would be the same as the manager: firm, and adamant in expecting hard work and discipline. We were right – to an extent. As a coach, he stood by his principles, but he was three times more demanding!

We drew Iceland in the play-off. Niko prepared us well for the two crucial matches that would take us to the 2014 World Cup. In the away match we were under a lot of pressure, but we got a good result, 0–0. In the rematch, Mandžukić scored in the 27th minute for a 1–0 lead, only to be sent off 10 minutes later. The referee, Björn Kuipers sent him off after a challenge on Johann Gudmundsson in the middle of the pitch. Despite being a man down, we achieved a victory and celebrated yet another successful World Cup qualification. Back then, I didn't expect Iceland to make such fast progress, as shown by their series of outstanding performances at UEFA Euro 2016. Their never-give-up mentality, together with technical progress and experience, brought great results. I had huge respect for them even before they settled the score with us in the 2018 FIFA World Cup qualifying campaign. They won first place in our group and directly qualified for Russia. We had to go through the third play-off qualification round since I joined the national squad, the fifth altogether in Croatia's history. It's interesting how teams' destinies intertwine. We beat and lost to England, Ukraine, Turkey and Iceland. We shrouded each other in mourning – and then settled the score.

Ciao, Carlo!

I was on my well-deserved summer holiday when I heard the news that Carlo Ancelotti had officially taken over as the new Real Madrid coach. I knew him well, as he did me, because he'd wanted to bring me to PSG. Now, our paths were finally crossing in Madrid. Ancelotti came as a trophy-winning coach, with a reputation as a UEFA Champions League specialist. From the moment I entered the world of Real, the story of the European title was always at the back of my mind. It had been 10 years since the team's last successful final in Glasgow. Real had won their ninth title with Zinédine Zidane smashing that fantastic winning goal against Bayer Leverkusen. And as fate would have it, Zidane was Ancelotti's assistant during his first season with Real. It was a symbolic link between the ninth and much-coveted 10th European title. *La Décima* was almost an obsession.

Ancelotti proved to be a cool guy. He never gave the impression of being a man with 12 major trophies under his belt – with AC Milan, Chelsea and PSG. He was the league champion in Italy, England and France; with Milan he had won two Champions Leagues and one

FIFA World Club Championship. After the temperamental Mourinho and all the turbulence surrounding him, Ancelotti's calm nature was a welcome change. He seemed relaxed, avoided arguments and was always ready to talk to you. We liked him from day one. The atmosphere was less tense, and we could focus on our work. During the pre-season tournament in the United States, we looked good. Ancelotti wanted the team to launch timely counter-attacks, to play a game that was aggressive and vertical.

On a personal level, my work with him couldn't have begun better. During his presentation, the journalists asked him to compare Andrea Pirlo and myself, and Ancelotti made it clear that he thought highly of me.

'They are different, Pirlo's position on the pitch is strictly defined, while Modrić is more mobile and dynamic.'

That came as a great tribute because Pirlo was a fantastic midfielder, and Ancelotti had helped him transform into a playmaker whose style and stature had changed the way we saw deep-lying midfielders.

I felt the coach was happy with the way I trained and what I showed during the first pre-season matches. I had a good spring behind me, but was aware that for a new boss I had to build my status from scratch. Ancelotti is a quiet guy, but, on those rare occasions when someone rubs him the wrong way, he can let himself be heard. We had a good start to the season – we enjoyed a series of five consecutive wins and a draw in La Liga, and then in the Champions League we swept the floor with Galatasaray, 6–1. I had just one poor game, in our only draw, against Villarreal, and for the next match Ancelotti benched me. I was angry because I thought it wasn't fair – *as if it was only my fault we hadn't won.* But I didn't let it get to me; I used it as a motivation to prove I deserved my place in the first team. I was on the bench for *El Derbi Madrileño.* Atlético won 1–0, and Ancelotti brought me on at the beginning of the second half. From then on, I was an indispensable member of the starting line-up. We had great chemistry. Ancelotti is a true professional, and used to be a top-level player, so he has a good understanding of the dynamics within the dressing room. He treats everyone fairly, and he is more than anything a good man and someone you can always count on. I remember one detail from when he had just come to Real. We had just returned from the United States. Madrid was empty; the heat was unbearable. My family was back home in Croatia, at the seaside, enjoying themselves. I had two days off, which wasn't enough to travel to Zadar and back. I stayed home and watched TV.

And then Ancelotti's phone call caught me by surprise. '*Ciao*, Luka! It's Carlo. What are you doing?'

I told him I was just relaxing, nothing special. There was not much to do. My family was in Croatia, so I was all alone.

'All right then, come over for dinner. My friends and I are going to this new restaurant in my neighbourhood. I hear it's great,' replied Carlo, who had a reputation as a true gourmet.

I gladly accepted his unusual invitation. It was a nice gesture, and also an expression of respect for me as a player. We met at the restaurant and spent a couple of hours in pleasant conversation. With his assistants, we talked about football – Real, but also about the Croatia national team. We also talked about life, family, our habits. I think this approach – his ability to make a decision he knows will not please his player but at the same time to invite him out for dinner – is what brought Ancelotti so much success. He never ruled with an iron fist, he never imposed his attitude on anyone or distanced himself from the players. On the contrary, his vast knowledge gave him an authority that inspired the players to follow him. I think his choice for his assistant coach also speaks to his personality.

Zinédine Zidane is a Real legend, one of the best players that ever walked this earth. Some might feel threatened by his charisma, but not Carlo. Until then, I knew Zizou only by reputation, but during that unforgettable season, I would get to know him personally. He seemed calm and quiet, always discreetly staying in the background, but he was unable to hide – his charisma simply shone through. He would play with us in training, and if you hadn't known who he was, you'd have assumed he was one of the players. One of the star players! The way he controlled the ball, how he passed . . . Wow! Zidane was there if you needed someone to talk to; he was always smiling and in a good mood. He was in charge of training sessions, but when tactics and team selection were in question, he wouldn't impose. That's when Ancelotti took charge.

In the first part of the season, with excellent performances from Gareth Bale, Dani Carvajal, Isco and other new players, we looked powerful. In the first 28 matches in La Liga, we recorded only two defeats, against Barcelona and Atlético Madrid. We had just picked up momentum and were aiming for first place when we suffered a shocking home defeat, again to Barça. We had the lead twice, at 2–1 and 3–2, but then Sergio Ramos got sent off, and Lionel Messi scored two more goals to complete his hat-trick and lead his side to a 4–3 victory. The defeat hit us hard, and we lost to Sevilla three days later. These results would prove a key factor in losing the title. In the end, Atlético Madrid came out on top, three points ahead of Barcelona and us.

We soon settled the score with Barcelona in the final of the Copa del Rey on 16 April, 2014, at Mestalla in Valencia. We were level at 1–1, following goals by Ángel Di María and Marc Bartra, when Bale made a blistering run. He picked up the ball just inside our half, went past the scorer Bartra at full speed, at one point actually running off the field, and then slotted the ball through José Manuel Pinto's legs from six yards out, for a 2–1 victory! What a sensational goal, what a run in the 85th minute of an extremely difficult game! We were ecstatic in our celebration at Mestalla because we had secured a huge victory, winning only our second Copa del Rey trophy in 20 years.

La Décima

In our UEFA Champions League group we won all our matches – against Galatasaray, Copenhagen and Juventus – except in Turin, where we drew

2–2 against the Italian team. In the round of 16, we beat Schalke into the ground by scoring nine goals in two matches. In 10 Champions League games, we had scored a total of 29 goals, conceding just seven. The media kept fuelling hopes of *La Décima*. The win in Gelsenkirchen was Real's first victory on German soil in 14 years. Everyone said that was a sign.

Two weeks later, our opponent was Borussia Dortmund. Judging from previous experience and their style of play, we couldn't have had a worse opponent. Jürgen Klopp's team was very dynamic, quick in transition, and physically superior. They played Klopp's trademark strategy of *Gegenpressing*, or the tactic of trying to win back possession of the ball *immediately* after losing it. It's a high-pressure tactic that relies on speed, discipline and stamina. However, in the first leg, we took a convincing 3–0 victory, even though they had their chances. The ease with which we won made us feel relaxed, and deceived us for the return match. In the 17th minute of that clash, we had a chance that could have sealed our big advantage, but Roman Weidenfeller saved Di María's penalty. That galvanised the home side, supported by the impressive 'Yellow Wall' – the always packed and extremely noisy north stand. In the deafening roar of Signal Iduna Park, Marco Reus' two goals by the 37th minute gave Dortmund a 2–0 lead.

Here I want to return to the wheel of fortune – it always keeps turning! In the previous season we had tried to cancel out their three-goal first-leg lead for a *remontada* in Madrid. Despite having our chances at 2–0, the third goal that would take us to the final simply didn't come our way. Now, it was they who had a 2–0 advantage, but in the next 53 minutes, despite their chances, they couldn't score the third goal needed to complete their comeback and give them a chance to advance into the semi-final. We took it as another sign of fate being on our side. Every year in the Champions League there is a critical factor defining which teams make it through to the very end.

In the semi-final we faced the reigning European Champions and the strongest strongest German side, Bayern Munich. They were led by Pep Guardiola, in his first job after his Barcelona era. Guardiola was the main reason why most people saw Bayern as favourites to win the Champions League. In both matches their attack was led by my Croatia teammate Mario Mandžukić, yet it was quite clear the style of play implemented by Guardiola did not suit Mandžo.

The first leg in Madrid was tense. Karim Benzema scored in the 19th minute for a 1–0 lead, and by the end of the match the result hadn't changed. Our slim advantage led the public to believe Bayern would make it to the final for the second time in a row. On the other hand, we thought 1–0 was a good result. We conceded nothing, and in a knockout stage this is always a big advantage. We also knew Real had scored at least once in all our away matches in the Champions League since 2010. The only exception was our quarter-final in Dortmund.

The fans at Allianz Arena witnessed a true Real Madrid rhapsody. In the 16th minute Sergio Ramos turned my corner into a lead. Four minutes later Ramos once again flicked a header behind Manuel Neuer, while Cristiano Ronaldo scored the third following a fantastic Di María–Benzema–Bale counter-attack. Bayern couldn't recover. In the 90th minute Ronaldo drilled a free-kick under the wall for a historic 4–0 victory in Munich!

That match made us believe this was our year. We could almost touch *La Décima*. Earlier that spring, the club had decided to release a new official song. A well-known music producer and a tremendous guy, RedOne, gathered the whole team in his studio and we recorded *Hala Madrid y Nada Mas (Let's Go Madrid and Nothing More)*. Singing, we felt so powerful and elevated. After the final, it would become the ode of *La Décima*.

The last match in La Liga ended in a 3–1 victory against Espanyol. However, the title went to Atlético Madrid, our opponent in the Champions League final, a week later in Lisbon. Having beaten Barça in the final of the Copa del Rey, we were now looking forward to getting even with our local rivals for losing the championship. After our Munich victory, we couldn't wait! The week before, excitement was at its peak; the feeling was phenomenal. I received calls from all sides to secure tickets. If I'd had 1000, it still wouldn't have been enough! I wanted all of my family and close friends there at Estádio da Luz – the Stadium of Light – right there beside me. As always, Vanja took responsibility for the 'Lisbon Action'. If it had been up to me, who knows who would have arrived and where?! Besides, I was completely focused on the match.

We had already arrived in Lisbon at our hotel when Vanja called me: 'I've taken care of everything, but there's a problem. I'm running a fever. Everything hurts, and the doctor told me not to travel.'

It was simply unimaginable. We were on the verge of fulfilling our dreams, just one more step, and the most important person on this and all other of my journeys wouldn't be there?!

'Vanja, do whatever it takes, you just have to be in Lisbon.'

Vanja took her cold medicine, drank gallons of tea, and called me the next morning before the match, 'We're here, Luka, in Lisbon. Everyone's accounted for!'

What a relief! All the victories, all the triumphs and trophies mean nothing to me if those I care about are not there with me.

I slept well the night before the final. Usually, I have no problem sleeping before an important match – I may even have a good nap after a matchday lunch. This time, I wasn't so cool. I couldn't wait. Playing in the Champions League Final is every player's dream. I wasn't scared or worrying about whether we would succeed – it was just excitement before such a big match.

In the hotel before the match, Carlo Ancelotti gathered us in the conference room. They had a wonderful surprise for us. On the big screen they played a video showing the families of every player sending words of support. It was so loaded with emotion that, for a second, I felt like crying – and I wasn't alone. We were all touched – and psyched. President Florentino Pérez encouraged us to give our best; It was obvious he badly wanted this trophy. We were aware that this was our first final after 11 years of drought. Real had been waiting for this elusive 10th title far too long. We knew victory could bring us immortality: in the fantastic history of Real Madrid, our names would be written in golden letters.

The bus ride from the hotel to the stadium was spectacular. There were crowds of fans on the streets, and a holiday-like atmosphere that was getting noisier and more intense as we inched towards Estádio da Luz. And there, at the approach to the stadium, a river of Real supporters threw a fantastic welcome for us. Even now, I get goosebumps.

In the dressing room, you could feel it immediately – the atmosphere was different. No one was joking around, as we usually do; we were anxious, serious, focused. We encouraged one another, hugged and drew from each other's energy. I recall Sergio Ramos, the seasoned professional who had played in many finals and big matches. He now approached me and I saw a different look in his eyes: 'Luka, you're very important to us. We need you at your best!'

Xabi Alonso, my experienced partner in the midfield, was absent through suspension. Ancelotti played a team with three midfielders – Sami Khedira behind Di María and me. He wanted us to be quick and vertical; he stressed we needed to be aggressive since we were playing against an opponent who relied on this very same quality. Atlético Madrid had already proven in La Liga that they were a tough nut to crack, difficult to break down. Yes, we had destroyed them in the semi-final of the Copa del Rey – 3–0 at Bernabéu and 2–0 at Vicente Calderón. Several weeks later, we had drawn 2–2 in La Liga during another away game at Calderón. However, Atlético were a tricky opponent, and they had memories from the previous season. The Lisbon final was being played almost on the anniversary of their victory in the 2013 Copa del Rey Final. Back then, they had been better, beating us on our home turf at Bernabéu.

'Luka, drop half-right, then get in the middle, between the lines,' was one of Ancelotti's instructions. He added, 'Whenever you get the opportunity, win as much space as you can with the ball at your feet. Get in deep.'

This was his fourth Champions League Final. As Milan's coach he had won two titles, against Juventus and Liverpool. The first time he won the Champions League in Manchester, Milan beat their Italian rivals on penalties. Two years later the wheel of fortune turned on them against Liverpool. In one of the most spectacular matches ever, Milan had a 3–0 first-half lead, but the Reds made a fantastic comeback and won on penalties. Two years after that, Ancelotti and Milan settled the score in Athens, where they beat Liverpool 2–1 and reclaimed the title.

All those experiences taught Carlo to remain calm, and he tried to pass his composure on to us. However, all the sweets he ate during the match made it clear that he was pumped full of adrenaline!

In the fantastic atmosphere we fought a real battle on the pitch. In the ninth minute, Diego Costa, who had been carrying an injury, signalled to the bench and had to be replaced. And then, in the 36th minute, after a corner kick, Diego Godín gave Atlético a lead! Standing not far from the goal, I watched as the ball flew towards the net and I hoped Iker Casillas would get to it in time. He didn't. It made me feel bad because, until that point, we had been in good positions on the pitch. We'd practised how to react to their free-kicks and corners, because that was their strength, and then in the final we conceded following a corner. But we never stopped believing we could bring ourselves back into the game.

At half time we got together and encouraged each other to keep going. The second half confirmed our drive, but for a long time our efforts failed. Then Ancelotti made his move and changed the tactics. Fifteen minutes into the second half he brought on Marcelo and Isco, and 20 minutes later Álvaro Morata. The substitutes brought fresh energy; we pressed Atlético into their penalty box. They were on the ropes – but we just couldn't score. Tensions reached their peak. The referee signalled five minutes of injury time. For us, the minutes were flying by; for Atlético, it must have felt like years. In the third minute of stoppage time we won a corner. I passed short to Dani Carvajal, who passed it back to me. I sent the ball to Isco; he passed it over to Di María on the far side, whose cross skimmed off one of the Atlético players and fell by the near post. I jumped to reach it, David Villa blocked me, and the ball rolled off him for another corner. Within a minute I won yet another corner, and this time I decided it was up to me to deliver the perfect ball into the penalty box. I was calm, but the atmosphere could be cut with a knife – like this moment would change everything. I could tell the ball's trajectory was right, and, when I saw Ramos leap up into the air, I knew it would end up in the net. Everything came together perfectly. As simple as that.

I was beside myself with happiness. We had scored right in front of our fans, and the explosion of joy was unbelievable. I ran like crazy – first back to our half of the pitch, and then towards the pile of players by the corner flag. I simply threw myself on them. I have watched the goal countless times since. The clock showed 92.47. For many, it's the moment that changed the course of Real Madrid's history. Being part of it is just phenomenal. Every time I watch that passage of play, I get anxious: *what if I hadn't crossed it so well? what if Sergio had connected an inch to the left or if the ball had hit the post?* But it went in. I get goosebumps every time the images remind me of those moments.

Before extra time, Ancelotti gathered us in a circle. We huddled together and encouraged each other: we knew we had them. Ramos' equaliser had crushed them. I knew exactly how they felt – I had gone through the same thing in the UEFA Euro 2008 quarter-final against Turkey. You can practically taste the victory and then, in the last moment, the opponent scores! It's a devastating blow. There's nothing harder than that. And so, when Bale scored for a 2–1 lead, they simply fell apart. Goals from Marcelo and Ronaldo were a sign the party could begin.

When Björn Kuipers signalled the end of the match, I threw my arms in the air and thought: *the dream has come true!* And then I offered my hand to the Atlético player near me. I understood how he felt, but my joy was so great I couldn't wait to let my emotions run free. From the day I joined Real, *La Décima* was our obsession. At the first press conference in Madrid, they asked me what I thought. When I first travelled on a plane with Real, I learned that José Mourinho always chose seat Number 10, a sign of his dedication.

The euphoria after the match was understandable. I brought Ivano down to the pitch. He was sleepy and tired; he was just four and it had been a long day for him. But I perked him up enough to take a photo with the trophy. I had to have that moment with him and keep it for eternity, so that one day he knows how big and important that evening was.

The dressing room was on fire. Florentino Pérez was there. I never saw him both so happy and so touched. The footage from the VIP box shows clearly what the trophy meant to him. I never saw him jump up so euphorically as he did to celebrate the goal that took us to extra time. Real legends who had won the Champions League in the past also came to the dressing room. Raúl was among them. The day before the final, he approached me and said, 'There's a lot of it riding on you for this final!' It wasn't a burden. On the contrary. I love responsibility and I hate the feeling of not being important. The words of such a legend inspired me to do my best and play at the level required for such a historic feat.

It took a while to reach the airport and our plane. We kept running late; we were partying, we deserved it. I let myself go too. I was among the last to get on the bus. I got in, sat behind the wheel, and honked in honour of *La Décima*. On the plane, at 32,000 feet, I juggled the ball, sang and danced. I had a couple of shots of whiskey – I simply had to! I was thrilled. Everyone watched me and laughed because they'd never seen me like that. We arrived at Cibeles Square in Madrid just after 5 a.m. I thought there wouldn't be many people because it had been six hours since the game and it was cold, but Cibeles was packed. That filled me with energy, and I went on singing even harder, even though I had lost my voice. As I'm almost tone-deaf, maybe it was for the best! But the fans kept singing – they chanted my name on a couple of occasions. I must have seemed crazier than the rest. This was my first Champions League and the most exclusive club trophy – and it was the first time I saw the square full of jubilant Madrileños. It would happen again, more than once, but *La Décima* was exceptional and one of a kind.

The World Cup in Brazil

After the Lisbon final, the celebration of *La Décima* did not end at Cibeles. I caught maybe two hours of sleep and then joined the rest of the team for a day of celebrations. There were receptions at various institutions, countless supporters in front of city sights, ceremonies, speeches, acknowledgements.

In the evening, the party moved to Bernabéu, where the stands were packed with euphoric fans. It was spectacular. Even before this, I was left speechless when I learned that more than 80,000 people had gathered at the stadium to watch the Lisbon match on giant screens. I saw videos from all over the world showing fans reacting to the equaliser and our subsequent victory. It was phenomenal to see such an explosion of emotions – and humbling to have brought so much happiness to all those people, to all the Real fans from all over the world. Many think we play football for money. We are professionals who play football for a living, that's true – and it's a good life, full of privileges. However, nothing can make a player happier than experiencing such fantastic emotions and sharing them with their fans. Without all this, football would have no story. And that's why it was the least of my problems – or rather, no problem at all – to keep a promise I had given before the final.

After one training session, a lot of players were in the showers. This is when we chat and comment about what's happened in the club: the usual team talk. Now the topic was what each of us would do if we won *La Décima*.

'I love my hair, but if we take the title, I'll shave my head.'

My teammates laughed, and Álvaro Arbeloa said he couldn't wait to win, and then he could cut my hair himself!

So, in the morning when I returned from Cibeles, I called my hairdresser to come to my house and give me a haircut. I had to keep my promise, but I wanted to avoid Arbeloa's expert hands! When I showed up in front of my teammates, almost bald, they dropped to the floor amid laughter and cheers of approval. I felt strange without my hair, like the cold could get in anywhere. But it was worth it!

After all the informal and formal celebrations I felt exhausted. I needed rest and a lot of sleep. However, Croatia had to prepare for the World Cup in Brazil. I joined my teammates at the end of the preparations, just before the friendly against Mali in Osijek. The Osijek Stadium was packed, the atmosphere upbeat. I played the final 15 minutes of the match and the 15,000 supporters gave me a warm welcome. It was their recognition for the victory in the UEFA Champions League, as well as their expression of support ahead of Brazil. Croatian fans love their national team, and during the World Cup or Euros the whole country is in a special mood. Expectations are always high. The fact that for years we'd failed to make our fans happy troubled me deeply.

Two days after the victory over Mali we travelled to Brazil. A long and challenging season at Real was behind me, and also a stressful qualification campaign with Croatia. I was looking forward to the tournament in a country that had given so many fantastic players to the world of football. Brazil has always been a country of creative, playful football and of magicians with the ball – that's just part of the mentality that has led them to be crowned World Champions five times – more than any other nation. We were curious about a World Cup held in the country that's so passionate about football.

After our arrival, we played in the last pre-tournament match against Australia. Nikica Jelavić's goal gave us a victory, but our performance was far from convincing. We weren't worried, because the thing that mattered was our performance in the first match of the tournament itself. Croatia opened the World Cup against the host Brazil. What an honour and an opportunity to show our best. More than a billion and a half people were said to be watching the game. Amazing!

The regime in our camp was rigorous: Niko Kovač introduced a Spartan drill. Every morning we had tests to measure the level of lactates in our blood, something we weren't used to. In my opinion, such a strict regime strained morale – and morale is vital when the national team gets together. However, the manager insisted.

There were other tensions: some of the players were not happy with their status, and they complained about the manager's selection. In all my years playing for the national team, it was in Brazil that our morale was the worst.

Nevertheless, we played well in the opening match against the hosts in Sao Paulo. We took the lead in the 11th minute when Marcelo, my teammate from Real, scored an own goal. We held our ground the whole time, although Neymar levelled the score 18 minutes later. But we were cut down by a penalty awarded by the referee in the 71st minute. We thought his call was unfair and we had no strength to get back into the match. The hosts' third goal in stoppage time only confirmed their victory.

In the second match we beat Cameroon with less trouble than expected. We played in Manaus, at the Arena da Amazônia, under extreme weather conditions. The air was humid and heavy; just standing on the pitch made you all sweaty. It was difficult to breathe. We gained a 1–0 lead when Alex Song was sent off for hitting Mario Mandžukić and this opened our path to the convincing 4–0 victory. Despite this, I felt the decisive match against Mexico would be a struggle. In their earlier matches we had seen that they were well-organised, tough and very competitive. On the other hand, we seemed to have run out of steam, like a team without energy and compactness. There was a lot of criticism towards Niko Kovač for selecting Ivan Rakitić and I as the playmakers; the pundits said it just wouldn't work. In Croatia everyone is an expert, and this reminded me of the discussion about the Boban–Prosinečki–Asanović midfield who played for Croatia's 'Bronze Generation'. Time has proved that Rakitić and I can be more than efficient in the middle of the field.

In Recife, against Mexico, the weather was once again humid and wet. We played at the right level for only about 15 minutes, and then the Mexicans outplayed us completely. We had no answer for their aggression and speed. They took a well-deserved 3–1 victory. Mexico only needed one point to advance to the next stage. We were eliminated, and, based on our performances, we didn't deserve more than that.

The critics could now vent their frustrations – the papers were full of all kinds of stories and photos. Like the one after the defeat against Brazil when paparazzi photos of naked players having fun by the pool leaked into the press. Pure nonsense. We were alone in the camp and, after the sauna, we went into the pool to cool down. Nothing unusual.

The day after Mexico we returned to our base. The camp in Praia do Forte in Bahia was fantastic; the hosts and employees even better. Before we travelled back to Croatia, Niko Kovač organised a final meeting. Some players were angry and there was a lot of criticism. The return was sombre. We had been eliminated at UEFA Euro 2012 two years earlier, but still went home with our heads held high because we had played well. In Brazil we did badly in every aspect. As far as my performances are concerned, I was awful. The tournament in Brazil was my weakest set of performances in my 14 years wearing Croatia's shirt. Against the hosts, I did more or less alright, but against Cameroon, I deserved a zero – and against Mexico, two zeros! I didn't shy away from admitting as much when we returned to Croatia. I was one of the most experienced players on the team and I had to take responsibility. An exhausting season was no excuse. I was terrible, and that was it.

A Season of Injuries

After the World Cup I needed a holiday. Surrounded by my family and friends, I regenerated at the seaside. I came to the pre-season camp fresh and looking forward to new challenges. Real had signed James Rodríguez, who had been excellent with Colombia at the World Cup. They also brought the German Toni Kroos, the new World Champion, and Keylor Navas. On the other hand, Ángel Di María signed for Manchester United, Álvaro Morata joined Juventus and Xabi Alonso chose Bayern Munich.

Xabi and I had a great relationship. I admired him as a player and adored him as a person. He is one of those people you look up to: calm, a real gentleman, confident, a man of firm character. We kept in contact even after he left, and he is still a dear friend.

I was sure Real would perform miracles during this season. We had a strong team, good morale and a real expert on the bench. *La Décima* gave us confidence and lifted the burden off our shoulders. Perhaps it even made us somewhat complacent, because before the international break in September we suffered two unpleasant defeats. We opened the season by beating Sevilla in the UEFA Super Cup. A week later, we played in the Spanish Super Cup against Atlético. The match at Bernabéu ended in a 1–1 draw, and they won 1–0 in the return match at Calderón. Mario Mandžukić scored a goal. He had just arrived at Atlético and he immediately gave us hell. At the time, my relationship with Mario was cold (but I'll return to this later).

In La Liga, we tasted defeat in the second match, 4–2 against Real Sociedad. When we came back from the international break, we lost for the third time, as Atlético beat us 2–1 at Bernabéu. It forced us to reset – and that defeat triggered a fantastic series of wins and the breaking of all kinds of records. We won 22 matches in a row across all competitions. We extended our winning streak to 10 consecutive wins in the UEFA Champions League. More importantly, we played fantastic football. One of the best periods in Real history coincided with my outstanding form. I played the best football of my career. For Real as well as Croatia, I felt I had reached my peak.

The team was brilliant. After Bale was injured, Ancelotti opted for a 4-4-2 formation instead of the usual 4-2-3-1 or 4-3-3. He put Kroos,

Isco, Rodríguez and I in the middle, Benzema and Ronaldo in attack, and behind us were Ramos and Pepe, Carvajal and Marcelo on the flanks. Our game was sensational: technically superior and to the taste of the demanding Real crowd. In October, we confidently won in the first *El Clásico*. Despite Neymar giving his side a 1–0 lead, Barcelona were defeated at Bernabéu 3–1. By Week 10 we were sitting at the top of La Liga. The media were so impressed they started calling us the best team in the club's rich history. Some claimed we were better than the famous team from Alfredo Di Stéfano's golden era. To be compared with that fantastic generation was phenomenal. Unfortunately, trouble lay just around the corner.

Throughout September and October 2014, Croatia played fantastic football. Niko Kovač refreshed the team, bringing new faces to its ranks, and Stipe Pletikosa, the veteran of many battles in the previous 15 years, said goodbye. We opened with four wins, three of them in the UEFA Euro 2016 qualifiers: Malta, Bulgaria and Azerbaijan fell easily. On 16 November, Italy waited for us in Milan with Antonio Conte at the helm. The *Azzurri* were our main competitors for first place in the group. They took the lead in the 11th minute. Nevertheless, we played well, and soon brought the game to the hosts. Four minutes later, we equalised thanks to Ivan Perišić's outstanding goal. I was convinced, given the course of the match, that we would win. However, for me, by the middle of the first half, the game was over – and with it all football activities for the following four months.

I was in the centre of the pitch, intending to pass the ball to the flank with my left foot. My position was slightly awkward, and when I hit the ball, the pain cut through the upper part of my quadriceps. I had never had major problems with my muscles, yet this seemed serious. After our doctor and physio treated my leg, I slowly got up and thought everything would be alright. I wanted to continue the match – it never crossed my mind to leave the pitch. But in the very next minute, Italy counter-attacked along the left flank, and I sprinted to catch my opponent.

That's when my leg gave up. It felt as if something in my muscle snapped; I lay writhing in pain, assuming the worst had happened. *Should I have stopped as soon it had happened? Did sprinting tear everything there was to be torn in my muscle?* All of this went through my head.

There were 7,000–8,000 Croatian supporters at the stadium, and they created a fantastic atmosphere. As I limped to the bench, supported by our team doctor and physio, they gave me a standing ovation. I felt like crying from all the pain, but the fans' reaction lifted my spirits, at least a little. Whenever injuries or health problems keep me away from the pitch, I'm miserable. I watched the rest of the match from the bench. Ivan Rakitić took the reins of the game and together with Marcelo Brozović and Mateo Kovačić, who came in to replace me, dominated the midfield. We played well and were the closest to victory. But suddenly, our rhythm was disrupted. A small group of fans in the Croatian stand started throwing flares onto the pitch. The referee, Björn Kuipers, was forced to stop the game for 10 minutes. We were worried that the match would be suspended and that the crowd trouble could jeopardise our Euro 2016 campaign. The game ended 1–1, but the fear of drastic punishment from UEFA now burdened the team.

In the morning, I took the first plane out of Milan to Madrid. Carlo Ancelotti called me before take off; he asked me how I felt and what the doctors had said. While I was still waiting at the airport, Florentino Pérez also phoned to encourage me. He told me Real would take care of everything. It was difficult to make a reliable diagnosis before a CAT scan. When we were back in the dressing room in Milan, Boris Nemec, our experienced team doctor, told me that it seemed I had torn the proximal rectus femoris tendon in my left thigh. The only positive about the injury was that it needed no surgery. But when they told me it would take at least four months to recover, I broke down. It was a huge shock, though I soon calmed down. I remembered one of the many wise things Michael Jordan said: 'I've failed over and over and over again in my life and that is why I succeed.'

The rehabilitation process was demanding. I started at the Valdebebas Centre at 9 a.m. and finished by 4 p.m. There was a lot of speculation in the media that the injury could jeopardise my career. I was almost 30 years old at the time and another similar injury could've ended my playing career. I didn't even consider such an outcome. My focus was to recover as quickly as possible and my goal was to come back onto the pitch at the beginning of March, before a full four months of rehabilitation. Of course, I didn't want to put any pressure on the doctors and hurry them up. Instead, I dedicated myself to the gruelling drill and, once any trace of pain and risk were gone, to getting the green light to get back on the pitch.

Vanja, Ivano and Ema were by my side, and they helped me through that difficult period. As I had spent my birthday with the national team – on 9 September, we played against Malta in Zagreb – Vanja decided to surprise me and take my mind off the injury and rehabilitation. She organised a small party for my birthday at a hotel in Madrid. She invited some of my friends as well as my teammates – Ramos, Pepe, Marcelo, Carvajal, Casemiro, Bale, and Kovačić, and we celebrated long into the night.

Real Madrid also made a big gesture that showed their support during this difficult time. Even before we won the Champions League, they had opened talks about extending my contract. It had been just a year and a half since I had come to Madrid, yet the management wanted to offer me a new deal. I accepted, of course, because I was enjoying my time at Real. This had a strong psychological effect: when I needed it most, the offer of a new, improved contract showed that they believed in me.

It gives me great pleasure to say that Real Madrid amended my contract on several occasions, and every time it was they who initiated the talks – a clear sign they were happy with me.

In December, I travelled to Marrakesh with the team, and this time supported them from the stands as they lifted the FIFA Club World Cup trophy. After my injury, Real continued to put in great performances, winning in La Liga and the Champions League. I missed playing in such an excellent and attractive team, but I was sure I would recover in time to join them in the pursuit of all the season's trophies. However, what happened next put an end to my hopes.

In the first match after the New Year's break, we unexpectedly lost in Valencia. Three days later, Atlético defeated us 2–0 in the Copa del Rey round of 16, while the return match at Bernabéu ended in a 2–2 draw, which meant we were eliminated from the first competition that season. We bounced back with five straight wins in La Liga, but then another catastrophe at Calderón meant we once again hit bottom. In *El Derbi Madrileño* in February, Atlético smashed us 4–0. The defeat was a hint that the team's form was on the decline. The media began calling for my return, and there was a lot of drama and questions about why I was still not ready. The real truth is that my recovery was going as planned, within the timeframe announced on the first day of my rehabilitation process. People at the club also started asking when I would be coming back, because they saw my training had become more intensive. But those were individual training sessions, and I needed more time to join the team.

That finally happened at the end of February, when the doctors gave me the green light. What a relief! On 10 March, 2015, in the match against Schalke, I replaced Sami Khedira in the 58th minute. The crowd gave me a standing ovation, and I felt as if I was born again. But it was a different kind of reality from the one in November. A week before, Real had lost two points in a home match against Villareal, and then all three points in Bilbao. We were still challenging at the top of the table, but our confidence was shaken. My return to the pitch was marked by our first Champions League defeat that season. We had beaten Schalke 2–0 in the first leg in Gelsenkirchen, but in the second leg we were in a lot of trouble and our progress into the next round was brought into question. Schalke had a 4–3 lead in the 84th minute, and were just one goal away from causing a huge upset. Luckily, we endured and made it through, winning 5–4 on aggregate. But it was a real struggle.

My own form was at a high level – I'd recovered completely and was fresh and eager to play. That was obvious on the pitch, and I think it gave the team more confidence. An important *El Clásico* at Camp Nou was ahead of us. Barcelona had taken first position, and we had dropped to second place for the first time in 16 matches. We played well – they took the lead after a free-kick, but we levelled after a tremendous passage of play. I provided a throughball for Karim Benzema, who backheeled a pass for Cristiano Ronaldo, who touched it with the tip of his boot and sent it into the net. Phenomenal! We had a couple more chances, and Gareth Bale's goal was ruled out because of an offside. Then, in the 56th minute, practically out of nothing after a long ball, Luis Suárez skilfully placed a shot into the top corner. Up until the 60th minute or so, I had enough energy, but then I started to feel the consequences of a long absence. Barça were quick to create chances from counter-attacks, and we had our own, but the match ended in a 2–1 win for Barcelona. By the end of the league campaign, Real had recorded nine more wins and a draw, but Barcelona kept top spot and won the title. Another battle, much more important than our earlier exit in the Copa, was lost.

Meanwhile, I lost the battle too. We were playing against Málaga at Bernabéu and in the 60th minute, during a challenge in the middle of the pitch, I was caught out of step. The opponent kicked the ball hard and my leg together with it. The pain shot through my leg and I left the pitch immediately. The crowd kept cheering me on, but the news was terrible: the medial collateral ligament of my right knee was strained, and I would be sidelined for at least six weeks. I had just come back, played in nine matches in 38 days, and now I was out again! I just couldn't catch a break. Two serious injuries, six months away from the pitch, and Real kept losing on all fronts. The last chance was the Champions League, but Juventus came out on top in the two semi-final matches. To add insult to injury, the decisive goal in the 1–1 draw in the second leg was scored by Morata, a former Real Madrid player now at Juventus. I did everything to try and be fit for this important match, but it was just an illusion. The season that had started like a dream ended up as a nightmare.

El Grande

During the summer holidays I didn't allow myself to relax too much. I exercised and swam in order to heal my ligament. I wanted to be fit for the pre-season, so that I could reach the required level when the campaign started. Two days after the end of the season, the club announced that Carlo Ancelotti was no longer the Real coach. I felt bad because Carlo is a great manager and an excellent person who simply ran out of luck. We lost two championships after coming so close, lagging just a point or two behind the winners, and all of that despite a plague of injuries. We won the European and the FIFA Club World title, the Copa del Rey and the European Super Cup. We played excellent football and broke a string of records. But all of that wasn't enough to keep Ancelotti in charge for the third season in a row. That's the reality at Real Madrid – if there are no trophies, someone has to be held responsible. Such are the rules of the game: Real Madrid can't settle for average, the goals are always set high. I stayed in contact with Ancelotti, and we still have a good relationship. I'm thankful because he trusted me and gave me the reins of the team. During his time at Real, I made some important steps forward in my game and I matured as a player. Professional players of the Spanish first and second divisions recognised this and voted me the Best Midfielder in the 2013/2014 La Liga. Considering the competition of top-class midfielders in the Spanish league, that was a huge recognition, and one I won again in 2016. Meanwhile, professional players from around the world also included me in the FIFA and FIFAPro World Best 11 for 2015.

At the beginning of June that year, Real announced the appointment of Rafael Benítez as the new head coach. I didn't know much about him, only what I had read in the papers. Xabi Alonso told me he was a very studious coach and, based on his experience from his time under Benítez at Liverpool, believed he was a good solution for Real.

Our pre-season tour took us to Australia and China. My first thought was that this wasn't a good idea, because we would be spending a lot of time on the plane. It drained the team, and that could be felt in practice. In one of the matches we played in China, our opponent was Inter Milan, with Marcelo Brozović and Mateo Kovačić. I watched the game from the bench, which allowed me to focus on Kovačić's excellent performance. Real won 3–0, but Mateo was the talk of the town. After the match, we were flying to Shanghai, where we would play against AC Milan.

On the plane, I told President Pérez, who was also impressed by Kovačić, 'We should bring him to Real.'

I saw the president was intrigued by Kovačić's performance, but he replied, 'Maybe next year.'

'Someone else will snatch him,' I insisted.

After dinner, I passed by President Pérez's table. I mentioned Kovačić once again, and this time it was clear he was interested. Cristiano Ronaldo also praised his performance and suggested that Pérez should also bring Ronaldo's countryman William Carvalho. Benítez, who had arrived from Italy, where he had coached Napoli and had the opportunity to experience Kovačić's potential first-hand, also spoke highly of him. A couple of days after we returned from the tour, José Ángel Sánchez, the Real Madrid CEO, came to the club's camp. He asked me what I thought about Mateo, not just as a player, but also as a person. I told him I thought the best of him on both counts, because he was an excellent young man and an exceptional talent. I also remarked that Real should sign him as soon as possible. It was clear Real had set the wheels in motion to bring Kovačić to Madrid. Within three weeks after the match in China, he signed for Real! I was happy we would be teammates both at the club and for the national team.

Our first impressions of Benítez were positive. He had history at Real Madrid, having played for Castilla, Real's reserve team, and also coached them at the very beginning of his career as a manager. Understandably, he was highly motivated to prove himself in his city and at his club. Benítez was a true professional: he organised everything to the smallest detail, and insisted everything that had been agreed should be honoured. It soon became apparent that this would be a problem. He wanted to change the style of our game, stubbornly introducing his ideas and insisting on technical corrections, even with the most experienced players. It was evident that this style of leading a team, more appropriate for a schoolteacher, would not work at Real. Things went wrong. During the opening weeks of the season we had relatively good results, but our playing style was not good. Results fluctuated wildly, and many players were unhappy with their status. Inevitably, the team lacked the necessary energy. At the beginning of November we suffered two defeats in a row, one worse than the other. We lost 3–2 in Sevilla and then came a real debacle in *El Clásico*: Barcelona smashed us 4–0 in the middle of Madrid! For the rest of the season the team could find no answer to the problem, and the pressure on the manager grew. And that's why, to be completely honest, I was not surprised when the club decided it was time for a change.

After the match in January in Valencia, which we drew 2–2, it was announced that Benítez would no longer be our coach – and that Zinédine Zidane would replace him. In my fourth year at Real, he was my fourth coach. As a kid, I'd admired Zidane's skill; later I got to know him as Ancelotti's assistant, and now he was manager. The atmosphere in the dressing room got livelier and, at the same time, more serious. We all knew him as Ancelotti's quiet and discreet assistant, but also as a man who was positive and always encouraging. The players all had a special respect for him. He had the charisma of a footballing legend.

We started winning immediately, and our game became more convincing. Zidane wanted us to be simple and direct – he insisted on moving the ball fast and switching sides, and wanted our game to be as vertical as possible; to attack and defend as a team. We accepted his ideas right away. However, many were surprised by his decision to work on our physical condition parallel to the matches. Zidane was convinced we lacked fitness, and developed a plan that would allow us to recover. To be honest, our summer pre-season tour in Australia and China was mostly spent on the plane. We had a series of matches and not much time to go through basic training. Considering that Real plays every three days and that most of the players also have to play for their national teams, it's clear that the lack of basic physical fitness takes its toll during the gruelling season. It wasn't easy to play and go through a parallel fitness programme, but the end of the season proved the coach had made a wise decision.

The team responded to Zidane superbly: everyone was satisfied because he knew how to motivate each player and make him feel part of the team. Cohesion within the squad is an essential precondition for a team to reach its maximum. Zidane gave everyone a chance to prove themselves, and this made everyone feel important. We had tactical analyses where he showed us what we needed to do. The results were good, but in the first part of the season we had fallen too far behind. It was a pity, because with Zidane at the helm we lost just one La Liga match, at home against Atlético. The real snag was the draws against Málaga and Betis. We had 17 wins in 20 matches in La Liga under Zidane. Following the defeat against Atlético, we went on to win all 12 games until the end of the championship – and we played excellent football. Particularly impressive was our 2–1 victory against Barcelona at Camp Nou, where we showed our supremacy.

In the UEFA Champions League we convincingly eliminated Roma in the round of 16 and then complicated our situation in the match against Wolfsburg. We lost 2–0 in the away match, but then Zidane led us through the first successful *remontada*, our 3–0 in the return and an advance to the semi-final.

That victory was a serious declaration of our ambition to win the European title once again. Our opponent in the semi-final was strong: Manchester City stayed in the game until the last whistle. The away match ended in a goalless draw, while in the second leg they scored an own goal, which secured our narrow yet crucial win.

Two years after the historic night in which we had won *La Décima*, we were once again in the Champions League Final – and we were up against the same opponent: Atlético Madrid.

After the depressing first half, the second half of the season was happier. But, once again, expectations were high. The Champions League is a competition that causes a huge adrenaline rush, for players and fans. The fact that Real Madrid is the most successful club in the history of this competition confirms that the Champions League is part of its DNA.

Reaching their second Champions League Final in three years clearly showed that Atlético Madrid had advanced to the next level. Since 2011, with Diego Simeone at the helm, they had won seven trophies. When it came to the finals against Real, they had beaten us in the Copa del Rey and the Spanish Super Cup finals. They were also the 2014 La Liga champions when we finished three points behind. In that same year, they were just minutes away from a fantastic accomplishment and their first double crown in history: La Liga and the Champions League. All of that points to the greatness of our city rival, and the outstanding level of Madrid football.

We travelled to Milan, where the final was played, aware that this was our last chance of the season to win a trophy. Most of the media and the public believed that this time the goddess of football would be on Atlético's side. We had a huge respect for our opponents, but we were convinced we were a better team. This, of course, we had to prove on the pitch.

The final was played at San Siro, one of the monuments of modern football. With endless crowds of people gathered around the ground, our arrival at the stadium's underground parking space was simply spectacular. The experience from the 2014 final helped me to keep my cool in what felt like days before the match could begin. And then the referee blew the whistle to start the match. Just as had been the case two years before, it was physically and tactically demanding. Milan was extremely hot and the air was humid, draining our energy and making it hard to focus. However, we took the game to Atlético and, after several dangerous situations, took the lead in the 15th minute. Toni Kroos crossed the ball in and Gareth Bale flicked it to Sergio Ramos, who smashed it into Atlético's net! Our fans in the north stand celebrated such an excellent opening.

Atlético, however, had a better start in the second half, and in the 48th minute Pepe challenged Fernando Torres and the referee pointed to the spot. But Antoine Griezmann smashed the ball against the crossbar. For Atlético, I think this had a strong psychological impact. Yet we soon faced a huge handicap too: in the 52nd minute Dani Carvajal had to leave the pitch due to injury. He was vital to Real's game because his runs down the right wing and his speed contributed to our direct style of play. Dani burst into tears because he knew what his injury meant: he was leaving the pitch in the Champions League Final, and would also now have to miss UEFA Euro 2016.

By the mid-second half we'd missed a couple of good chances to take a 2–0 lead. Benzema, Ronaldo and Bale could have saved us all the trouble, but they were just unlucky. As often happens, we were punished. Atlético pressed on and, in the 79th minute, Juanfran found Yannick Carrasco with a right-wing cross for the equaliser. Now it was the fans in the south stand celebrating. The match went to extra time, which was very difficult for our side. We were more fatigued; Bale had cramps and my thigh felt tense. Atlético had more energy, but from today's perspective, it seems they lacked the courage to win the match in regular time. They sat back and closed off all routes to their goal, as if they were waiting for the penalty shoot-out. Yet another ordeal.

Zidane asked every player if they were ready to take a penalty. I said, 'Yes' then he chose the five penalty takers and I wasn't among them. I think his plan was to use me for the sudden-death rounds, as the sixth taker. It was difficult to watch the shoot-out – the suspense was unbearable.

It's a real game of nerves; it can't be practised. Taking penalties in training sessions is one thing; taking them in front of 80,000 people at the stadium with so much at stake is a whole different game. It's crucial to remain as calm as possible and focus on the kick. Some players pick the side and the way they are going to take the shot before they step up to the ball. Some wait for the goalkeeper to move. Some aren't sure what to do, so they improvise. This, in my experience, is the riskiest thing to do.

In this case, all the penalties were taken superbly. Even the one that determined the winner – an inch or two to the right and Juanfran's strike wouldn't have smashed against the post. When that happened, we knew the victory was in our pocket. The decisive penalty was Ronaldo's responsibility and, under such circumstances, Cristiano never fails to demonstrate incredible focus and confidence. He knew his shot could bring us the trophy; he knew what was at stake, yet he was so composed and sure of himself. So admirable! When we saw the ball in the net, we simply exploded, just as we had two years before in Lisbon.

But someone's happiness means someone else is left devastated. That's why I immediately went to the Atlético players, who were in tears. They came so close, yet the prestigious title – the major one missing in their rich club treasury – had slipped through their grasp. Watching them cry reminded me how difficult such moments are.

And that's why you should enjoy it when luck smiles on you. Our families joined us on the pitch of the legendary stadium. We celebrated by throwing Zidane up in the air. I had come to Madrid to win trophies and, after the glum predictions following my first season at Real, now I could take pride in two Champions League trophies! Fantastic! But that wasn't all.

The next morning, we arrived at Cibeles and were once again met by crowds of fans. That's a real spectacle, every time it happens. After celebrating with the fans, we went to a club and had a private party to commemorate *La Undécima*.

Zidane had made it. This was his first time as the head coach of Real Madrid, and he'd just won the European title. At one point, I watched him celebrate the title in his typical fashion – discreetly. Yet he emanated a unique energy. When a great player becomes a trophy-winning coach, he has an entirely different aura from everyone else. Zidane went through all the steps at Real: player, icon, technical director, assistant coach, Castilla coach and finally the first team manager. And on every step of the way he was *El Grande*. That's how everyone in Real saw him. When he took charge, he understood the demands of a great club like Real. That's why he insisted we improve our physical condition. And that's why training sessions under Zidane were the most difficult for me since I had become a professional footballer. A lot of running, but also playing football.

I got to know his angry side too. He raised his voice at me more than once, especially when I played a wrong pass. Zidane would gesture and make his thoughts plain. Something along the lines of: *Come on, Luka, what are you doing?!*

We had an outstanding relationship from the very beginning. He would invite me into his office and ask me how I felt, if something was bothering me. He would ask what I thought about how we had played and he would explain some of his ideas if I didn't understand them. As a player, you feel special when the coach respects you and asks your opinion. Still, his approach and the fact that he saw me as one of the key players in the team never made me complacent. On the contrary, it motivated me to work even harder and prove I deserved such status.

Zidane asked me to start acting like a leader because he thought he saw it in me. He wanted me to take it onto the field, to talk with my teammates more, to organise them on the pitch. He said I understood the game and my teammates followed me. He also insisted I should shoot from distance and participate in the attack.

'When I was a player, my approach to the game was similar to yours. I was too reserved to take the initiative. So, I understand your position, but I'm sure you can and have to be a leader.'

Zidane encouraged me to take more responsibility. During our first conversation after he had taken over the team, he told me something that truly impressed me. It went more or less like this: 'Luka, you have to know your value. You're in the category of the players who can win the Golden Ball.'

This was the trophy he had won back in 1998, and before he said this, even to imagine myself listed among the top three, let alone winning the Ballon d'Or, seemed surreal. Now he made it sound like something that might happen. Zidane never says something out of politeness, and his words made me feel as if I had already been nominated for the award. Still, it never occurred to me that his prophecy would come true.

There were days when his methods didn't agree with me. He limited my game time – if it were up to me, I'd play in all the matches, in all the competitions, even in friendlies. I always want to play. But Zidane had his own ideas and he saw them through. Good that he did, too. His rotations allowed me to remain fresh and stay at my competitive maximum.

**

With two Champions League titles and a total of six trophies since my arrival in 2012, I felt like a king in Madrid. Not only because of my professional accomplishments but also because my family was fulfilled. We had been happy in London too – the first two years we lived in London like a couple, and then Ivano became the centre of our world. When we left London, Vanja had a hard time adapting to life in Madrid. She was pregnant with Ema and her pregnancy needed to be monitored, which meant she often had to travel to Zagreb, where she gave birth. It wasn't easy to adjust to life in Spain. But, as I have already mentioned, Madrid is a terrific city, and it soon grows on you. It's not a megalopolis, the traffic is bearable, and the city is well connected. People are open and kind, respectful, and this type of mentality agrees with us. We lead a relaxed life and enjoy the Mediterranean cuisine we are used to in Croatia. The city has everything you could wish for. In London, our social life wasn't great, while in Madrid we have made lots of friends and have a nice group of people around us. Marcelo, Varane, Ramos, Navas, Nacho, Vázquez, Bale are my teammates, but also family friends. We celebrate our children's birthdays and other occasions together. When Ivano started school, we also got to know his classmates' parents. Vanja became friends with our neighbour Sara, our children's paediatrician. It's important that Vanja has someone who can jump in if she needs some help. It makes everything easier, both for her and for me, especially when I'm away.

The food in Spain is excellent. My favourite food is *pata negra*, a type of Spanish ham. I also like *paella*. At home, we mostly eat Croatian dishes. I love *sarma* – cabbage rolls, beans, stuffed peppers. Every time our relatives or friends from Croatia are coming for a visit, if they ask us if we need something, Vanja says, 'Bring some cabbage for sarma; we can't find the right kind here.' She loves to cook, although with three children it can be a hassle! However, every day we have two cooked meals. It's a gigantic task, especially since we have to pay special attention to my sports diet.

The school system in Madrid is well-organised and on a very high level. Ivano and Ema attend the American International School. Since nursery school, they have spoken English. At home we use Croatian, so they are fluent in three languages: their mother tongue, English and Spanish. It gets lively at home when it comes to languages. I was thrilled when Ema could use all three languages at just three years old. It's funny to see Ivano and Ema playing in English – and fascinating that, even though they are so little, they switch from one language to another depending on the situation. Sofia is still little, but we want all three of our children to know Croatian, and to have English and Spanish as their second and third languages.

Because of all this, once my career is over, Vanja and I can see ourselves living in Madrid. Just as Luís Figo and his wife Helen have done. When they visited Croatia in the summer, and on some other occasions, we talked about their life in Madrid. Their children feel at home here; they go to school and have their friends. Although Luís and Helen often travel for business and regularly visit Portugal and Sweden, Madrid is their home base.

I can't tell what will happen one day when I stop playing, but Vanja and I decided to buy a house in Madrid. What encouraged us to do so was the first contract extension I signed at the end of 2014. It was a clear signal we could stay at Real a while longer. After two years of intensive searching, we managed to find a house that suited us perfectly. It's in the same neighbourhood we had lived in until then, La Moraleja. The school, the nursery school, shops, restaurants, cafés, several of my teammates living nearby – all of these were important factors that helped us choose our home. Another imperative is that our training ground is close. When I played in London, I got used to living close to the training base, where I spent a lot of time. We don't go downtown all that often, and when we do, the traffic doesn't bother me as much as it did in London. However, it's important Valdebebas is just a couple of minutes away.

Our children love it when we go to Croatia. For them, Zagreb means they are going to see their grandma, Vanja's mother. When we go to Zadar, they look forward to seeing my parents. But, of course, after a while, they want to go back to where they feel at home. For them, that's Madrid, our house and our routines, their friends from school and Ivano's football practice. At first, we found it odd when we were in Zagreb or Zadar and Ivano would ask when we were going home, meaning Madrid. But that's the way it is. They have a different childhood than we did. I know they will love both Croatia and Spain, and have more opportunities to live their lives according to their wishes.

What has changed since the first couple of months of living in Madrid is that I've become much more popular with the fans – not only in Spain, but elsewhere too. That's the Real effect. When I played for Tottenham – that is, when I was part of a strong and globally recognised English

Premier League side – people seldom recognised me in the street or approached me to take a photo or sign an autograph. After winning the Champions League, I felt a drastic change. It became more difficult to go out in the city, or play with my children in the park, because in two minutes there would be a crowd of people around me. For example, Vanja and I visited Paris on several occasions. The first time we went there, maybe two or three guests recognised me at the restaurant and asked to take a photo with me. When I came back to Paris after the Champions League success with Real, people kept stopping me in the street, and when I went to a restaurant, most guests wanted a photo or an autograph. I have never rejected anyone – popularity is a sign you've done something right. Taking a photo or giving an autograph is a chance to show the fans and everyone else interested in football that you respect their passion. Football is a special sport. Without the fans' passion, it wouldn't be what it is.

Falling in France

With the second European club title under my belt, in the summer of 2016 I travelled to Croatia. We had yet another chance to achieve something big. The UEFA Euro 2016 was taking place in France where, 18 years before, Croatia had won the bronze medal at the 1998 FIFA World Cup. People were saying this was our chance to step out of their shadow. I didn't feel the bronze casting a shadow on us, I didn't see it as a burden; on the contrary, it was a source of inspiration. I wanted to bring yet another celebration to everyone in Croatia – and the burden was the fact that we had yet to do so. This time, I felt we were ready to take it one step further. We had an excellent team; our form and confidence were at a high level.

Before leaving for France, the annual award ceremony for the best Croatian players and coaches took place in Zagreb. It's a traditional event organised by the Croatian Association Football Union and *Sportske Novosti*, the oldest sports magazine in Croatia. I have been voted the best Croatian player seven times in a row. This recognition is dear to me, because it comes from my colleagues and experts, players and coaches from the Croatian Football League. Also, I'm truly honoured that the awards have been handed to me by legends of Croatian football, such as Robert Prosinečki, Slaven Bilić, Zvonimir Boban and Dario Šimić. In 2016, I won the trophy for the fourth time and hoped this would be an introduction to the successful European Championship and an even more successful end to the season.

I arrived at Croatia's camp well rested and ready, a huge change compared to the World Cup in Brazil two years before. I was enthusiastic and hungry for success. When you win trophies, your appetite only grows stronger. I was ready, as were my teammates, for a big result.

At this tournament, I expanded the list of the rituals I go through before coming out onto the pitch. I think every player has some such routine. From the beginning of my career, I have always put on my left boot first. My parents gave me a gold chain with a little cross for my 18th birthday; I always take it off just before warm-up, and I always kiss the cross. Since France 2016, I wear special shin guards. On one are photos of my wife, our children and Jesus; on the other are their names. Every time before stepping out onto the pitch, I kiss them too.

In the first match, we beat Turkey 1–0. I scored the decisive goal, we were dominant, and we opened the tournament with confidence. But instead of celebrating, we got the news that our captain, Darijo Srna, had lost his father. It was a huge shock. Darijo and I have been friends for years. Our families always spend part of our summer holiday together, so I knew his father was seriously ill. I also knew what Darijo was going through because he was very close to his father. He immediately travelled to Metković, his home town, to attend the funeral. Many people came to pay their respects and I was glad that my parents were among them. The tragedy mobilised us, and we wanted to show what Darijo meant to us. Although it would have been understandable if he had stayed with his family, the captain did not leave his team: he came back to France and led us in the second match against the Czech Republic. The whole world was touched when, during the anthems, tears flowed down his face. His grief just had to come out. His father had wanted him to play, no matter what. Darijo kept his promise and was one of Croatia's best players at the tournament.

We swept the Czechs off the field with Ivan Perišić and Ivan Rakitić scoring for a 2–0 lead. Soon after the second goal, in the 62nd minute, I had to leave the pitch. My adductor muscle had been troubling me ever since the UEFA Champions League Final in Milan. I had been carrying the injury, and the strain of two matches was once again making itself felt. In the 76th minute, the Czechs pulled a goal back. Then, four minutes before the final whistle, flares were thrown onto the pitch from the stand containing our fans and the referee stopped the match. Constant problems with some of the fans had us fearing riots and possible grave consequences for the national team. This disrupted our mindset and our focus. The fans were protesting against the people in charge of the Croatian Football Federation and their way of running things. They were convinced that the Croatian Football Federation did not treat everyone the same and put the interests of the privileged few first. I think it's all right to fight for your ideals, but I couldn't understand the way in which it was done. Something that brings harm to the national team cannot bring good to anyone.

Unfortunately, in the 89th minute, the Czechs were awarded a penalty, and they levelled the score. Despite the draw, we secured our passage into the second round, which meant there was no pressure on us in the final group game against Spain. So, after consultations with the coach Ante Čačić and the team's doctors, it was decided that I should skip the match. Had it been necessary, I would've played; I already felt better, but it was important to spare my leg a bit more. We could see a clear path to the semi-final. Had the results been as people expected, in the round of 16 we would have played against Iceland. After that, our opponents would have been Poland or Wales. These were good teams, but they were not stronger than us. However, it didn't happen. We beat Spain, 2–1, but the unexpected outcome of other matches brought us a more demanding opponent – Portugal. We always found it difficult playing against them and had never beaten them. And unfortunately, that tradition continued.

We looked better on the pitch but missed a couple of chances and the game went to extra time. In the 116th minute, Perišić smashed a shot against the post. Just a minute later, Portugal scored on the counter-attack! And there you go, we cried again. The defeat got to me because I was sure we had everything to make it to the very end. It's hard to say why we didn't, although our performance wasn't as good as in the group matches. Portugal were afraid of us, choosing a very defensive strategy and relying on counter-attacks. For them, things needed to work out just the once, and they did – and that was it. All those details – when one team doesn't concede because the ball hits the post, and then they get lucky and the ball bounces to the opponent's feet to end up in the net – show that many things have to come together to become successful. It's as if Portugal were meant to become European Champions. Their game wasn't particularly impressive, but who cares about impressions when you win the trophy? I was happy that Cristiano Ronaldo, my teammate from Real, led his team to a great result. I know what it meant to him.

In the end, while we were in tears, Ronaldo approached me and tried to offer me consolation. He told me that they had feared us, and said to themselves: 'If we eliminate Croatia, we're going all the way.' So it proved. They got to celebrate, while we got nothing but disappointment once again. We failed at the first step after the group stage, just as had happened in Austria against Turkey back in 2008. After eight years of yearning for success with Croatia, nothing had changed. As always when the national team fails to produce a result, all fingers were pointed at the team's manager. Čačić had led the team in the group stage when we looked good and against Portugal when we were less convincing. We failed together, he as a manager and we as a team.

At nearly 31 years old, I questioned if it made sense to continue playing for the national team.

Still, I was convinced the result we all strived for would come sooner or later. I had faith in the team's quality, and I believed fortune had to favour us once. No team can get to the top without luck. We learned that in France.

After that tournament, Darijo Srna said goodbye to the Croatia shirt. He played a fantastic Euros and then left. As a vice-captain, I took his role. When I was a kid, I had dreamed about one day becoming Croatia's captain. Now the dream had come true. It was a great honour and an even greater responsibility. As the first among the equals, you have more responsibilities: you lead the team and you make sure that anything that could affect the team's performance is at the right level. But even at that moment, I obsessed about finally making it to the top. I wanted my team to leave a mark in history. I didn't want to make peace with the fact that after so many years in the national team I would conclude my career without a real result – one for which we would be remembered, just as the names of the members of the 'Bronze Generation' from the 1990s are a shining reminder of one of the greatest achievements in the history of Croatian sport.

CHAPTER EIGHT

I spent the summer at our house in Zadar. I love it when we get together after we haven't seen each other for a while. My parents, my sisters, Vanja's mother and grandparents, our relatives, our friends, we all get together during the summer. We also visit those who cannot come to Zadar. That summer, I drove to Zaton Obrovački, Kvartirić, Obrovac. After I won the second UEFA Champions League with Real earlier that year, I saw it as the final confirmation of the team's value. I kept telling myself it was a miracle to win two European titles in such a short period. Most of the players or coaches who had tasted this only once told me it was the peak of their career. I already had two titles, and I thought, *Why should it end here? We could win the third Champions League.* Every next trophy would be a bonus to the already sensational feeling of being part of Real's golden era. All of this made me exceptionally calm during my summer holiday. I had entered the fourth decade of my life and 14 professional seasons were behind me – eight of them in the most competitive football leagues. This is to say that I had a lot of experience – I had been tested in many battles – and the string of team and individual accomplishments gave me a sense of fulfilment. The only thing missing was success with Croatia, and I was determined never to give up.

Once you turn 30, a moment comes, I guess spontaneously, when you look back at your career. And you think about what you haven't yet accomplished and what you can do to change this. In a footballer's career, the knowledge that time cannot be stopped only intensifies the feeling. After your 30th birthday, the talk about your age, about being past your prime and finishing your career, becomes inevitable.

Probably because I never cared much about what other people said about me, I didn't allow such thoughts to weigh me down. I have always been realistic – I guess that's the result of all the good and bad things I had gone through since my childhood, as well as the fact that I had to mature quickly. I learned to deal with problems and obstacles, to be tough, but also to appreciate all the good things and take pleasure in my success.

When I achieved the first big breakthrough in my career, and fully proved myself at Dinamo and the national team, there came a reminder of how cruel life can be. It was 2008 and a tragic event stole from us our friend Hrvoje Ćustić. He adored football, his hometown of Zadar, and dreamed of becoming a professional football player. He was two years older than me, a great player and an even better person. In the 2004/2005 season, we played together for Croatia under-21s. As an older and more experienced player, he was always there to help those younger and less experienced than him. But one day, in a match between Zadar and Cibalia, one ordinary duel proved fatal. He fell and smashed his head against a concrete wall right next to the touchline. A concrete wall right next to the touchline?! Such absurdity was difficult to grasp. To lose your life on a football pitch, during a top-flight match, in the 21st century, and for such a bizarre reason. Hrvoje succumbed to his injuries in Zadar Hospital five days later. He was just 24 years old. His funeral was too sad to describe.

Zadar's goalkeeper during that fateful match was Danijel Subašić, one of the greats that Zadar gave to the national team. We used to play together in the youth teams at Zadar, and Hrvoje was Danijel's best friend. I know how much he misses him. During every match, under his shirt he wears a t-shirt with Hrvoje's picture on it. It's an expression of true friendship and the feeling of attachment to a sorely missed friend. My parents are friends with Hrvoje's family, and I'm in touch with them often. We regularly see each other in Zadar, and I often see Svetko, Hrvoje's father, who's fighting to keep Zadar football afloat.

In February 2014, when Real were finding the momentum to win *La Décima*, my parents called to tell me Tomo Bašić had died. I owe my career to him. He believed in me when no one – except for my family, and especially my father – thought I could play serious football. With his attitude and the firm conviction with which he defended it, Mr Tomo helped me build the foundations of my self-confidence. I will never forget him. He left this world at 77 years old. His funeral was scheduled three days before a very important match: Real were playing against Schalke in Gelsenkirchen in the Champions League round of 16. It never even crossed my mind not to go to Zadar and attend his funeral. When I went to ask Carlo Ancelotti to allow me to go home, I had already ordered a private plane. I knew the coach would let me leave when I explained, but I also knew that he would ask me to come back right away. In one afternoon, I flew from Madrid to Zadar and back. I had to say goodbye to Mr Tomo. Three months later, when I lifted the Champions League trophy, he was one of the first people who came to my mind on the Lisbon turf. I thought how nice it would be if he could see it and take pleasure knowing that, in my case, he proved a wise prophet.

Bašić's trust was important because it filled me with confidence. Once you have that, you can deal with all the difficulties in your career and your life. Nevertheless, I have learned it is important to keep your feet firmly on the ground even when things are going your way. The risk of losing your footing is at its greatest when the euphoria of success has taken hold. This is why I like to talk about such moments with friends who have a deep understanding of everyday life. I love to read about it, and then think it through.

I've had some painful periods in my life, but have learned to react when things are not going as expected and to try and change things. That's how I came to an understanding I consider very true: *the best things in life never come easy.*

During the holiday before my fifth season at Real, I drew a line. I did this not only because I wanted to tally the score after my 30th birthday, but also because this was a moment of great happiness in my career and my life. It could have led me to relax, satisfied by having made it. But I knew what was in store if I wanted to continue to be successful. And I wanted that with all of my heart. If the experience at Real has taught me anything, it's that winning a trophy only makes you hungrier. You can never get enough titles and the honours that come with them.

I've never lacked motivation, not at 20 or even when I turned 30. The only difference is the conditions in which things happen. As the years go by, you need to train more. It's essential to care for your body and your diet, to avoid injury, to rest. And yes, it's crucial to put all the trophies and awards away so you can focus on what's ahead and not recall what it used to be like. Despite the doubts that age, or the loss of power and agility, might provoke for someone else, I never questioned my motivation. Winning the second Champions League after the bad start to the season only reminded me how nice it feels to win. Elimination from the Euros only strengthened my desire to taste victory with Croatia, as I had done with Real Madrid.

As the pre-season drew near, I knew I was returning to more or less the same group of players. Álvaro Arbeloa, a veteran of many battles, left and I will always remember him as a dear friend who offered a helping hand when I had just arrived. Young, fresh forces came, such as Marco Asensio, while Álvaro Morata returned from Juventus. I was confident we had a great, competitive team, with two excellent players at every position. We were fully accustomed to the coach – in the first six months with Zinédine Zidane at the helm, we had almost caught Barcelona at the top of the table.

During the pre-season, we seemed ready for great things. The training was hard because it followed a very demanding programme designed by Antonio Pintus, a conditioning expert. Zidane insisted on physical fitness because he considered it the prerequisite for outplaying the opponent and allowing our qualities to shine. He also knew that the heavy schedule of participating in five competitions, together with international appearances for our national teams, would not allow space to make up for what we had lost during the summer preparations. However, this time we did an excellent job. We felt we were ready for a big season. We were driven by the ambition to finally, for the first time since my arrival at Real, win the Spanish championship. An additional motivation was to become the first team in history to defend the Champions League title.

We couldn't have hoped for a better opening to the season. The first trophy was under our belt! In the European Super Cup we beat Sevilla 3–2 after extra time. By 15 January we had put together a streak of 11 wins and four draws in La Liga. Our first defeat came against Sevilla, which, in a sense, closed the circle. In the same week, we also lost the Copa del Rey match against Celta, which led to our elimination in the quarter-final. It was a moment of weakness, but it didn't disrupt us. In La Liga, and the Champions League, we maintained our winning performances.

I think one of the most important factors in that season was Zidane's idea to rotate the players. When a team has so many top-class players as was the case with Real, it's difficult to keep everyone happy. The atmosphere in the dressing room depends on the level of satisfaction of players from the 12th to the 20th position. Zidane included all the players in the competition; he gave everyone a chance to feel important and to contribute to the team's success. We were a band of brothers. We played 60 club matches during the season, and the coach used 27 players. The rotations helped us to stay fresh and strong for the end of the season, and the final result showed just how prudent and wise Zidane's decision had been.

Zidane's tactics were clear: he asked us to defend and attack with equal intensity, and without tricks. The simpler your game is, the more difficult it becomes for the opponent. He insisted we maintain a high pressure, which wasn't always easy to accomplish. We were slow to close our opponents, which could cause us problems. The overall quality of our game compensated for this, as well as the individual qualities of our players. But, as so often happens when things are going well, problems were waiting just around the corner.

In mid-September, we played against Espanyol in Barcelona. I got kicked in the knee, and immediately felt sharp pain. I have a high pain threshold, so I continued the match. I played in the next two matches, against Borussia in Dortmund and at Las Palmas. Interestingly, both ended in a 2–2 draw, although we had a lead of 1–0 and 2–1 in both games and conceded in the last few minutes of the match. We lacked concentration. In Dortmund, my knee played up again. It was a clear sign I had a problem that would require a thorough check-up. As soon as we returned to Madrid, I went to have an MRI. The scan showed a piece of cartilage had chipped off as a result of the injury I had picked up in Barcelona. The chip was moving around my knee and causing pain. The doctors recommended an arthroscopy to resolve the issue, and I expected to be out for a whole month. I wasn't depressed, even though it was the beginning of the season. Injuries usually involve a gruelling period before coming back to the pitch, but this time everything went without a hiccup, and I was soon fit to play. I came back on 6 November in a match against Leganés. Zidane didn't want to force anything and insisted on reintroducing me gradually – and my performances soon reached the desired level.

The team had gathered momentum by the time we travelled to Japan to play at the FIFA Club World Cup. After beating Club América 2–0 in the semi-final, in the final match we faced the persistent and tenacious Kashima Antlers, who took the game to extra time. The Japanese even had a 2–1 lead, but then Cristiano Ronaldo first levelled and then, in the first period of extra time, scored two more goals for a 4–2 victory. We knew the match would be difficult due to the time difference; it was a tough tournament, and we had lost sleep. The Golden Ball for the best player deservedly went to Ronaldo. With one goal in the first match and a hat-trick in the final, he finished the tournament with four goals in two games. I also took a trophy back to Europe – I won the Silver Ball.

In La Liga, we were fighting for first place, while the Copa del Rey exit to Celta was a temporary blip. I didn't play in the return match because of my injury. On the other hand, we handled the Champions League competition well. In the round of 16, we eliminated Napoli without much stress. However, in April, we were scheduled to meet Bayern with Carlo Ancelotti and Xabi Alonso. That was more than stressful. True, it didn't look like that after the first match: Bayern took the lead at Allianz Arena, but Ronaldo scored twice in the second half and secured our victory. Bayern are a big club, with top-class players and coaches, and you can never drop your guard, regardless of where you are playing and what advantage you bring into the match. So we knew the return match at Bernabéu wouldn't be simple, but I never thought we would have to go through so much trouble and come so close to being eliminated! They took the lead at the beginning of the second half, but Ronaldo levelled 14 minutes before the end of the match. Just two minutes later, Sergio Ramos scored an own goal, and it became clear we were in for a difficult evening. Six minutes before stoppage time, Arturo Vidal earned a second yellow and was sent off. We entered extra time a man up – and Ronaldo once again scored two goals to restore our lead, before Asensio netted the fourth to confirm our victory. We had advanced into the next round, though not without trouble. Bayern complained about the refereeing, but I'm convinced that it was the better team who progressed into the semi-final. Ronaldo had scored five goals in two matches against Manuel Neuer, an outstanding goalkeeper.

In the semi-final, we once again faced Atlético Madrid. Zidane had decided we would use the 4-3-1-2 diamond formation until the end of the competition. The team performed well with Isco behind two strikers, Karim Benzema and Ronaldo. Since the quarter-final Ronaldo had been on fire, and he only confirmed his fantastic form in the first match against Atlético. We put in a tremendous performance, crowned by him with yet another hat-trick. The 3–0 victory made us feel we would have no problems in the return match. Maybe that's why we did. At Calderón, carried by their sensational supporters, Atlético took an early lead of 2–0! They punished us with their most dangerous weapon, set-pieces. In the

Signing contracts: Luka and Real Madrid president Florentino Pérez. 27 August, 2012.

Flying to Madrid: Luka and his parents.

Luka with Vanja and their son Ivano on the Santiago Bernabéu pitch for his official unveiling at Real Madrid.

Luka scores his first goal for Real Madrid, against Real Zaragoza, 3 November, 2012.

Celebrating with the fans at Santiago Bernabéu. In the beginning, Luka wore the number 19 shirt.

Luka's father looks anxious during the 2014 UEFA Champions League Final against Atlético Madrid. Real triumphed 4–1 and, in doing so, secured a record 10th title in Europe's elite competition (*La Décima*).

Luka celebrating his first Champions League title and Real's *La Décima*, and the promised haircut.

Luka lifts the UEFA Champions League trophy after Real Madrid's 12th title in 2017.

Real Madrid's players after winning the 2014 Copa del Rey.

Luka celebrates his first La Liga title with Karim Benzema and Sergio Ramos, in 2017.

Luka with Carlo Ancelotti.

Luka with José Mourinho after Mourinho's final match at Real Madrid.

Thumbs-up with Zinédine Zidane.

Luka and Mateo Kovačić, close friends playing for Real Madrid and Croatia's national team.

Celebrating with Sergio Ramos, the Real Madrid club captain.

Luka takes a selfie with Gareth Bale, Mateo Kovačić and Toni Kroos.

Luka and Cristiano Ronaldo pictured together. They played alongside one another for six years.

Luka with Gareth Bale, after winning his third UEFA Champions League title in 2017.

Luka and Vanja with
Real Madrid teammate
Marcelo and his wife
Clarice Alves.

Luka with Francesco
Totti, one of his
role models.

Luka embraces
his fellow midfielder
Andrés Iniesta during
a match between
Croatia and Spain.

The Modrić family: following the birth of Luka and Vanja's youngest daughter Sofia.

All of Luka's No. 10s: in Real Madrid and Croatia shirts before the 2018 FIFA World Cup in Russia.

'Hearing the Croatian national anthem always gives me goosebumps.'

Luka celebrating his superb strike against Argentina at the 2018 FIFA World Cup. Croatia won 3–0.

Luka with Mario Mandžukić, his footballing comrade for more than a decade.

The clash of the No. 10s: Leo Messi and Luka during the Croatia v Argentina 2018 FIFA World Cup match.

Luka shares an emotional moment with Croatia coach Zlatko Dalić.

Luka celebrates with two of his children after defeating England to reach the 2018 FIFA World Cup Final.

Croatia's line-up for the 2018 FIFA World Cup Final: (back row, l-r) Dejan Lovren; Ivan Strinić; Mario Mandžukić; Ante Rebić; Danijel Subašić; Ivan Perišić (front row, l-r) Marcelo Brozović; Domagoj Vida; Ivan Rakitić; Šime Vrsaljko; and Luka Modrić (captain).

Croatia players and staff celebrate as 2018 FIFA World Cup runners-up. They were defeated 4–2 by France in a dramatic final in Moscow.

Winning the Golden Ball at the 2018 FIFA World Cup in Russia. The greatest honour at a moment of great disappointment.

Croatia's national team showing off their FIFA World Cup silver medals.

A moment's rest for the Croatia captain.

Euphoric scenes in the main square in Zagreb as the Croatia national team return home after the 2018 FIFA World Cup.

A homecoming celebration with his two sisters, Jasmina and Diora.

A selfie with the fans.

The 2017/2018 UEFA Men's Player of the Year award ceremony.

Luka with Zvonimir Boban at the Best FIFA Football Awards ceremony. Boban is one of Luka's idols and was a member of the 1998 'Bronze Generation', who came third at the 1998 FIFA World Cup.

And the Ballon d'Or to complete the collection!

Luka and Vanja with Predrag Mijatović and his wife Aneta at the Ballon d'Or Gala.

Luka and Davor Ćurković, his agent.

Luka with his family after the Ballon d'Or award ceremony.

Zinédine Zidane, Marcelo, Luka and Raphaël Varane at the Ballon d'Or event.

Real Madrid
teammates
honouring Luka
for winning the
Ballon d'Or.

A party for
the winner.

All in one place: the individual
awards and trophies won by
Luka in 2018.

12th minute we conceded after a corner, while in the 16th they scored from a penalty. The situation was serious, but this was our season; we were simply too strong. Three minutes before the half-time break Isco took the ball, punched away by the goalkeeper after Toni Kroos' shot, and sent it into the net. The goal was preceded by a fantastic piece of play by Karim Benzema, one of the most talented players I have played with. On the left-hand side, right by the goal line, in the space the size of a napkin, he dribbled past no fewer than three Atlético players and passed the ball to the oncoming Kroos. Atlético could no longer hurt us. They needed three more goals to eliminate us, which proved an impossible mission. In the span of four years we were getting ready for our third Champions League Final – the second in a row with Zidane on the bench!

Before the clash against Juventus in Cardiff, we faced a couple more important challenges. Ahead of us were three matches to secure our triumph in La Liga. After losing 3–2 in *El Clásico* at Bernabéu, we recorded six consecutive wins. We scored 22 goals and conceded just five in that spell. The average of 3.7 goals per match was a clear indicator of our form. We simply flew over the pitch, our outstanding physical fitness allowing us to impose ourselves. We played the last match of La Liga in Málaga and, thanks to Ronaldo's and Benzema's goals, took a 2–0 victory and won our first Spanish championship title since I had arrived in Madrid!

The feeling was new, yet magnificent once again. The welcome in Madrid was fantastic; the crowds of fans at Cibeles were sensational and we could enjoy the celebrations as much as we wanted because the Champions League Final was still two weeks away.

During my eight years in Madrid, Real have won no fewer than 16 trophies yet only one La Liga title so far. Considering the club's size and the quality of its players, this doesn't make sense. I have often heard the same question: why are Real so dominant in Europe but cannot manage the same in domestic competition? I think the main problem lies in the continuity and focus required during the 10 months of the Spanish league. We fluctuate often and sometimes let ourselves think that the season is long, so we'll have enough time to make up for what we lose. But that's just wrong. Barcelona are dominant in La Liga because they don't miss out on any opportunity, regardless of the opponent, to win three points. And they always know how to take advantage of our setbacks. During my eight seasons at Real, they've won five titles. I think the coach's role is vital in maintaining the team's focus and the continuity of performance. Coaches are important, both when you are winning and when you are losing.

Zidane proved he knew how to keep the team focused and how to distribute the load during the season. There were times when I wasn't happy with his decision to rest me, but it turned out he was right. I have already said his greatest strength lies in simplicity: he doesn't say much, but he says the right thing. He never raises his voice, he doesn't raise a storm, but his authority is evident. He is also a great motivator – he used to show us video compilations of our games and wins. Before the matches, he would get us psyched to the max – especially before the most important matches.

The 2017 Champions League Final in Cardiff was scheduled for 3 June. Two weeks without matches after the end of the Spanish championship brought the risk that our form would drop, but the coaches prepared a programme focused on this particular match. Zidane had spent five wonderful years playing for Juventus. There he had won the Ballon d'Or and five major club trophies, becoming an icon, before signing for Real, where he became a legend. This is why he was well acquainted with the mentality of the Turin club, and fully understood their determination to put an end to 21 years of expectations in Europe's premier club competition. Zidane is not keen on long meetings and prefers short analyses. He shows the team the most important points of the opponents' game, and indicates their weaknesses. That season, Juventus' performances in Europe were fantastic: before the final, they had conceded only three times and scored 21 goals, almost two per match. They were the favourites to win the title.

Their dominance in Italy was total and in Cardiff they had won six consecutive Serie A titles. Two years prior, they had played in the final and lost to Barcelona. Their obsession was now, finally, to conquer Europe.

Unfortunately for them, our ambition was just as strong. Real Madrid had won the last double crown back in 1958. It was our chance to repeat the success of Alfredo di Stéfano's fantastic generation, and that's why unifying the European and the Spanish title after 59 years of waiting seemed so important to us. Not only that, beating Juventus meant setting a new standard of success in the Champions League. Real Madrid would become the first club to defend the Champions League title. That's a lot to be psyched about! When the adrenaline starts rushing like this – I know it from experience – no opponent can outplay you.

The final once again saw the usual share of excitement and arrangements – the frenzy for tickets, family and friends getting ready to travel to Cardiff. When this happens, I'm completely calm. Vanja is a master of organisation. Her arrangements and preparations are so thorough that our expeditions of family members and friends always arrive at the destination without the slightest hiccup. I have nothing to worry about. When preparing for an important match, this is a huge plus.

Finally, the day of the match at the Millennium Stadium arrived. The atmosphere was magic, as is usually the case in the Champions League Final. Juventus opened with a couple of dangerous attempts that Keylor Navas neutralised. Then, in the 20th minute, Ronaldo got an excellent return ball from at the edge of the box and turned it into a 1–0 lead. It's important to emphasise one factor that proved decisive for this match, and clearly demonstrated Zidane's wisdom. In our preparations for the final, he pointed out that Juventus were great in defence and difficult to break down, but they did have a weak spot: their poor reaction to return balls. The first goal made this vulnerability evident.

Just seven minutes later, Juventus scored to level. Mario Mandžukić hooked in an overhead kick and scored a fantastic goal! But it didn't throw us off. On the contrary, the whole time I had a feeling that we were the better team and certain to win. In the second half, my hunch came true. We outplayed Juventus completely. On a personal level, after a solid first half, I put in an excellent performance in the second – not only because I assisted Ronaldo for 3–1, once again delivering a return ball. I felt that the team and I could do whatever we wanted. And we did, winning 4–1 and making history. The first double crown after 59 years and legends such as Di Stéfano, Francisco Gento and Raymond Kopa. The first defending Champions League champion. The third European title in four seasons. What a story!

I was speechless. After all the victories during all the years in Madrid, it's fascinating how every new trophy offers new inspiration. That is one of Real's greatest allures. There's always a new level to reach and then surpass – something no one else has achieved, something unattainable to others. The celebrations that followed after Cardiff were fit for kings: receptions, the hero's welcome at packed Cibeles, celebrating with the fans at Bernabéu. We had been there not even two weeks before, yet they rejoiced as if it had been a long, long time ago. I savoured every moment of it. As if I knew happiness wouldn't last long. Even so, I never thought the moments that followed would be so difficult.

Leaving Madrid, I caught myself thinking that Cardiff was not the team's zenith, and I believed we could win more trophies. I knew Pepe, James Rodríguez, Álvaro Morata and Danilo were leaving, but I also knew the club would find excellent players to replace them. Its high aspirations mean that a club such as Real Madrid needs a wide selection of players. In June, I had another decisive match ahead of me – Croatia's away game against Iceland. In the first part of the 2018 FIFA World Cup qualification campaign I played only in the opening match, against Turkey in Zagreb. It ended in a 1–1 draw, although we were dominant and had couple of shots against the post and also against the crossbar. Then, due to the knee injury, I skipped the matches against Kosovo and Finland, which my teammates won. I came back just in time to play one half against Iceland

and to conclude the year with the third successive win for Croatia. In the only match in the spring, we won a difficult, yet deserved, victory against Ukraine led by Andriy Shevchenko. Nikola Kalinić scored for us. We were in a comfortable situation, more or less, sitting at the top of the table, with a clear outlook to qualify for the World Cup without a stressful play-off round. The match in Iceland was decisive: a draw would allow us to take a massive step towards first place in our group. But our performance was poor – we seemed helpless, sluggish, ineffective. The home team was no better. It seemed the match would end in a draw – a fair result considering how both sides had played – when, typically, we lost concentration. After a corner in the 90th minute, an Iceland player jumped and bumped the ball with his shoulder straight into the net! We lost, which meant Croatia would have to take a difficult road to qualify for the World Cup. What until the day before had seemed simple – a direct route to the World Cup – was suddenly brought into doubt.

Gloomy Days

A difficult period followed, but not because of football and the national team. Two days after the match in Reykjavik, I was called to testify at the Osijek County Court in a criminal trial against several officials from Dinamo Zagreb, my former club. Zdravko Mamić was the principal defendant. I testified and told the court everything I knew about the transfer fee paid by Tottenham to Dinamo back in 2008 and about its distribution among the parties involved. I also talked about the business arrangement between Mamić and myself. Everything that happened at the trial, my testimony included, is public knowledge. The process has still not been concluded.

My testimony raised a storm of disapproval in Croatia. The public thought my testimony supported Mamić's defence. The fact is, I only told the truth. As for the distribution of the transfer fee, I followed what was stipulated by the agreements that all parties had signed. Once again,

I repeated that I was ready to return the part of the transfer fee that had been given to me if the court determined it to have been illegal.

My testimony caused a public outcry, the likes of which has never been seen before in Croatia. Brutal insults came from all sides. Offensive graffiti appeared all over the country, even in Zadar, my hometown. Threats and vulgar messages were all over social media, and all were then published and underlined in the press. It was a nightmare that had somehow become my reality – as if I had committed a murder, and I was the country's biggest problem. This was devastating – there's no other word to describe it. In the course of a single day, I became the most hated person in Croatia. This was a completely new experience in my life, and it struck me hard. My family and closest friends remained my biggest support. I knew how hard it was to endure all that was happening to me. I was especially worried about Vanja, who was pregnant with our third child, and her pregnancies were risky. I feared that the stress would impact her health. My parents were also miserable. I tried to calm them down, insisting that everything would be alright.

This national rage seemed to me to be an injustice, especially when it escalated. The animosity towards Zdravko Mamić has a long history, and after my testimony failed to favour his critics, they directed their anger against me. I can't get into the reasons behind all this. For 12 years now I have been living and playing abroad. Back in 2008, when I left, it was a different time.

By that point, Mamić was an important factor in my career. I have never denied this – nor do I intend to do so. When I was a young player, he helped me to prove myself – just as he helped others. Some became successful, some less so, some didn't even have a career. The fact is, it's up to every footballer, once he is given a chance, to prove his value and his capabilities on the pitch. Of course, the support of coaches and teammates matters, but after this moment I can say, without false modesty, that I take the most credit for everything that happened in my career. Both good and bad. There were others involved in my subsequent transfers, but these inevitably depended on my own performance and behaviour. This, of course, does not lessen my gratitude to all who helped me in my career in one way or another.

I decided to distance myself from everything that was going on in Croatia before the start of the 2017/2018 season. I needed peace for two reasons. First, I needed to rest after the exhausting campaign just gone; it had been an enormous mental strain that drained me of energy. I took my family and spent a week outside Croatia, then, upon our return to Zadar, our close friends joined us for a short cruise around the Adriatic. The second reason was to evaluate my future position in the national team. Some people, whose opinions mattered to me, doubted that I should continue wearing Croatia's shirt. The problem wasn't my approach, but the fear that the negativity would impact my performances and be a burden for the whole team. This possibility, that the national team could suffer because of me, forced me to consider my position and make a decision. Was I going to remove myself from the team, or was I going to face the dissatisfaction of the fans and an angry public and give everything I have to contribute to Croatia's success?

I knew I hadn't done anything wrong, so I quickly decided to stay and fight just like I had done before; to try and make the dream we had dreamed for so long come true. I felt relieved. I was aware that many things could go against me, but I was even more determined to do whatever lay in my power to take this crucial step forward. I was sure that Croatia had a great group of players who just needed a bit of luck to achieve a big result. My conviction was based on the experience of past European Championships and World Cups, but also on the fact that our group was mostly made up of players who would be arriving in Russia at their peak. For most of us, it was clear that this was the last chance to do something big for Croatia. Another detail was important too: we played for big clubs and many of us were key players in the most challenging leagues and European competitions. I knew these things made a difference and they were a clear sign of the team's overall quality.

ver, the final part of the qualifications for Russia 2018 took a
n. The first match, against Kosovo, on 2 September, 2017, was
suspended in the 22nd minute because of extreme weather conditions
and a waterlogged pitch. The game had to be rescheduled, and we never
even considered that FIFA would decide to play the very next day. But
that's exactly what happened, mainly because our next match, against
Turkey, was due just three days later. The match against Kosovo was
rescheduled for the next day, and the date of our following game against
Turkey remained unchanged. In just 48 hours we were supposed to play
the remaining 68 minutes against Kosovo, then travel to Eskişehir and
stand up against the motivated Turks!

We failed to convince against Kosovo. They put up a tough fight,
and we weren't able to break through their defences. But then, in the
74th minute, we were awarded a free-kick. I crossed the ball into the
penalty box and Domagoj Vida jumped high to direct a header into the
net. Finally! Three points were all that mattered; the rest could be
forgotten. On the other hand, this was my first match in front of a home
crowd after the turmoil of two-and-a-half months before. There were
around 7,000 people at Maksimir and their greeting was friendly. That
meant a lot.

Two days later, in Turkey, we lost 1–0. The home team had fanatical
support, but, objectively, they seemed a weaker team than in the previous
years. We had our chances, but we failed to take them. I think the referee
even failed to award us a penalty. Our opponents took their one chance
in the 74th minute and this decided the final result. The following
matches would show that Turkey were not strong enough to qualify for
the World Cup, but this offered us no comfort. We plunged into another
crisis right at the end; it's as if we must always complicate our situation
to the maximum.

The two matches at the beginning of October would determine our
destiny. The first was against Finland in Rijeka, then a game in Ukraine
followed. We were considered the favourites against Finland, but it was also

important that Iceland did not beat Turkey. We thought the Turks wouldn't miss out on the opportunity to secure second position, and Iceland had beaten Ukraine, making them a contender for first place in our group. There were many possible combinations, but we found ourselves in serious trouble before the final match of the qualifying campaign.

The day before the team gathered to prepare for the matches against Finland and Ukraine was 2 October. As my teammates arrived in Zagreb, I was by Vanja's side. This was the day she gave birth to our third child. At Petrova Maternity Hospital, under the watchful eye of their tremendous staff, everything went without any problems. After Ivano and Ema, we became proud parents to Sofia. The next morning I travelled to Rijeka with the rest of the team.

When you have children, you often talk about their character and who they take after in the family. From my angle, it seems Ema is just like me: she's a lively child just as I was when I was little. Ivano is calmer and quieter; he takes after his mum. We still have to see about Sofia. When they grow up, I would love them to have their mum's kindness and sense of justice, and my fighting spirit and the desire to fight for their dreams. And I want them to have their mother's good looks!

As far as my participation in their everyday life is concerned, I spend every free moment with them. Of course, my frequent absences mean my role caring for our children cannot be compared with Vanja's. And she has to be fully dedicated to them even when I'm at home, because my thoughts are elsewhere – due to football-related problems, tiredness, injuries or the stress before important matches. Vanja recognises when I'm in a bad mood, and her understanding lifts the burden from my shoulders. When I don't have any responsibilities at the club or with the national team, I spend a lot of time with the children. I take them to school and pick them up afterwards. Ever since Ivano has started to play football, I take him to his training and wait until he's done. When they were just born, I would wake up at night to change their nappies, and give them the bottle or whatever they needed. I did this mostly with

Ivano, because we were alone in London and Vanja needed to take a break every so often. With Ema and Sofia, this wasn't necessary because we decided to hire a nanny to help Vanja recover and look after the children.

At Rujevica Stadium before the match against Finland, Davor Šuker, the president of the Croatian Football Federation, presented me with a special shirt to commemorate my 100th Croatia cap. Nike made a shirt featuring the design of all the shirts I had ever played in. It's truly exceptional. The milestone made me really excited. It seemed like only yesterday I had dreamed about playing just one match in Croatia's shirt, and now I was ready for my 100th appearance. Only Darijo Srna has more caps than me. But, unlike that special moment, the match against Finland was torture. Despite seizing the initiative and dominating possession, we weren't creating many chances, and those we did, we failed to take. In the 57th minute, when Mario Mandžukić finally scored, I thought we'd start to relax and play better. The opposite happened: we retreated and, afraid of conceding, we allowed the Finns to become more dangerous. I'm not sure why. We were punished in the 90th minute, just as we had been when playing Iceland, and Finland's goal shook the national team.

It was a colossal blunder, but it was also a confirmation that our form had been dropping throughout the autumn. For this team and the level of quality it possesses, that wasn't expected. When we are in shape and focused, we can play against anyone. But, when this is not the case, anyone can cause us trouble. When the referee blew his whistle, we all knew something would have to change. The atmosphere in the dressing room was depressing. In the evening, Davor Šuker sat down with several of the more experienced players and told us he had decided on replacing the manager. The next morning, we learned that Ante Čačić was no longer head coach. Zlatko Dalić was his replacement.

I hadn't met Dalić before, but I liked his approach. It was impossible to make drastic changes because the day after the match against Finland we were flying to Kiev to face Ukraine. The team just needed a boost of confidence, good morale, and the belief it was possible to win. Perhaps it seems simple now, but considering that there wasn't enough time to prepare for the match, that we needed a win, that we had a new coach and our confidence was shaken, things couldn't have been more complicated. Dalić talked to us a lot, both at practice and in the hotel. He showed he believed in us. He said we had loads of quality and we just had to show it on the pitch, now when it was most needed. He filled us with confidence. The atmosphere in the team changed radically, and you could tell every player was determined to win. The draw against Finland got to us, as did the change at the helm, but I think our biggest motivation came from the fear we could miss the World Cup. The more experienced players, me included, knew this was our last chance.

At one point, Dalić explained his tactics: 'I see you as an attacking midfielder, behind the strikers. I want to rid you of defensive tasks.'

I said the only thing I could've said: 'I'll play wherever I have to.'

I think Dalić's biggest contribution was the way he prepared the players mentally for the match, which allowed him to get the most out of the team and its existing tactical set-up in such a short time. Vrsaljko was the left full-back, Vida the right, Lovren and Mitrović the central defenders. Rakitić and Badelj played as defensive midfielders, and in front of them were Kramarić, Perišić and me, and Mandžukić as the striker. He asked us to block the Ukrainian full-backs, because that was their strength. The idea was to control the match in the first half and take as few risks as possible, waiting for Ukraine to run out of steam and cave under the pressure of high expectations and their 70,000 fans in the stands – and then attack. During the first half, the home team were more dangerous, but we endured. In the second half, we picked ourselves up and showed our strength. We were on the rise, they were losing momentum, and our goal in the 62nd minute clipped their wings. I delivered a cross to Andrej Kramarić, who sent a wonderful header into the net. Ukraine were wobbling, and when Kramarić scored his second goal, this time assisted by

Ivan Rakitić, they were done for. Then, maturely and confidently, we brought the match to an end. Finally, we could relax. At least for a moment. We had been given a second chance. Upon my return from Kiev, one thought just kept running through my mind. Twenty years before in Kiev, Croatia had barely escaped elimination in a stressful second leg of a World Cup play-off. Back in 1997, in the first match in Zagreb, Croatia took a 2–0 win. Then, in the fifth minute of the return match at the very same stadium where we now took the crucial victory that would take us to the 2018 FIFA World Cup, Andriy Shevchenko's goal brought Ukraine close to overturning Croatia's advantage. Alen Bokšić levelled that match in the 27th minute and cooled down Ukrainian euphoria. At the same time, his goal fed the fire in which the subsequent bronze medal would be forged. Shevchenko, once a talented striker on his way to the heights of world football, now having just lost to Croatia as a head coach. Was this a sign?

I wasn't thrilled to hear who we had drawn in the play-off round. I wasn't afraid our game wasn't good enough to beat Greece, but I couldn't get my mind off their closed formations and their destructive play. I also thought about the fact that we were playing the first leg at home and that, if we didn't have a good start, the crowd would become restless, reflecting on the team. But on that evening at Maksimir everything was exactly the opposite; I could feel something new happening. Or, perhaps it was something we'd had before but lost along the way: an immensely positive morale! Our hearts were full at the warm-up when we saw the packed stands and we heard that well-known noise from the fans, giving us wings. We couldn't wait for the match to start. As if someone had let us off the leash, we ran onto the pitch wanting to bring joy to our fans and ourselves. After a long while, we were receiving unanimous support, and when this happens, there's no stopping us.

Greece didn't stand a chance; Croatia put in a phenomenal performance. As early as the 13th minute, from a penalty kick awarded after a foul on Nikola Kalinić, I gave our side a lead. Six minutes later, Ivan Strinić sent an ideal ball to Kalinić and he wonderfully backheeled the ball into the net. Maksimir was in a state of total euphoria! Then, in the 30ᵗʰ minute came a shock – Greece scored after a corner kick, something that was becoming our weakness. But, just three minutes later, we showed it was our time. We didn't sink – instead, our response was immediate. Šime Vrsaljko delivered a wonderful cross and Ivan Perišić sent a header into the net for 3–1. Right at the start of the second half, after another mistake by the Greek defender, Vrsaljko stole the ball and Kramarić scored for 4–1. We had dismantled the Greeks!

In such an atmosphere, with such support, we freed ourselves of all the frustrations, the burdens, everything that had been holding us back. We were flying over the pitch. My feeling is that on that evening everything fell into place and convinced us that we were strong. That we could go far. Of course, our new coach Dalić had been able to exploit more tactical initiatives, finally having the time to introduce his ideas – more at least than was available before the match in Ukraine. What he did showed once again how much he cared about the team's and the players' mental state. In the last minute, they called me off the pitch, Mario Pašalić coming on to replace me. I heard loud applause and the fans chanting my name. My heart was as big as a mountain. As I walked towards the touchline, I didn't think about the return match in Greece – I knew we were going to the World Cup. The only thought running through my mind was that this was our time. I just knew it; I lived for it. Something special was taking place. Suddenly, and out of nowhere, had come Dalić. Now everything was falling into place. People believed in us once again.

***

The first part of the new season with Real also had a terrific opening. In August we had a glamorous and demanding start – in the span of just eight days, the European Super Cup against Manchester United followed by the two legs of the Spanish Super Cup against Barcelona! The European

Super Cup took us to Skopje. On United's bench was the coach who had brought me to Real: José Mourinho. Earlier that summer, we had met in Los Angeles during our pre-season tour. Mateo Kovačić and I took a walk around Beverly Hills and noticed Mourinho coming our way. When he approached, he hugged me. We had a nice chat and shared a few laughs.

At the stadium in Skopje, where I had last played five years before when Croatia beat Macedonia, Real played an excellent game. The match ended in a 2–1 victory for us, but our performance was much more convincing than the result showed. We won the first trophy of the season, and it's always good to have a winning start. We did the same in the two *El Clásicos*. I didn't play in the first leg because I had been sent off in the Spanish Super Cup against Atlético three years before and I had to sit a match out in the same competition. Real won 3–1, and we were once again dominant in the return match at Bernabéu and triumphed 2–0. The result was 5–1 on aggregate – it had been a while since we had outplayed Barcelona like that. That only raised our expectations for the new season. However, our performances in La Liga fluctuated inexplicably. We lost points against clubs that were objectively weaker, at the bottom of the table. In October, it became apparent we were in crisis. Our performance in Madrid in the first match of a UEFA Champions League double-header against Tottenham was poor. The match ended in a 1–1 draw, but it seemed we lacked energy. Twelve days later we recorded an unexpected 2–1 defeat to Girona, who were 15th in the table. It was a bad omen: three days later, at Wembley, we lost again. Mauricio Pochettino's Spurs dismantled us 3–1. It was the first time playing in London against my former club. True, this wasn't White Hart Lane, which had passed into history because the new stadium was being built. Of all of my former teammates, only Danny Rose was still there. More than five years had passed, my attachment was perhaps not as strong, but I still had huge respect for Tottenham and their fans. We had a special relationship. True, the goodbye had maybe not been ideal, but nothing could erase the memories of four years I had spent at the club, watching their growth overlap with mine. Today, Spurs are a big club in every respect – they have a new top stadium, they have built a top-quality training centre, they possess an excellent team and coach, and their results rise continuously. In 2010, with me on the team, we won our first qualification for the Champions League. Nine years later, Tottenham played in the Champions League Final for the first time. It was a confirmation that Spurs had become part of the elite, a club fighting at the top of the English Premier League and regularly competing in the Champions League. The investment has paid off. The only thing missing to complete the project is a prestigious trophy, and for both the club and the fans I hope this dream comes true as soon as possible.

In mid-December 2017, we played once again at the FIFA Club World Cup in the United Arab Emirates. First, we played against Al Jazira, a tricky opponent. They took the lead in the 41st minute before we levelled in the 53rd, after my assist for Cristiano Ronaldo's goal. In the 81st minute, Gareth Bale scored for our victory. I was voted the Man of the Match. Grêmio were our opponents in the final, which proved to be another hard-fought match. Ronaldo scored a free-kick in the 53rd minute, and that proved to be the winning goal. A special jury voted me the Best Player of the final and the tournament. After the Silver Ball the year before, I had now won the Golden Ball – the first in my career! At that point, I didn't even dream that this could be the beginning of a fantastic string of trophies that would end with the Ballon d'Or. I think I played at the highest level in the tournament and I was happy my good performances were recognised. The award is usually reserved for attackers and strikers, and the fact that it was given to a midfielder only made it even more special. The trophy came at the end of an exciting year in which Real Madrid had won the first double crown after almost six decades of drought, and I was included in the Champions League Best XI for the first time. And all of this in the year of Croatia's successful qualification for the 2018 FIFA World Cup in Russia – a bumpy road and all the sweeter for it. It was a year that was also difficult for me personally because of the negative reaction to my testimony at Zdravko Mamić's trial. I thought about leaving the national team, but then we clicked, so I made up my mind and took even more responsibility as the team's captain and leader. Finally, and perhaps this should've come first, this was the year I became a father for the third time. I returned from the UAE to Madrid a happy man. But before the Christmas holidays, we had another clash against Barcelona in *El Clásico* at Bernabéu.

You Need to Fall Before You Can Fly

The stands were packed. *El Clásico* is the match that determines the rest of the season in La Liga. Barcelona had an eight-point advantage, and we had played a game less than them. The FIFA Club World Cup meant the match against Leganés had to be postponed until 21 February, 2018. Our calculations were clear: beating Barça meant closing in on their lead, to only five points behind, and a win in the postponed Leganés match would bring us to within just two points. In other words, everything was open. But you can't always get what you want; we learned that the hard way in this match, which started at an unusual time of 1 p.m. The visitors took the lead in the 54th minute, and, when Dani Carvajal handled the ball in the 63rd minute, that was the end – not only of this *El Clásico* but also of our ambition to win the title. Carvajal was sent off and Lionel Messi scored for 2–0 from the subsequent penalty. We tried to get back into the match, but the only change to the scoreline was Barcelona's third goal in stoppage time. Two days before Christmas, such an outcome ruined our mood. To be honest, even before the match, I'd sensed that this La Liga season wouldn't bring us much happiness.

I spent the holidays in Zagreb. For the previous two New Year's Eves club commitments meant that we hadn't travelled to Croatia. Mateo Kovačić and his wife Izabel had been with us, but these hadn't been big celebrations because we had to go to bed early, ready for the matches. Now we could finally celebrate the arrival of 2018 at home.

We spent the evening with our family and closest friends – it was wonderful. Among other things, I wished for 2018 to bring me more success as a footballer. It may seem exaggerated, but my goal has always been to be the best. When I was a young player, I wanted to prove myself as a professional footballer in Croatia. But I also hoped one day to play for a big European club and fight for the most prestigious titles. When I won *La Décima* with Real, my first thought was to win another trophy immediately – I didn't want to wait. Two years later, when we won the UEFA Champions League once again, I wanted us to be the first team to defend the title. I was convinced we could accomplish all these goals. When I look back at my footballing path from Dinamo and Tottenham to Real Madrid and the national team, that well-known proverb – *dreams come true for those who dare to believe* – seems entirely credible. I entered 2018 with such attitude and dreams, ever more determined to make all of my wishes come true.

But the year started badly: the match in Vigo against Celta ended up in a 2–2 draw, and a week later we lost a home match against Villarreal. A look at our La Liga standing was depressing – Barcelona had a 16-point advantage while we were sitting in fourth. We were seven points behind Atlético and five points behind Valencia. However, the worst was yet to come when Leganés eliminated us in the Copa del Rey quarter-final! All of this was very frustrating, because the cup could have been one of the trophies to wash away the bad taste of the unsuccessful season in La Liga. To make matters worse, we'd won the first leg 1–0 as visitors. The return match at Bernabéu was simply embarrassing. I don't want to demean Leganés' great achievement – they deserve all the credit for the fight they put up and for their historic result – but we entered the match with an advantage, at our stadium, against an opponent that was objectively below our level, and we simply shouldn't have allowed ourselves such a debacle! Once again, it proved that complacency leads to a fall. I played around 20 minutes in each of the cup matches because of a problem with my calf muscle. I was supposed to skip the matches because Zinédine Zidane wanted to spare me for the important clashes ahead of us, especially the Champions League round of 16 against PSG.

Real's crucial match of the spring part of the season was scheduled for 14 February at Bernabéu. We had been eliminated from the Copa del Rey and the race for the Liga title. The Champions League was the only trophy left – the last, but also the most glamorous chance to bring the season to a triumphant end. After we had drawn PSG, the prevailing opinion was that the Parisian team were the favourites. That was slightly odd. True, we had been eliminated from two title races and weren't showing much form, but we still had more or less the same team as the year before – a team with a lot of experience, especially in the Champions League. Despite our fluctuations throughout the season, we were still strong enough to eliminate anyone in the knockout stage of the Champions League. On the other hand, PSG had some outstanding players in their team. Their attacking potential was fantastic, with the likes of Kylian Mbappé, Neymar and Edinson Cavani. Still, PSG were also the team who had not managed to achieve a trophy-winning result in European competition, despite their immense investments.

The first leg was played at Bernabéu. We started the match well and had a couple of good chances, but their goalkeeper, Alphonse Areola, was excellent. They fought back, but until the 33rd minute there were no goals. Then, Adrien Rabiot took advantage of a ball cleared after a counter-attack and fired it into the net. PSG took a 1–0 lead, and at that moment I assume many people thought Real were done for.

If they did, that was a huge mistake! We never give up, no matter what happens on the pitch. In the 45th minute, Toni Kroos was fouled in the box and Cristiano Ronaldo levelled from the penalty spot. The battle in the second half reminded me of two heavyweights trying to knock each other out. We maintained an intense rhythm and in the 83rd minute, Ronaldo, helped by a bit of luck, scored for 2–1. Just three minutes later, Marcelo added another one for a 3–1 win. A tremendous match and vital victory! We knew it wasn't over, but we felt we were better and more compact. We knew Neymar's skill from La Liga, and Mbappé was simply astonishing: powerful, fast, fierce – and yet so young. In the return match, I was on the bench. I rarely had muscle problems, but this time I had to take a break. The medical team were clear: a month off the pitch was essential if I wanted to recover fully and be ready for the extreme wear and tear at the end of the season.

I came back a week early. This time the rest didn't bother me – I knew there would be some super-important clashes in the Champions League. I also knew I had to be ready for the World Cup. I saw the enforced break as an opportunity to catch my breath, rest and gather enough energy for what lay ahead. I wanted to win another Champions League. And then, I wanted to do something big with Croatia at the World Cup in Russia. My goals are always high, but in this year my determination was especially strong; as if I knew that this would be the year.

In the return match against PSG they weren't convincing. Neymar had picked up an injury – a huge disadvantage for them. In the 51st minute, Ronaldo turned Lucas Vázquez's excellent cross into our lead. The way they played, PSG had no chance of scoring the three goals they needed to take the match into extra time. Cavani levelled after some pinball action in our penalty box in the 71st minute, but Casemiro's shot gave us a 2–1 lead in the 80th minute. We deserved our advance into the quarter-final. The victory fuelled our hopes we could achieve a miracle and defend the title for the second time in a row, setting a new record of three consecutive European titles.

After Paris we had another away match in Eibar. I played the full 90 minutes in the 2–1 victory, providing an assist for Ronaldo's first goal. After the game, Zidane gave us a couple of days off.

Mateo Kovačić and I took our wives to Marrakesh to relax before the final part of the season. The step away from the daily drill came as a godsend. We had a wonderful time in Morocco, where we ran into Keylor Navas and his family. I returned to Madrid full of energy. At the time, countless media analyses mentioned my name as one of the players who could leave the club at the end of the season. It didn't bother me, especially as I knew this was just harmless guesswork. However, in my six years at

Real Madrid it was the first time this had been mentioned as a possibility. The main reason for this, the papers said, was my age, even though, in terms of physical fitness, I felt wonderful. The media need to tell their stories; when Real are going through a rough period, the foretelling of the management's next moves is all over the papers. Still, I was calm, very calm. At the same time, I was extremely motivated. Having returned to the pitch after the enforced rest, I put in some top performances. I think my physical and mental freshness was the decisive factor.

After a 6–3 victory over Girona, in which I recorded another assist, it was time for the international matches and Croatia travelled to the United States to play against Peru and Mexico. Because of my recent injury and the rehabilitation period, the club wanted me to prepare for the season finale in peace and not travel to the United States. But this was Croatia's only gathering before the preparation for the World Cup. Also, it was important for team spirit. I was eager to go because I was convinced we could do something big in Russia. I talked to Zlatko Dalić, explaining that I wanted to join the team in America, but that I also had to recognise that I was returning after injury. Playing in two demanding matches in four days, with a lot of travelling and little training, wasn't too sensible. We agreed it would be best if I played in the first match against Peru and then returned to Madrid. Dalić told me that other players were in a similar situation and they agreed to do the same.

The American tour was fantastic. The Croatian community in the United States gave us a wonderful welcome. We also got to watch Miami play against the New York Knicks. Many on the Croatia team are huge NBA fans. On top of everything, we got to meet Novak Đjoković, a fantastic athlete and a great person. The positive atmosphere around the team, and the opportunity to spend some time together and hang out as a group, strengthened our collective spirit. And then there was the match. There were around 46,000 fans at the stadium in Miami. Peru were better, more agile, faster, and they beat us 2–0. Peru are a very good team. At that moment, they were 11th in FIFA's rankings – in other words, better than us. As usually happens in Croatia, the defeat caused alarm. Although this was just a friendly match and the result wasn't a priority, the media turned it into a drama – especially after Dalić allowed Subašić, Mandžukić, Perišić, Brozović, Kalinić and I to leave. Rakitić was supposed to return to Barcelona too, but he changed his mind and stayed.

It was as if some people just couldn't wait for the opportunity to start calling us out. No one seemed to care that I, for example, had been out for a month because of my injury and was just returning to form. There were all kinds of comments in the media, but despite what many journalists may think, I don't get offended when they criticise me. The only thing I can't accept is insults and untruths. When journalists and pundits express their point of view and say that I, or someone else for that matter, have put in a lousy performance, that I am not a good player or something like that, I don't mind. Comments that don't go my way don't bother me. The media are just doing their job, and contrasting theories and analyses are part of it. So, when they criticised me for leaving the team in the United States, insisting that this wasn't appropriate for the team's captain, I didn't want to respond. I knew where that would lead, from one controversy to another. However, it did bother me when some other players publicly criticised those of us who had returned to their clubs. I didn't understand their point since they knew that this had all been agreed with Dalić. I'll tip my hat to anyone, but no one had the right to criticise me. In almost 13 years wearing Croatia's shirt, I had attended each and every gathering, even for promotional purposes, even when I didn't have to, and when the coaches had begged me to come for the fans and for the team's morale. I never once asked to be spared or treated differently. The only time I wasn't with the team was when I was seriously injured, when I had to have surgery or when I was coming back from an injury.

I was particularly disappointed when I read the comments of Vedran Ćorluka. He could've told me what he thought to my face, back when we were in the United States. On top of everything, he expressed his criticism at a press conference, which only provoked discussion in the media. Ćorluka and I are friends – we stood side by side throughout our careers, playing together at Dinamo, Inter Zaprešić, Tottenham and for the national team. We were inseparable. He was the last person I would expect to call me out like that, to attack me in public. He knew me better than anyone else, and knew too how serious I was about my responsibilities for the club and the national team.

At any other moment I would probably have let time take its course, let it wash away the bitterness. But we didn't have time for this, because then we wouldn't have good morale in Russia, and that was crucial if we wanted to achieve something big. I decided to sit down with Ćorluka before going to the World Cup, have a long chat and talk everything over. Whether he had been misunderstood no longer mattered; we agreed it was uncalled for and unjust. Talking turned out to be a good thing. I'm convinced that an open and honest conversation, when there is a need for one, is a key to a true and firm friendship. That's how it is with Charlie.

I talked about the epilogue of the US tour with Dalić too. He liked to consult the more experienced players, and me as captain, about all the more important matters. The purpose of the tour was to pull our ranks together and create good morale before the World Cup, but the tour ended up inviting a lot of criticism, which hurt the harmony within our group. In this respect, I thought his statement after our victory against Mexico was out of place: he called out the standard of the more experienced players. He said they should be concerned about their position on the team, or something along those lines, because younger players were coming and playing better and better. No one, he insisted, would make the team based on previous merit. He gave the example of Ante Rebić who, he argued, now had the advantage over Ivan Perišić – just like that and all of a sudden. Why? Because Croatia had won the friendly against Mexico, while, only four days before, with the apparently more experienced players in the starting line-up, we lost to Peru. This argument, using Perišić as an example, took me by surprise. He's a player who has proven himself, a powerful winger and a veteran of many battles – not only for his club, but also for the national team. Form is never constant, every player has good and bad periods, but Perišić – Perija as we call him – brings immense value to the Croatia national team. I told Dalić I was taken aback by such statements, and he insisted he had been misinterpreted. His intention was to motivate the players, all of them, to get ready for Russia. I told him that it wasn't journalists writing stories that made the US tour look bad. They were simply doing their job; they had the right to ask questions. The problem was that we, within the team, encouraged public criticism and ruined morale. I added that, according to my experience, things wouldn't turn out well if this continued. After this, when we gathered to prepare for Russia, Dalić held a very important meeting with the players.

Something had been troubling me on a personal level, and I was determined to clear up all the misunderstandings before the World Cup preparations. It was Mario Mandžukić. We have played together since 2007 when he signed for Dinamo. We spent a year together at Dinamo and we played side by side in Croatia's shirt for 11 years. Mario is a special type. Sometimes he seems grumpy; more often he is in a good mood. Those who don't know him might think he is always in a foul mood – but I have always known Mario as an outstanding man, with a big heart. I liked him from day one, although many people took a long time to understand him and see him like I did. We went through a lot in the national team.

When we played in Iceland, in the play-off qualification round for the 2014 FIFA World Cup in Brazil, I ran into Mandžukić in front of the hotel elevator. 'Let's go, Mario. Give it all today,' I told him. It was the usual pep talk you often hear during training or before a match.

His reaction took me by surprise: 'Leave me alone! Mind your own business.'

I thought maybe he was in a bad mood. As if he held a grudge against me, but I couldn't think of a logical explanation. We always had a good relationship; we kept in touch. But then . . . silence. Our relationship cooled. If I had known then what I know now, I would've gotten it straight right then and there, or at least during the next international break. But I took it against him; two strong characters sparked. The result? A short-circuit! To be honest, I felt bad about it, but I didn't want to make the first move. Neither did he. As teammates, we didn't have any problems; nothing changed on the pitch. Even off the pitch, our communication was normal, especially during team meetings and such. He congratulated me on winning my first Champions League – he knew the happiness it brought me because he had won it a year earlier with Bayern. So that wasn't the problem. Of course, within the national team, things can hardly work the same way they do at clubs, where players meet on a daily basis. Players change; the team is made of players who come from different clubs and environments, who have different attitudes and belong to different generations. Of course, you are closer to someone you know better, or who is part of your generation, so you spend more time together. Where everything comes together is, more than anything else, within the national team, sharing the responsibility and the honour of wearing your country's shirt. In that respect, Mario and I worked well. But I'd had a close, friendly relationship with him, and this stalemate – the pretence that everything was alright when it wasn't – troubled me.

As fate would have it, in the summer of 2014, Mandžukić had left Bayern and signed for Atlético Madrid. Once again, we were living in the same city and were rivals in the city derby, just like a long time ago when he had played for Zagreb and I for Dinamo. As soon as I learned about his transfer, I wanted to send him a message, but I didn't have his number. I don't think there's a player who changes his phone number more often than Mario! When I finally got it, I sent him a text message, congratulated him on the transfer and told him to get in touch if he needed help with finding an apartment in Madrid, or something else in the city – or anything at all. He replied, thanking me, and that's where it ended. Mandžukić stayed in Madrid for just one season. Real and Atlético met no fewer than eight times: twice each in La Liga, the Spanish Super Cup, the Copa del Rey and the Champions League. We played against one another in four matches – I missed the rest of them due to serious injury I had picked up in Milan with the national team.

During that year, Mario and I saw and said hello to each other only during those four matches. We were reserved and stayed that way in the national team too.

Before the World Cup in Russia, I decided to put an end to it. I knew this was our last World Cup and most likely the last tournament where we would play side by side. And one where we had the opportunity to do something big. Mario was one of the most important players in Croatia's team, both on and off the pitch. He had his quirks, we all do, but he is a straight-up guy. In some things we are similar – we are both somewhat introverted, we rarely show our emotions, we can be stubborn. But he is someone I would follow into any battle. Whatever happens, I know he would give his best, he would have my back and never abandon me. The only time he can fall short is when he is not in form.

I waited for the right moment to begin a conversation; I wanted to tell him how much I liked him and how sorry I was we weren't closer. I wanted to know what had happened, and why, for more than three years, we had failed to communicate like friends. We both knew this was our last big chance, and we knew how important it was to come together and unite. I told him I was sure that we were strong and that this was our moment. We had an open conversation and at that moment, the ice between us melted, this thing that had come out of nothing.

'I wasn't mad at you. I thought you were mad at me,' he said, and I told him the same.

So, there you have it: this is what a good relationship can come to if you don't talk. It shows once again that it's best to deal with what's bothering you immediately, especially if this involves relationships. There was an instant surge of positive energy between Mario and I.

Maybe I'm exaggerating, but I think it was stronger than it had been before. After Russia, and everything we went through, we will have a story to tell when we grow old.

The Race for the Treble

The spring in Madrid had its ups and downs. We tried to leave a better impression in the final 11 matches in La Liga, and in the end we had six victories, four draws and one defeat, where we lost 3–2 to Sevilla. We pulled ahead of Valencia and were sitting in third place in the table. However, Atlético were three points ahead of us and third place means little to Real. A sign of our good form was the season's last *El Clásico*, three weeks before the UEFA Champions League Final. The derby at Camp Nou had no competitive importance, but it was as intense as always. The tensions were palpable. Barcelona took the lead twice, and twice we drew level. As the season was coming to its end, our confidence grew.

Having eliminated PSG, we were sure we would once again make it right to the end of the Champions League. The draw for the quarter-finals had given us Juventus, and we showed dominance in the first leg in Turin. We beat The Old Lady 3–0, with two goals from Cristiano Ronaldo and one from Marcelo. In the 64th minute, we witnessed one of the most spectacular goals by the man who had scored hundreds: Ronaldo. His overhead kick following Dani Carvajal's cross was simply perfect – as was the moment and our opponent. He had been trying to score an overhead goal for a while, and now it had finally happened – against Gianluigi Buffon, one of the greatest goalkeepers of all time. The only thing more beautiful was the reaction of the Turin crowd, as everyone in the stadium got to their feet and applauded Ronaldo for a long, long time. From today's perspective, I think this was one of the main reasons Cristiano chose to move to Juventus three months later.

The result and our excellent performance in Turin probably made us too confident, and the return match almost turned into a debacle. Though we had struggled in home matches that season, our ordeal against Juventus was hard to imagine. The day before the match, the odds were proven not to be impossible. Barcelona arrived in Rome with a 4–1 first-leg lead, but at the Stadio Olimpico Roma put in a fantastic and fierce performance, and scored three goals, conceding none, and eliminated Barcelona from the competition. It was a sensational result. But we learned nothing from it. Juventus were brave and by the second minute they had taken the lead. *Trouble's just around the corner,* I thought, looking at our performance, and a second goal in the 37th minute only confirmed my fears! In both cases, it was Mario Mandžukić – my friend – who gave us hell! Two headers, two goals and two steps closer to causing a huge upset. Mario loved to score against Real: in 12 matches he scored five goals and made one assist. By the time Blaise Matuidi had scored the third goal in the 61st minute, we were in real trouble. We simply had to score, because every next goal conceded could mean saying goodbye to the Champions League. We gave it everything we had and then, in the last seconds of the match, we were awarded a penalty. Lucas Vázquez, who was alone in front of Buffon, ready to shoot, was pushed from behind. Juventus were furious, especially Buffon, the most experienced among them, and he was sent off. Their agitation was understandable, they were too close to upset, but the referee made the right call: the foul was obvious. Ronaldo didn't make a mistake, and we advanced into the semi-final.

The first leg against Bayern was played in Munich. 'Our' Carlo Ancelotti wasn't on the bench; he had been sacked at the beginning of the season. Jupp Heynckes, also 'ours' given that he had won the Champions League with Real Madrid back in 1998, came in to replace him. Bayern, with Heynckes in charge, had won a string of trophies and their last Champions League in 2013. The home team took advantage at Allianz Arena, Joshua Kimmich scoring in the 28th minute. Still, we played well and Marcelo levelled in the 44th. Marco Asensio, brought on at half time to replace the injured Isco, made it 2–1 in the 57th minute. That was the result at full time, offering us yet another huge advantage before the return match.

This time, bruised by our bad experiences against Bayern and in other home matches, we took the return match very seriously. Unfortunately, Bayern took the lead early, in the third minute, Kimmich scoring once again. It seemed that we were facing another ordeal, although Karim Benzema levelled in the 11th minute. At the beginning of the second half, after a massive mistake by their goalkeeper, Benzema added another goal to give us a 2–1 lead. Bayern kept attacking, though, and didn't allow us to relax. Quite the contrary, the match became even more difficult. I don't know why that kept happening, considering our team's quality and experience.

The crowd at Bernabéu always keeps pushing us forward, and that's understandable. But in a demanding match we should know better and take it down a notch once we have the advantage, rather than rush to score another goal. And then we conceded. James Rodríguez, our player on loan in Munich, levelled in the 63rd minute. Bayern, and James in particular, had a couple more chances, as did we, but the match ended in a 2–2 draw. We had teetered on the edge, but in the end we could look forward to the fourth Champions League Final in five seasons. Sensational! And well-deserved. There were complaints about the refereeing in the match, and when a referee's call goes in Real's favour, such criticism only becomes louder. There were several bad calls against us, but it almost always turns out people believe that the mistakes were done at our opponent's expense.

Another grand finale! I was once again going to Kiev, to the same stadium where seven months before I had celebrated victory with Croatia. This time, Real faced the legendary Liverpool – the club with a fantastic tradition, charismatic past and great names who had brought no less than five European Cup and Champions League titles to Anfield in their glorious history to that point. Liverpool, with Jürgen Klopp at the helm – and with my good friend Dejan Lovren in the starting line-up – who came into the game with a fantastic season behind them. It was a special match.

After three finals, I was less anxious before Kiev; the excitement was there, of course, but my previous experience allowed me to control it. For some of the boys this was their first final. When Zinédine Zidane played us a video with messages from our families, every player became emotional, but the first-timers were visibly moved. Anticipating this, Zidane had prepared another motivational video. He showed us the successes of the LA Lakers, Chicago Bulls, Boston Celtics – basketball dynasties who had ruled their respective eras and won multiple titles, showing fantastic dominance. I'm a huge NBA fan. Just as I'm a fan of NFL, especially the New England Patriots and Tom Brady, their phenomenal quarterback. When it comes to basketball, the Bulls are my favourites, because of the unique Michael Jordan – the king! Great champions, like Ali, Federer and Woods, the greats and legends who marked their respective sports, set completely different standards and inspired new generations. Earlier that spring, when Croatia had toured the United States, I was honoured to meet one of my idols, the three-time NBA champion Dwyane Wade, who played for Miami Heat. We exchanged shirts and hung out for a while.

His interest in European football surprised me; most people think Americans are not interested in the game. I learned this was not the case when I met Julia Roberts, the film star, who visited Bernabéu with her children and her husband, Danny. Even though she is a legend and we all wanted to take a photo with her, she was very excited to meet us. She was especially happy when she saw how much her children enjoyed the experience and how happy they were when they took photos with Real players.

Ahead of the Champions League final, Zidane's message was clear: the greats always find new motives to win new titles – this is what makes them great. They put in fantastic performances regardless of how many consecutive victories they have under their belt because they simply enjoy winning.

'Get out on the pitch and have fun. Take pleasure in football.' This was Zidane's main comment during the pre-match meeting.

Tactically, he was as straightforward as always. He wanted us to switch sides as quickly as possible because Liverpool always play high-pressure football; they dictate a high rhythm. It was vital to move the ball around quickly to break through their first line of defence and get into their half. We were ready. This was yet another match to go down in history – to make a new record and to inspire a legend about yet another golden Real Madrid generation.

We came out onto the pitch, where the Champions League anthem was performed by two musicians from Croatia, the renowned 2Cellos. The atmosphere was majestic, the stands packed.

Liverpool opened the match well. Their game was no surprise for us, fast and skilled. They were tough, but we stood our ground. Ronaldo and Benzema threatened on the attack, before in the 30th minute, something important happened: a setback for Liverpool. Mohamed Salah was injured and had to leave the pitch. It was such an unfortunate moment – he hurt his left shoulder falling in a tangle with Sergio Ramos and the injury was too painful to continue. There were all kinds of discussions about Ramos' tackle. People said he had injured Salah on purpose. What nonsense! Any football player knows it was an accident. When Salah got substituted, I thought we would have a more comfortable game on our hands. But I was mistaken. Just six minutes later, we lost Carvajal, who was very important for our style of play. Once again he was injured in the final; Dani just couldn't catch a break.

It was an extremely complicated match – a true battle, each team trying to outsmart the other. There were chances on both sides in the first half. In the second half we had an ideal start when Benzema pressed Loris Karius, the Liverpool goalkeeper, who tried to throw the ball to his defender and made a mistake. The Frenchman nudged the ball towards the goal and it slowly rolled into the back of the net. Benzema is a true fox; his awareness never fails to amaze me. Four minutes later we were back to square one – James Milner delivered a corner, Lovren was up highest to nod the ball down into the goal area, where Sadio Mané jumped at the opportunity and sent the ball into the goal!

In the 61st minute, Zidane sent Gareth Bale on to replace Isco. Three minutes later, Bale scored one of his most beautiful and most important goals. Marcelo crossed with his right, and Gareth performed an outstanding overhead kick from around 13 or 14 yards out and sent the ball into the top right corner, past the helpless Karius. The same players would be involved in the third goal, which finally decided the European Champions. Bale hit a powerful dipping shot from around 30 yards out and Karius got his hands on the ball – but it slipped through his fingers and into the net. One player celebrated his second goal in the Champions League Final, while the other, the goalkeeper, felt trauma. Such is football: joy and despair trade places. I was sorry for Karius, but delighted that we had accomplished another historic feat. Winning the Champions League for a third season in a row! No one besides us had ever won two Champions Leagues in a row, and now we had won a treble! It will take some time to surpass our dominance in Europe; Real Madrid had just won their 13th title. Our names would be written in golden letters, our place in history secured. No one could ever change this. This fantastic feeling stayed with me for the next couple of days.

I tried to comfort Lovren – he was devastated. But then it was time to celebrate. I had already experienced it, but the feeling was just incredible. My children joined me on the pitch, and the next day the fans threw us a fantastic welcome in Madrid – receptions and yet another party at Bernabéu. The only difference was that I wasn't able to fall asleep. There was just too much excitement, too many emotions, the heat, although I was so tired.

The only blemish on the whole story came from Ronaldo. While we were still down on the pitch, he hinted he was leaving Real Madrid! I never dreamed that could be possible. It was a time to celebrate, so I didn't ask him anything when I first heard. I thought maybe it was just a phase, maybe he was in a bad mood. I was sure it would pass. Though, when you say something like that in the middle of celebrations, you can't expect such comments to just go away.

Ronaldo was on his way out. And the surprises didn't end there.

CHAPTER NINE

Waking up in the morning at our home in Madrid is pure magic. It's almost always sunny and warm, and La Moraleja is so quiet. It's nice to come out on the porch, sit down, watch the plants in the park and enjoy the birdsong. Of course, when Ivano and Ema are at home and the weather is good, they will soon start jumping into the pool and playing. The quiet is then replaced by their cries, laughter, play. There's nothing more beautiful than seeing your children play without a care in the world. I truly enjoy our home.

On such mornings, Vanja and I love to look back at our life, and towards our future. We often talk about the events that brought us here. I think the fact that we talk to each other all the time makes our relationship so wonderful. We are not always on the same wavelength; we have our differences and can sometimes have heated arguments. That's part of marriage. Were it different, if we agreed on everything, it would be so monotonous! Our conversations mean a lot to me. It's easier when I can confide in her if something bothers me. Just as it's even nicer to share a good story. Sometimes, it is enough just to listen to her and think about what she is saying, especially if she knows better than I do. Sometimes I just need her to listen as I vent my frustrations, about football or something else. Most often, however, we simply have pleasant conversations.

After two days of celebrations and receptions after the UEFA Champions League Final, I finally caught some time to relax and look back at everything that had happened. I managed to catch some sleep too; the adrenaline had faded. On the day of the Kiev final, Croatia gathered in Zagreb and began preparations for the FIFA World Cup. Dejan Lovren, Mateo Kovačić and I talked to Zlatko Dalić and arranged to join the rest of the team on 31 May in Rovinj. We needed a couple of days to relax after the club season's finale. To be honest, I wasn't tired; the injury had forced me to take a month away from football during the spring part of the season. That's why I was still fresh and at my peak in this most demanding period. My fourth Champions League title had filled me with a super-positive energy. I knew that I was a member of the team future generations would call *golden*, just as Alfredo di Stéfano's generation had been called for more than 60 years. The Spanish newspapers and generations of Real fans had been talking in such terms even before our victory, knowing our team was capable of such a feat. And that had felt good. Yet the third consecutive European title, together with 12 other trophies I had won since my arrival at Real in 2012, was the true testament to the historic quality of this generation of players and coaches. That's why I felt so special after Kiev. Whatever happened next, I had achieved with Real what I had hoped and worked for, and nothing could change it.

Signing for Real in 2012, I was convinced I would win trophies. Real is just that kind of a club, destined for the heights. But who could have imagined this incredible number of trophies, filling me with so much pride? Who could have dreamed about winning more than 15 titles in the Los Blancos' shirt? Had anyone told me about this, I wouldn't have believed them. But now that I have won them all, I know.

That morning, Vanja and I, feeling an immense pride and joy, sat on our patio in Madrid, reflecting on this incredible story. And then, after a moment's thought, I blurted out, 'Vanja, you know what, I feel so well and I'm so motivated, I think we'll kick some butts at the World Cup!'

She looked at me in wonder, as if asking, *Where's that come from?* But there was no need for questions, I simply poured my heart out. 'That's just what I feel, and I've felt it for a while now. I just want Croatia to win something. It's eating me up on the inside. I used to think, just like everyone else, it'd be great to pass the group stage, but I'm convinced this will be our tournament. Don't ask me why, I just know it.'

If she hadn't known me, she would probably have assumed I was still hungover from celebrating the title! But if anyone knows my thoughts about something that seems unattainable at the moment, it's Vanja. So she didn't dismiss me with a wave of her hand, and she didn't tell me to stop fantasising. Such determination before Croatia's big tournament must have been something entirely new for her, but she hoped my expectations would come true, like other moments in my career.

Those three days with my family in Madrid filled me with energy. I knew I would be gone for weeks, and I had a feeling that weeks away from my wife and children could turn into a month or more. Separation never comes easily, but I went to Rovinj, where Croatia's team was preparing for the World Cup, full of energy and elation. I couldn't wait to join my teammates. Even before Rovinj, when we talked to one another, I sensed an energy that was different from previous tournaments.

As I travelled to Croatia, thoughts of the World Cup in Russia were interrupted by Zinédine Zidane's abrupt announcement that he was leaving Real Madrid! It would be an understatement to say I was shocked. It was now clear that Cristiano Ronaldo was also leaving, and this was the second big news to catch everyone at the club by surprise. Mobile phones were on fire immediately. I talked to many people, including Sergio Ramos, Mateo Kovačić and Javier Coll, the club official responsible for first team logistics. We were all shocked.

The news spoilt my mood. I was sad Zidane was leaving. We had clicked immediately, and I'm sure his advice and belief in me helped me become a better player. He was also a great person. I had looked on him not only as a coach but as a role model, and I felt I could learn a lot from him. When someone is as charismatic as Zizou, it's hard to accept that the relationship will become a thing of the past. Luckily, this was not to be the case.

Preparations for Russia

I joined my Croatia teammates in Rovinj on 31 May. I found them training at the Valbruna Stadium. We greeted each other on the pitch and got down to work. I don't want to bother you with the descriptions of our training sessions. I can only say that our preparations for Russia, in terms of tactics, fitness and technique, were at the highest level. These were my sixth preparations for a big international tournament. Since 2006 I had competed at three Euros and two World Cups. In those tournaments our best results were achieved in 2008 in Austria and Switzerland, and in 2016 in France. Both times we passed the group stage. Unfortunately, that was as far as we got because Turkey and then Portugal eliminated us in the first knockout stage. At the World Cup in Germany in 2006, and eight years later in Brazil, we were eliminated in the group stage. The worst result was the World Cup in 2010, when we failed even to qualify for the final tournament.

This was Zlatko Dalić's debut in every sense. As a player he'd never had the honour of wearing Croatia's shirt. Nor had he coached the biggest Croatian clubs, Hajduk and Dinamo. But for our preparations he seemed confident and self-assured. I think his almost youthful passion and evident joy at being able to lead Croatia was a decisive factor that helped inspire the whole team. Before every big tournament, we were, of course, motivated and enthusiastic, but this time the atmosphere was special. Usually we announced our belief in achieving a good result. This time, however, we said nothing, though we were absolutely sure.

I'm sure Dalić's psychological preparation played a crucial role in this. From the very start, we had a good rapport – we simply clicked, and this led us to believe that Russia could be *our moment*. Another critical factor was the support of the public and the fans. After the match against Greece in Zagreb – the qualifying play-off round – the positive reactions and massive support we received, like in the time of the 'Bronze Generation' of 1998, filled us with tremendous energy.

Dalić invested a lot of effort into creating a good atmosphere. Our stay in Rovinj and then Opatija was well thought out, with the right amount of relaxation outside the training sessions. There was one evening in Opatija that is lodged in my memory. We went out for dinner and had a perfect time. Is this something we had never done before? Of course, it wasn't. Was this something extraordinary? Of course not. But it was special because we became closer as a team. We were together the whole time; no one stood apart or tried to single themselves out. And, most important, as far as I'm concerned at least, this wasn't just for the sake of it, the order of the day – it was sincere.

The opponents we faced for our preparation matches offered an excellent challenge. A match against Brazil is always sensational – and it's an excellent opportunity to assess where you stand at that moment. We played at a high level for about an hour. We lost in the final third of the match – the result was 2–0 to Brazil – but our form was promising.

The match against Senegal demonstrated that African teams could be very dangerous if we allowed them to get going. In light of our clashes against Argentina and Nigeria in Russia, these matches served their purpose and prepared us for the challenges ahead. The game against Senegal, which we won 2–1, was played in Osijek, the city in Slavonia where the delighted crowd once again showed us that Croatia was standing behind us and believing in us. That gave us a great impetus before our departure for Russia.

An important moment during the preparations was a meeting Dalić held in Opatija. We were just back from Liverpool, where we had played against Brazil. There, at Anfield, we saw the first act of *The Nikola Kalinić Case*. Here's what happened: when he learned he wasn't in the starting line-up against Brazil, Kalinić reported a back injury. Dalić was convinced that what was really hurt was his ego.

'The team comes first, Croatia's interest comes before your personal interests, you all have to understand this. It is the only way. If we join forces, we could do something. Whoever doesn't want to be here, whoever is not ready to help the team, whether it be for one, five or 10 minutes, speak now. We need positive energy, not tension.' This is how Dalić made it clear that he wouldn't tolerate, 'any undisciplined behaviour'.

I talked to Nikola. We had a physio treatment together. He complained about his status. He was convinced he was in good form and he should have an advantage over other attackers on the team.

I listened to what he had to say and told him: 'The coach has the right to choose players as he thinks best. Mandžukić is a beast, he plays well for Juventus, he ploughs the pitch for the full 90 minutes, non-stop. But if you think you're not ready for everything that's in front of us at the World Cup, I think you should speak your mind and make it clear immediately.'

Nikola was positive: 'It's not easy. I'm aware that I'm competing against Mario, and that he's in a better position, but I'm patient. I'm here and I'll help as much as I can.'

I believed the crisis would blow over. Generally, I was very optimistic about everything during the preparations. I saw that Ćorluka, Mandžukić, Rakitić, Subašić, Lovren, Vida – the so-called senators – had that special glow in their eyes. It was as if we were saying, 'Guys, this is our last chance. Let's not blow it.' Not that we ever said that out loud. By contrast, I thought a lot about my role. I told myself, 'You've got to be the captain, in every sense of the word. Be the leader who is going to encourage your teammates, lead by example, and motivate everyone to give their best. The captain who is going to listen if someone has something to complain about, but also the captain who is going to make it clear to anyone who stands out in a negative way that it has to stop.'

In this respect, Dalić's attitude was crucial. From day one, on the eve of our match against Ukraine, we established a good coach–captain relationship. We talked a lot. His was the position not of a boss whose every word must be obeyed, but of a coach who wants to hear what the most experienced players are thinking and then make his decision. I

231

have said it already: after more than 13 years in Croatia's shirt, I think the central element of the coach's job is to create good morale in the team. In those few days the players are together for the international break, it's difficult to come up with serious tactical solutions. It is especially devastating to try subjecting the players to a club regime because in such a short time it can't create the desired effect. What is needed is to establish good chemistry in the dressing room, choose a formation that is the most suitable for a match ahead, and motivate the players with a positive approach. And Dalić proved to be very successful in this. After we saved our necks in the qualifiers against Ukraine, and then dismantled Greece in the play-off, the team felt his positive energy. That's why the players followed him.

There were those who believed that Dalić was indecisive, or that he paid too much attention to what the players wanted – simply because he understood our point of view. I heard all kinds of stories about the players, and how we worked against past managers and had them sacked if we didn't like their methods. Those know-it-alls – and there were many of them around and even within the team – often singled me out as the mastermind. I guess it made their hollow story seem true. I got used to such lies and half-truths a long time ago, and never let them get to me.

Whenever someone asked my opinion, I was always honest – both at Real and with the national team. I never hide and I appreciate openness.

And that's how it was with Dalić – honest and open. He asked for my opinion as a captain, but he also asked Mandžukić, Ćorluka, Rakitić, Subašić, Lovren, Vida – the more experienced players on the team. He talked individually with other players. He organised meetings with all of us together. And then he would decide what was best. Sometimes he would accept our ideas, sometimes he wouldn't. The key thing is that it was always him making the decisions, as was only to be expected.

After Senegal, Dalić gave us a couple of days off. I used them to fly to Madrid because I knew I wouldn't see my family in a while. Not until mid-July, I hoped, regardless of how difficult it was to be away from them. I said this to Vanja, who organised a party for Ivano's birthday on the day of my departure.

We gathered in Zagreb on 10 June. On that evening I attended the sixth edition of the Footballer Trophy. Just like three days before, when the Croatian Football Federation had honoured me in Vukovar, the players and coaches of the Croatian First League voted me the Player of the Season.

The final stage of 'Operation Russia' began the following morning. The expedition gathered at the airport and the excitement was simply palpable. Just as noticeable was that we all wanted to arrive at our destination as soon as possible so we could make ourselves comfortable and change into tracksuits. We wore top-quality official suits, but players always feel best in their work clothes. That's why we asked Dalić to allow us to travel to the matches in our tracksuits, and not official suits.

The Croatian Football Federation officials chose a camp at Illychevo, about an hour's drive from Saint Petersburg, which offered comfort and ideal conditions to train and prepare for the challenges ahead. The Woodland Rhapsody, as the complex is called, had everything we needed: breath-taking nature, the lake, the forest, peace and quiet, and a pleasant climate. The staff were extremely kind and always at our disposal. They clearly wanted us to feel welcome, and were excellent hosts – as well as true fans. Like everyone else, I had my own room. (During international gatherings when I did have to share a room, it was almost always with Vedran Ćorluka.) Our training site was in Roshchino, some 15 minutes away from the hotel. It's easy to underestimate just how important training conditions and accommodation are; the team needs peace and quiet, and they need to distance themselves from anything that could disturb them or disrupt the team's daily routine.

My experience from the five previous tournaments taught me how important the first match is. At UEFA Euro 2008 and 2016 we beat the co-hosts, Austria, and Turkey respectively, gaining the momentum that took us past the group stage. At the two World Cups, in Germany and

Brazil, we lost both opening matches to Brazil and failed to advance to the knockout stage. Sure, at Euro 2012 in Poland and Ukraine, we opened the tournament with a victory against Republic of Ireland, but we also had two heavyweights in our group, Spain and Italy, which made it difficult to advance. If we include all the big tournaments since Croatia's independence, we can see that victory in the first match helped us to make it to the knockout stage. Defeat at the start always meant the team's path ended at the group stage.

The whole time, we found ourselves playing the numbers game, which only fuelled our hopes. Croatia were always successful when the year of the tournament had an eight in it. Back in 1998, at Croatia's debut appearance at the World Cup in France, we won the bronze. A decade later, in 2008, we were excellent at the Euros in Austria and Switzerland, and advanced to the knockout stage very convincingly, with three wins. Now we were playing at the 2018 World Cup – and we expected success.

Interestingly, Croatia didn't fare well in the years with a zero at the end of them. The only two campaigns where we failed to qualify happened in 2000, for the Euros in Netherlands and Belgium, and in 2010, for the World Cup in South Africa.

Luckily, the Euro 2020 qualifiers have proved all this is just mumbo jumbo!

Nigeria

We were extremely motivated to prove our worth in the first match in Russia and show everyone that our high hopes were not unfounded. Our opponent was tricky: Nigeria had some excellent players on their team, and if they worked together, we knew they could cause problems for anyone. We didn't feel pressure during those few days before the match. The main thing was the morale within the team. What I have already talked about became only more apparent in Russia. From one hour to another, from one day to another, we were a group – close, supportive of each other, motivated. After our meals, we would sit down and talk. We would go out for a walk and enjoy the beautiful nature around Woodland Rhapsody, or play some sport or a game. Dejan Lovren, Marcelo Brozović, Mateo Kovačić and I played fiercely competitive games of table tennis. Domagoj Vida and I regularly lost to Kovačić and Brozović at darts. We played FIFA on PlayStation, or watched games. What encouraged me the most was that almost no one chose to retreat to their room, to watch a film on their own. I think unity and closeness were a crucial element that led to our success.

Zlatko Dalić knew how to balance serious training with a relaxed atmosphere. Tension grew as the matches came nearer, and it was good that we changed our usual travelling routine. Dalić wanted us to travel to the host city two days before the match – a wise decision. It took us an hour by bus from Woodland Rhapsody to the airport, and then we would spend another couple of hours on the plane. Dalić wanted us to adjust to the new environment and have enough time to focus on the match. And afterwards, we never spent the night in the city where we played. That was smart too – after a match, players are tired, the adrenaline is still flowing and it is difficult to fall asleep. That's why we decided to go through this process on the plane or the bus; it allowed our bodies to escape the stressful situation, and gave us all the time we needed the next day to relax and freshen up.

When we arrived in Kaliningrad, I saw the tournament was being wonderfully organised – and was safe. We had a top-quality security detail in the camp and at the matches, everything was at the highest level. Of course, the atmosphere before the first match was fantastic: crowds of our fans in chequered shirts around the stadium, tremendous support from the stands. It was like playing back home in Croatia. The game followed the course we wanted. We stayed close and did not let them develop their game, especially on the counter-attack, given that they were very quick. Dalić asked us to pass the ball safely, to switch sides and move quickly, and when we lost the ball, to press immediately and regain possession. We put in a solid performance, especially since it was the first match, and won 2–0, which meant we fulfilled our first goal: winning the opening game to ensure less pressure in the clash against Argentina. I thought I played well – not because I scored a penalty, but because I felt strong and focused.

After the match, Ćorluka came to me and said, 'Luka, we've got a problem.'

There was a new development in *The Nikola Kalinić Case*.

The moment I heard, I knew it wouldn't be pleasant. That first time, in Liverpool, when we played against Brazil, Dalić had expressed his dissatisfaction with Nikola's behaviour. What now? Charlie and I went to see Dalić, who told us he had wanted to bring him on at the end of the match, but Kalinić told him, through his assistant Ivica Olić, that his back hurt. Dalić had had enough and now wanted to send Nikola home. We suggested it might be better to sleep on it and decide in the morning. Dalić agreed. It was better we take pleasure in our first victory and the surge of positive energy around the team. The atmosphere created by the fans in Kaliningrad was absolutely fantastic. I hoped – as did other players, and I'm sure Dalić expected it too – that Kalinić would do something tomorrow to try and soothe the coach's anger. It was only reasonable. So Dalić waited until the evening. Then, when nothing happened, he sent Olić to tell Kalinić to leave the camp the next morning and go home. Around 10 p.m., Kalinić called me on the phone and asked me to come to his room. He told me what Olić had said, and I saw he felt really bad about it. Ivan Perišić, Ivan Strinić and Ante Rebić, who spent the most time with him, were already there. They were sorry too, but they were aware Nikola had made a huge mistake. He's a great guy and an excellent player who realised only then just what he had done. After talking to Dalić and Olić, he saw there was no way back.

The situation was extremely unpleasant, and we were one player short for the rest of the tournament, but it didn't harm morale within the team. In fact, the players rallied and came together as a group. The happiness caused by our victory over Nigeria had a lot to do with it.

Argentina

The next day at Woodland Rhapsody we turned all our attention to the clash against Argentina. We were very excited. In footballing terms, Argentina are a superpower: they have Leo Messi, they've won the FIFA World Cup twice. After Brazil at my previous two tournaments, this was the greatest opponent we had faced in the eight matches I had played at the World Cup. The clash against Argentina brought back some special memories: in March 2006, I had made my debut for Croatia during a match in which Messi scored his first goal for Argentina.

We couldn't wait to come out onto the pitch and find out how we measured up against them. We were facing an opponent who are always one of the favourites to win the tournament – a true test of our hopes of doing something big in Russia.

We had watched their match against Iceland, and we saw we could compete with them. Should we waste words talking about Messi's genius? No, it's obvious to all. Just as we knew that he was carrying by far the greatest responsibility and, with it, the huge burden of Argentina's hopes and expectations for the title. Given my position in the national team, I had some idea how Messi felt: the expectations on our team are always closely connected with me. All kinds of things could be heard and read in this context about my contribution to the team. Some said I didn't care about Croatia and that I saved my efforts for Real. What can I say about that?

I've never agreed with opinions placing too much importance on individual players. I've watched many great teams, and read a lot about celebrated clubs and their stars, and I think no one can say that this or that player was a decisive factor in winning a tournament or a championship. Football is a collective sport, and no individual can make up for the weaknesses of his team, no matter how talented or extraordinary he might be.

The unbearable pressure on Messi only made Argentina's situation even more difficult. Besides, Messi's Argentina were very close to winning the title in Brazil back in 2014. The story of whether he is greater or as great as Diego Maradona should not be brought down to one goal in the final – the goal he didn't score against Germany in the showpiece in Rio de Janeiro. A phenomenal player is not enough; the whole team must put in an outstanding performance and only then can we expect everything to fall into place for the ultimate victory. And even if all these pieces are in place, events can still take a wrong turn.

***

Nizhny Novgorod was the site of our great clash. There weren't as many of Croatia's fans as in Kaliningrad, but there were enough of them to create a fantastic atmosphere once again. Of course, we had considered the best ways of stopping Messi. I had played against him in many *El Clásicos,* as had Mateo Kovačić. Leo is unstoppable when he makes a solo run and quickly changes direction. Defend him one-on-one, and he's just off and away. So, it made more sense to put him up against the zone and prevent him from getting the ball, forcing him to come back deep to receive it. Two more players on the left side, Ivan Strinić and Ivan Perišić, lay in ambush. It was phenomenal – that's the only expression I can use to describe the plan, and it's execution, which stopped such an incredible player.

The game was balanced: Argentina kept possession and, in the first half an hour, they created a couple of dangerous situations in front of our goal. Perišić and Mario Mandžukić also had some big chances. We were good, and I was sure we would be even better in the second half. I could feel us rising to the occasion. The key moment was the first goal. It's true that Willy Caballero, Argentina's goalkeeper, made a mistake and misplaced a pass, but the mistake was provoked by Ante Rebić's tenacity and vision. He pressed the goalkeeper at a moment that seemed all but lost – and forced Caballero to make an error. Rebić is a special character, and that's probably why he scored such a tremendous goal. I suppose most players would first try to bring a high ball under control, but not him. He smashed the volley and scored! From then on, carried by our euphoric supporters, we simply flew up and down the pitch. We destroyed them in the second half, and the final 3–0 scoreline clearly showed the difference between the two teams.

We needed that big victory; I needed that performance. I scored for 2–0, and the goal was almost an exact copy of the one at Old Trafford back in 2013 when Real were playing against Manchester United. But back then I wasn't celebrating so much because we still needed another goal. On this occasion, though, I simply erupted. Seeing the ball in the net, I was as happy as a child. It's fantastic to score such an important goal against such a great opponent at the World Cup and then run to your fans, who are going wild in the stands, and celebrate with your teammates and coaches on the bench.

We had a real party in the dressing room. We celebrated because we had qualified for the last 16 and, already after the second match, we had accomplished our minimum goal. We let our hair down and had a beer or two after the match, but we didn't take it too far. The big party was yet to come. Beating Argentina wasn't as simple as it may have seemed, and it gave us faith. We were dominant. Those on the pitch as well as those on the bench, we all played our part. This is the unity that matters; without it, even getting in the position to think about outsmarting your opponent on the pitch is impossible.

Beating one of the tournament favourites in a high-stakes match served as the catalyst for what came later. The team's reaction after celebrating on the bus taking us to the airport showed our maturity. At first, we were singing songs chosen by various DJs, especially by Mandžukić and Domagoj Vida, but then we quickly turned down the volume and talked about the rest of the tournament.

The staff of Woodland Rhapsody gave us a warm welcome. Our phones were on fire from all the messages of support, while video messages from Croatia gave us a hint of the euphoria in our homeland. Even when I was just a child, I thought about the generation of 1998 and the feeling they must have had when the whole of Croatia came out on the streets and squares to celebrate their achievements. Argentina allowed me to feel the reality of this emotion for the first time. I felt – and other players said the same thing – connected to all of our people, in Croatia and abroad.

After every match, I always called Vanja and the children and my parents. Their happiness spurred mine. I felt I could go through and beat anyone on the pitch. I was as psyched as ever, and I kept thinking I could do anything I imagined on the pitch.

We spent the day after the match against Argentina in the peace of our camp. Dejan Lovren, Šime Vrsaljko and I went for a walk to the lake. We sat down and chatted. Dejan and Šime are very close; they just have to look at each other and they immediately burst out laughing. They were having a good time together – but this conversation was serious. Whenever we talked about our ambitions at a big tournament, it always came down to our wish to pass the group stage and win the first knockout match at least. Considering that there are only about 4 million people in Croatia and a small base of about 120,000–130,000 football players, qualifying for 10 out of 13 possible tournaments in the 28 years of our independence is simply fantastic. For example, Italy weren't in Russia – and they are a footballing nation with four World Cup trophies. But one of the most exciting things in football is that David can beat Goliath. And that's why whenever Croatia qualifies for a big tournament, there's an ambition behind it; we are not there just to participate. After 1998 and the bronze medal, expectations are always high, but with the exception of our debut year at the World Cup, we'd never managed to pass the first step after the group stage. So, we thought, what matters is to cross the first step, and then the path will open to the very end. Vrsaljko, Lovren and I concluded we were ready for that path; we felt we were strong enough to fight for the medals. We never thought we could slip and fall, and we didn't feel the pressure of previous unsuccessful attempts.

In the first stage of the competition, we got one day off. Everyone said Saint Petersburg was beautiful, and it was only an hour away from our camp, but no one was in the mood to relax; all of the players used this day off for individual training sessions. The gym was packed. Never in the 14 years wearing the chequered shirt have I seen so much self-initiated individual work. We were completely focused on what lay ahead of us.

Iceland

Next was Iceland. We had often met in recent times – this was my fifth match against them in as many years. They'd made progress too, and had beaten us a year before in the qualifications for this very tournament. A country on a distant island, with just 350,000 inhabitants, they have every right to be proud of their team. They needed a victory against us: if things fell into place in Group D, they could come second in our group and advance to the knockout stage. By now, we had made it through, but it never crossed our minds to relax. Our morale was simply too good, and we didn't want anything to disrupt this. No one would hold it against us if we lost but still, every wrong move brings something negative, always.

Zlatko Dalić said he wanted to save me for the knockout stage, so I would get 20 minutes or so of playing time. It was as if he'd read my mind – I understood that starting on the bench did me good, allowing me to catch my breath. But I'd also noticed something else, both at club level and for the national team. When my continuity is disrupted – for example, when the coaches make me skip a match for fear of injuries – my rhythm in the next match is slightly off. That's what happened against Turkey in 2008 after I had skipped the third group match against Poland. The same happened in 2016 during the Euros in France when I didn't play in the third match against Spain. In the next match, against Portugal, I was out of rhythm. That's why I need to get at least some playing time in competitive matches to stay in shape. However, two days before the match, Dalić changed his mind. He explained that nine new players would be brought in, the ones who had earned this with their work, behaviour and responsibility. He concluded it would be good for their confidence if I led them as their captain.

'They're more confident with you on the pitch.'

I said, 'Yes'. I always want to play, even when everyone tells me it would be wiser to skip a match. We played against Iceland in Rostov-on-Don. It was extremely hot, a new moment in Russia. The atmosphere in the Rostov Arena was terrific – and chequered. Our team, with nine new players, Ivan Perišić and I, performed well on the pitch. Everyone was motivated; each player took advantage of the slightest space to show off his skill and write his name in history. Milan Badelj scored a fantastic goal and gave our side a lead, but Iceland levelled in the 76th minute from a penalty. I had already been substituted because Dalić decided to give a third of the match to Filip Bradarić, the only member of our team who hadn't played yet. Only Dominik Livaković, our third goalkeeper, wouldn't get at least a minute of playing time in Russia – but time is a young goalkeeper's ally. Iceland searched for another goal, and then, as so often happens, they conceded in the last minute: Perišić counter-attacked and smashed the ball into the net! For the first time in our FIFA World Cup history, we had won all nine points in the group!

It was a well-deserved bonus for the players who contributed from the bench. They played well, which was already a plus, but the victory made them feel fulfilled – they had contributed to Croatia's winning streak. I talked to Vedran Ćorluka about it. That was our first talk since it became evident his role at this championship was to be a substitute.

We'd joined the national team together back in 2006, and until Russia he had the status of an indispensable member of the first team. In the year before the World Cup, he'd ruptured his Achilles tendon. It was a serious injury that required complicated surgery and a lengthy recovery period. Those were difficult moments for Charlie because he was fighting against time – his desire to play at the World Cup made him want to return to the pitch and get back in shape as soon as possible. It wasn't certain Dalić would include him in the team; Ćorluka had to prove he was fully recovered and able to endure the competitive pace. He returned to the pitch at the beginning of March. I encouraged him because I knew how much he wanted to play at the World Cup in Russia, the country where he has become immensely popular playing for Lokomotiv Moscow. He is the team's captain, they won the Russian Premier League just before the World Cup, and he's also won three Russian Cup titles. During almost eight years in Russia, he's gained the status of a legend.

He managed to recover. It's not easy to get back in shape in just three months, following eight or nine months away from the pitch. But Dalić chose Domagoj Vida and Dejan Lovren as the central defenders. This wasn't easy for Charlie to accept, but he remained positive. He had been a key player for a long time, but he put the team's interests before his own and not once did he create even the slightest problem. He showed his character and greatness. At past tournaments, some players found themselves in similar situations and then complained about it, spoiling the atmosphere. Except for Nikola Kalinić, everything in Russia was perfect. This approach, where every player on the team remained positive, open and honest, was one of the foundations of our success.

Denmark

There were five days before the first knockout match, where our opponent was Denmark. I'm already used to the frenzy about tickets at European and World championships – especially if we are playing against better-known opponents or at smaller stadiums. But what happened in Russia just before our match against Denmark was unprecedented. It was mad! No matter how organised you are, no matter how well you plan, when the euphoria kicks in, it's all in vain. I had booked 30-50 tickets for each of our knockout games, depending on the match. If it had been possible to get more after the quarter-final, I would have reserved them. Even so, I gave away everything I got. I spent about €100,000 on tickets in Russia. And I wasn't sorry: please God, let it happen again!

My parents flew to every match from the beginning of the championship. They had a lovely time, and I was happy for them. They're retired, they worked their whole lives, raised three children, and looked after the elder members of our family. When I earned some money at Dinamo, I told my mother to quit her job and dedicate herself to the family, and find some time for herself. She didn't want to hear about it, and my dad was even worse. After I signed for Tottenham and was making good money, I finally managed to talk my mother into retiring. My father was in the military and retired after 42 and a half years of service. He more than earned his retirement.

Vanja and I discussed how we were going to approach the tournament – Sofia was too little to travel, and Ivano and Ema had school, so we made a plan: 'You'll come to Russia with Ivano and Ema after the round of 16.' She laughed, because I'd made it clear I was convinced we would pass the group stage and win the first knockout match. I missed my wife and children a lot. Luckily, there was FaceTime.

The preparations for Denmark were more or less the same as before. Dalić warned us of their strengths, and their dangerous set-pieces. We practised our defence. Dalić asked us to close the midfield and force their centre-backs to build up play. They were a tough team, they didn't concede often and they played good football. They also had some good individuals on their team – particularly Christian Eriksen, their offensive creator with excellent crosses and set-pieces. But watching their previous matches, I was convinced we were better and could beat them.

The days before the match were slow, partly because our anxiety and expectations took their toll. After all, we were standing in front of an obstacle that Croatia had not overcome in the past 20 years. After the euphoria in Croatia, after our excellent performances in the group stages, we faced a real danger that the whole story would come to an end. Just as had happened at seven previous tournaments. It wasn't hard to imagine the reactions: we would be marked as 'Modrić's loser generation'.

I made special preparations for the tournament, especially mentally. Of course, I didn't neglect my physical fitness and preventative measures. I had a couple of injuries during the season, which forced me to miss four or five matches, but it also kept me fresh for the season's finale. For the past few years, I've been training with Vlatko Vučetić, a professor from the Faculty of Kinesiology in Zagreb. It makes me feel stronger, and in Russia the adrenaline kept me in a superb rhythm.

The start of our match against Denmark was a nightmare – we didn't even have a chance to get to our positions and they'd already taken the lead! It was the first minute of the match, and their left-back Jonas Knudsen had a throw-in. Their defender somehow got to the ball, took his shot, and the ball went through many feet, deflecting off Danijel Subašić along the way and slowly into the net. We had practised how to defend against Denmark's set-pieces, but we weren't prepared for long throw-ins. Generally speaking, our reactions to set-pieces were our weakest point. Who knows what the history books would say now about Russia 2018 were this a stronger part of our game?

We didn't sag – and this was perhaps the first game when we became aware of our mental strength. We reacted promptly and quickly levelled the score. On this occasion, we got lucky – just as they had done a few minutes earlier – because the ball ricocheted off their defender's head and Mario Mandžukić confidently swept a shot beyond Kasper Schmeichel. In the fourth minute, the score was already 1–1. Who would've thought that it would not change for the next 116 minutes? It wasn't a good game to watch; both sides were too aware of the match's importance. Denmark surprised us with their long balls and throw-ins. Everything else went as expected. The pressure got to us and our performance wasn't at the same level as before. The high stakes took a toll on them too.

It was also hot in Nizhny Novgorod. A lot of humidity in the air made us expend more energy and it made it hard to focus. For me, this was the most difficult match of the tournament. My teammates said the same. Experienced analysts always say a team has to overcome one critical match if they want to reach the final. It's nice to talk about it when everything turns out well, but surviving those 120 minutes and the penalty shoot-out – it was very stressful! If you lose, it's drama and tragedy, like Vienna in 2008. If you win, ecstasy.

From the day I signed for Real Madrid, there was more and more criticism in Croatia about my game. People seemed to think, probably because I was a member of such a famous club as Real, that I should play some out-of-this-world football, especially in Croatia's shirt. After I had adapted to Madrid football, especially after the vital clash in Manchester, the Spanish media mostly showered me with compliments. The fans supported me, my teammates and coaches respected me and, without false modesty, I kept putting in outstanding performances. At the same time, I was criticised in Croatia for not scoring enough goals, for making few assists and for being too reserved. In Spain, everyone praised the quality and the importance of passes I made or decisions that helped set up an attack, especially when these led to a goal. In Croatia, all of these were given an ironic term – 'pre-assist'. Some coaches only encouraged such opinions. When Croatia failed to deliver the desired result, criticism was directed mostly at me and what I deigned to call a football alibi. With every failure, we were 'Modrić's losers'.

On the other hand, for the past seven years in a row, Croatian players and coaches have voted me the best Croatian footballer. The fans in the stands were also positive – even more so, in fact. Such a contrast was more or less typical until the autumn of 2017. That's when it all changed for me. After the criticism that erupted following my testimony at the court in Osijek, I questioned my position. I knew things would be much harder now, but I loved playing for Croatia too much to step away without yet another attempt to do something big. I found some new inner strength and told myself, 'Enough! Deeds, not words! It's now or never!'

In the autumn of 2017, Croatia started losing points, yet the fans grew ever fiercer in their support for me. The media praised me more than before. Despite our defeat in Turkey and the draw against Finland, they said I was among the few to play at a high level and insisted that the rest of the team should look up to me. I think this was the first time anyone in Croatia had written about me in such a way, and I found it odd. I did play well, but even so we had lost four out of six points. What happened? From today's perspective, it seems the public recognised I had changed and took a different view of me. After everything that had happened, I decided to assert myself as a leader. When all the negativity rained down, I realised this: *Before my career in the Blazers' shirt comes to an end, I'll give everything I've got to achieve something special with Croatia.* I dug my heels in. I think that was obvious during Ante Čačić's last three matches, against Kosovo, Turkey and Finland. And the public was exhilarated after the three tremendous matches under Dalić against Ukraine and Greece. All the pundits, as well as people close to the national team, praised both the new head coach and me as the 'true leader of this generation'. I have to acknowledge that such a turn of events also meant that I was partly to blame for what had happened previously: it shows I hadn't known how to assert myself, or hadn't been convincing enough as a leader. Both in the team and on the outside. Now there was no way back – I knew the public expected me to give it all I had. The fans came back, and the atmosphere was positive once again. I wasn't allowed to disappoint them. They wouldn't tolerate it, and they would never forget.

***

While waiting for the penalty shoot-out with Denmark, all the responsibility, burden and risk seemed to be packed into that one moment. The adrenaline kept running through my veins, but I needed it because with it came resolve and courage. I missed a penalty in extra time, but even before Dalić ran up to me to encourage me to take a penalty in the shoot-out, I had already decided: I couldn't let down either my teammates or myself. What message would I have sent if I had been scared by the responsibility? What kind of a leader would I have been had I crawled into a mousehole while my friends faced perhaps the biggest trial of their careers? Someone said it seemed like I didn't know where I was at that moment. I knew alright. I knew very well where I was, what I wanted, and especially what I risked.

If Denmark eliminated Croatia, we would once again be called losers. And if we lost, I would be the guilty party. They would have every right to think as much, too, because in the 116th minute I'd missed a penalty. So, if I didn't now take the penalty in the shoot-out, and then we lost, I would've failed everyone in Croatia, myself included. What's more, had I missed the second spot-kick, then the biggest loser of all time would be me. And, since there were still people angry with me for my testimony, I would become one of the most hated people in the country's history – for all time and with no way back.

I was aware of what was at stake, but at that moment, I tried only to calm myself down. My teammates helped – they encouraged me. I knew they were having a hard time because we could've won the match in extra time, and I saw they sympathised with me. I felt I owed them; I felt I owed everyone.

Just for a second, let's go back to that penalty miss in the 116th minute. It's a wonderful action: I receive the ball in the centre of the pitch and see Ante Rebić making a run into the penalty area. I send the ball through as he storms into the box and rounds Schmeichel. We all see the ball in the net, but the Danish defender brings Rebić down. The referee awards a penalty. I never watch the opponent's keeper on a matchday. However, earlier that day, Marjan Mrmić, our goalkeeping coach, had shown Danijel Subašić and I how the Danish players took their penalties, and how Schmeichel reacts to a shot – he dives a moment before the shot itself is taken. I'll shoot down the middle, and he'll already be in the corner. I put the ball on the spot; I'm holding the keys to open the door that has been closed for us for the past 20 years. There are a couple of minutes before the end of the match and I don't believe they can score. Maybe they might even concede the third goal from a counter-attack. I run up to the ball without looking at him. But, in a fraction of a second, I change my mind and send the ball to the side. No way – Schmeichel saves the ball and holds it in his hands! Later, in the videos – and I watched them who knows how many times – I saw he moved early. Just as he always does. But I didn't take the shot as I usually do. One thing is certain, I will never watch goalkeepers save penalties before a match again.

As Schmeichel holds the ball in his hands, as his teammates and fans cheer and call out his name, and as his father Peter jumps around the box with happiness, I'm devastated. I wanted to crawl inside my own skin. *Can this be possible? Is it 2008 and all the drama all over again? No, it can't be.* I react immediately. In the past, I would perhaps have drooped, but this time I had had enough. In the last five minutes of the match, there was only us on the pitch. That showed the team's spirit. We were ready for big things, I could feel it in my bones. Unlike Vienna and Turkey, I saw my teammates believed in success. I could see it in their eyes. Drama, once again, but this time it wouldn't close the circle of 10 years of torture and misery.

'Come on, let's win this for Luka! He pulled us up, we have to do the same for him.'

This is what Ivan Rakitić yells out in the huddle in the centre circle. We all cheer one another on and here we go. Subašić saves the first shot – we have the advantage. Schmeichel saves Milan Badelj's kick and we're level once again. They score, Andrej Kramarić ties. The Danish score another penalty and have a 2–1 lead. I leave the huddle and walk towards the spot. If I miss, and they score for 3–1, it will be almost impossible to come back. I can't possibly miss two penalties at such an important moment. It will haunt me forever. I'm calm when I put the ball down on the spot. Everything comes down to this. I'll come back with the shield or on it. At that moment, I'm focused; I'm sure I'll score. As I approach the ball, out of the corner of my eye, I see Schmeichel has moved to his right before the shot and I shoot down the middle. It's in! The ball passes right by his extended legs, and it's in the net! What a relief. As I walk back to the centre circle, I smack my head in anger. *Why didn't you shoot like this in the 116th minute?*

Now it's the Danish player's turn, all the weight is on his shoulders. Subašić saves – the second, heroic act of his legendary story. Josip Pivarić misses the opportunity to give us the lead, and now Schmeichel is close to becoming a Danish legend. The fifth penalty is left. Their striker takes the penalty in a similar way as I did; Subašić gets down just like Schmeichel did when I took the shot, but Subašić's legs are an inch longer, an inch that changes history. Everything is now up to Rakitić. He's the last taker, just as he wanted. In Vienna back in 2008, he missed the penalty, just like I did. Destiny owes him one. All eyes and hopes are on him. He seems as if he already knows he has scored! He places the ball in the net with such ease and picks it up in his hands as if we're at training and then slowly, as if nothing special has happened, turns towards us. What nerve! Of course, we all erupt with happiness. We run towards Rakitić, towards Subašić, towards our fans. We jump all over one another, hit by an elbow or foot. It doesn't hurt, we feel no pain, we're in seventh heaven! I need to hug and kiss all of my teammates. *You saved me! If we'd lost, the guilt would've haunted me for the rest of my days.*

The celebration on the pitch reflects the agony we have endured. Without a doubt, it's the most important match of this generation. We're beside ourselves; we've passed the first knockout stage. All our frustrations are gone. We have the opportunity to write golden pages in football history. We wave at the fans and I get goosebumps – I can only imagine the atmosphere in Croatia, everything must be on fire. The 1998 genie is out of the bottle, and everything reminds us of the bronze path. Except that now I'm here, on the pitch. I'm no longer some kid trembling in front of the screen, watching those older than me hopping around with happiness, jumping into the sea and celebrating Croatia's victory. Now I'm playing and I'm shaking with excitement. I hug Subašić. He doesn't have to save another shot ever in his life; he did his thing, he's a legend. He cries with happiness and reveals his t-shirt with Hrvoje Ćustić's picture on it. I feel a lump in my throat. I shout, 'Thank you, Suba, thank you!' He's the one who's led us here! I'm too happy to think about the Danish players. This is their Vienna; this is their tragedy and it's going to haunt them for a long, long time. Football is like this – dramatic. It brings joy to some, misery to others. Sometimes the line separating heroes from losers is very, very thin. On that evening, Subašić became a legend. Schmeichel has to wait his turn.

The dressing room is on fire. For the first time, the Croatian president, Kolinda Garbar-Kitarović, joins us in the celebrations. She congratulates each player – it's obvious she's moved. She tells us Croatia has erupted. People are in the streets; everyone, every single person is celebrating. Unity! This word has been said many times in our era, but here, in Russia, we truly live it for the first time. What a feeling!

This time we stayed in Nizhny Novgorod. We didn't go back to Woodland Rhapsody, and our hotel was a rhapsody of celebration: songs and joy everywhere. There was no sleep before the morning. We just couldn't sleep, the adrenaline was still rushing through our veins. We cracked open the heavy door, we got rid of the burden of the disappointing seven European and World championships. We glanced at the medals for the first time and we wanted the moment to last.

Just before morning, I tried to close my eyes, at least for a little while. The scenes kept coming back. I remembered all the changes in my approach. I recalled the confidence all of the players showed. I thought about coach Dalić and what a perfect match he was for us. I imagined what would've happened if the penalties had gone the other way. The scene was stronger than me, although I was aware it only kept me awake. Before I managed to fall asleep, I once again went back to our group hug before the match against Denmark. Traditionally, when we come into a huddle, the manager says his final words, and then the captain. After this, the captain shouts: 'For the win!', and the team responds: 'Croatia!'

However, this time I needed to say something else: 'Today we're playing for ourselves, for our families, for our children, for all of those who stood by us through all the suffering. This match is our final! Mark my words, if we win today, the next stop is the final!'

I believed what I said and I wanted to make the team believe the same. With these thoughts running through my mind, I finally found peace and fell asleep.

Russia

In Sochi on the Black Sea, with a temperature of 30 degrees Celsius, we waited for Russia. There were six days until the quarter-final. Even though it was hot, we felt too good to let it bother us. We had fun watching other matches. Everything is easier and nicer once you know you have made it through to the next round. Coach Dalić gave us a half-day off and in the evening, as if by arrangement, almost the whole team gathered in a restaurant. We had dinner together and watched the match between Belgium and Japan.

As time went by, we focused on Russia and analysed their game. Dalić and I talked about our tactics a lot, and he treated me as his right-hand man. So if there was something I didn't consider a good idea, I could say as much. He was ready to hear everyone out and never stopped anyone from expressing his opinion. He wasn't vain or dismissive and he never thought he endangered his position by discussing tactics with his players. He once said that his players had the experience of playing for the biggest clubs and competing in some of the toughest football leagues in the world, so why not take advantage? I agree with him – that's a huge plus and the players should share their experiences, both about the upcoming opponents and their own team. Ivan Rakitić talked about Lionel Messi, Vedran Ćorluka either knew or learned everything there was to know about the Russians. When we had played against Ukraine, Darijo Srna's insight and advice were extremely valuable. Dalić listened, soaked everything in, thought it through and then made his decision. Sometimes he accepted our ideas, sometimes he didn't. His word was final – just as it is supposed to be. Positive chemistry.

By the eve of the clash against Russia, we had spent 42 days together. There was no need for special tactical preparations. We knew what the coach expected from us; only slight details changed. We talked about the Russians, analysed their game, and worked on set-pieces, especially on defence. We focused on the zone defence, with a 4-3-2 block attacking the crosses. It seemed it could work well, but only if all the players were on the same page. During training sessions, it was more or less okay, but we had failed to do what we agreed in previous matches.

Dalić explained his plan for how to start the match: he wanted to play with two attackers, Andrej Kramarić and Mario Mandžukić, with Ivan Perišić and Ante Rebić on the wings, and Rakitić and I in the middle. Dalić expected the Russians to use a more defensive approach, and he knew they didn't have a player on their team whose speed and agility could cause us problems on the counter-attack. He told us to allow Artem Dzyuba to receive the ball, and to avoid duels with him because that was his strength. Aleksandr Golovin was always lurking behind to break through. We had an attacking formation, and Dalić wanted to press high and weave the net around Igor Akinfeev's goal.

There were 45,000 people at the Olympic Stadium in Sochi. Naturally, most of them were Russians. They were delighted by their national team, especially after they had eliminated Spain. Russia exceeded all expectations, and now their fans were on fire. The Russians left a great impression as hosts, and in general they were extremely welcoming and friendly. From our first day at Woodland Rhapsody, their treatment was fantastic. They celebrated our every victory with us. Perhaps they were in our debt after 2007, when our win against England helped them qualify for UEFA Euro 2008. We felt an immense respect at every step of the way, and they rooted for us in every match – except, of course, when we played against their team. In all our other matches, before and after, I had the feeling that most of Russia was on our side. One detail after our win against the host nation sticks in our memory.

The clash in Sochi was complicated – our performance in the first half was below our abilities and Russia's offensive approach caught us by surprise. They kept us under pressure, preventing us from building our play from the last line. And then the player I had known from Real suddenly stepped up. We had played together for a while for Los Blancos and we had a good relationship. Denis Cheryshev had been humble and quiet, and an excellent player. Now he took the ball in front of me, I didn't manage to kick it out of his feet, and he hit a tremendous shot from 20 yards out and into the top right corner. While the Russians were euphoric, a thought ran through my mind: *Not again! Now we're chasing to catch up?!*

Eight minutes later, Mandžukić sent in a fantastic cross from the left side for Kramarić, who skilfully headed it into the goal! Once again, a timely response to our opponent taking the lead. In the second half, Dalić made an excellent move, bringing on Marcelo Brozović instead of Perišić in the 63rd minute. Now we had an extra pair of legs in the midfield and our game immediately became more balanced. We dominated, had possession and created chances. This second half saw one of our best performances at the tournament. This is what I often say: at one point, when the match is being decided and can go to either way, you need a manager whose decision will lead you to success. Dalić's call was an excellent and timely move.

Extra time. Another 30 minutes of added play within a week. Šime Vrsaljko and Ivan Strinić, two full-backs who ran up and down the pitch the whole time, were feeling the consequences. Strinić left the pitch first; he just couldn't take it anymore. Vrsaljko had knee problems throughout the tournament. I admired how he endured it all. He had to go off a couple of minutes into extra time. Ćorluka took Domagoj Vida's place at centre-half, and Vida moved to Vrsaljko's position – two heroes who created our second goal in the 101st minute. I took the corner, Mandžukić made a block, and Vida rose on the penalty spot and headed the ball towards the goal. Ćorluka was right in front of the goal, basically in the way of the ball, but he made a smart move and let the ball pass through and into the Russian net! We celebrated as if the goal would bring us eternity, the goal for the semi-final. And then another disastrous move: Josip Pivarić, who had replaced Strinić, handballed and gave Russia a free-kick on the right side of our penalty area. Could there be anything worse for us than a free-kick in such a dangerous area? Yes, of course. A cross, Mário Fernandes rising high and heading the ball into the net, 2–2! We were level again. Now the Russians celebrated like mad, and I just couldn't wrap my head around it – it had happened again. I was at the centre spot ready to kick off, but instead of passing it to the side, I hit the ball with everything I had and sent it towards the touchline. I was so frustrated what had we put ourselves through again?!

Penalties! Again! I was one of the takers – and once more I would take the third penalty. I felt we were focused, unnerved. They were carrying the expectations of the whole of Russia on their backs. They missed the first shot – that is, Subašić saved. Brozović scored in reply. Then they scored, and Akinfeev saved Mateo Kovačić's penalty. We were back to the start. But Fernandes, who had levelled the score in extra time and taken the game to penalties, missed the goal entirely. Now it was my turn. It was a bit easier than against Denmark, especially because we had the advantage on account of their miss. I aimed low and left, but Akinfeev dived quickly, flew to the side and got a hand on the ball. The ball hit the post, rebounded, and looked like it would bounce out. For a fraction of a second, I stopped dead in my tracks, petrified, but out of the corner of my eye I saw

Subašić. He was standing parallel to the goal line and waiting his turn, and now he threw his arms into the air. When I saw the ball settling in the net, I threw my arms into the air too. We had the advantage. No one was going to miss anymore. Vida scored a fantastic penalty. And Rakitić?! What can you say about him? Those were his moments. He routinely placed the ball in the net for yet another decisive penalty kick and we were free to celebrate once again. Croatia were in the semi-final!

Our Russian hosts greeted us in the hotel upon our return from the stadium. They applauded – just like the fans at the stadium, even though overcome by sadness for their team and their missed opportunity. Wonderful people!

The party went on: there was singing, dancing, unbridled joy. Total euphoria. Our mobile phones were once again on fire from all the messages. There was no need to check the video messages – we knew that Croatia was burning; everyone was on the streets. I almost felt like crying from happiness, but we needed to sing, to celebrate.

I'll never get over Euro 2008 and those sad, sad minutes at Prater Stadium in Vienna. Just as I will never forget that goal in the 120th minute and the penalties – it is the sorest wound of my whole career. Back then, just like today, I was convinced we were ready to fight for the title. But how could I have said that after everything that had happened? Who would've taken me seriously? Ten years later, there was no need to say anything: Croatia were FIFA World Cup semi-finalists. Just like in 1998! It took some time to realise this was real and not a dream!

England

We now moved to Moscow. Even before the match against Russia, we knew we would play against England if we made the semi-final. They were a team to watch; it was a different England, young and full of energy. I knew everyone wanted tickets. Luckily, Vanja was once again there to take care of things. She prepared the list, organised the trip and it was up to me to make sure everyone got their ticket. I needed more than 100, but it was a miracle I managed to get even 50. My family and closest friends would be by my side. That meant a lot. Vanja arrived with Ivano and Ema; we were finally together. I hadn't spent any time with my children since Madrid, when I was packing my bags to join the team.

We didn't have much free time. There were three days left before the match against England. After dinner, we had a couple of hours to spend with our families, and then the team retreated into the quiet of our separate floor in the hotel. We were exhausted, and there was little time to recover. We weren't as nervous as we had been before the match against Denmark. We had qualified for the semi-final and now we had two chances to fight for the medals. We had already exceeded all expectations, no matter what happened next. This made us calm and allowed us to form a clear picture of what we wanted to do. And that was to win!

We had played five matches in three weeks – if we add two periods of extra time, that's two-thirds of yet another match, plus the enormous pressure of two penalty shoot-outs. No other semi-finalist had had to go through this. We felt that price before playing England: Subašić, Lovren, Strinić, Perišić and Vrsaljko didn't train because of their injuries. Mandžukić did, against our medical team's advice. The night before the semi-final, Rakitić got a fever. And to make things worse, the morning before the match Rebić said he was unfit to play as his neck was stiff. The doctors and physios played their part – this was their match, so to speak, and their performance was simply phenomenal. They pulled off a miracle and managed to patch everyone up enough to play. Vrsaljko was in the worst condition – his knee had been troubling him for a while and during the championship the pain was unbearable. Luckily, he's as tough as they get, one of the Zadar boys, and he doesn't give up. I told him, 'You've got to bite the bullet and do whatever it takes, this is a once-in-a-lifetime opportunity!' He knew what was at stake, and he held out to the very end.

Coach Dalić revealed his idea for England: a 4-4-2 diamond formation. That meant one striker out, and an extra midfielder in. We had our reservations, to say the least. Dalić wanted to bring in Mateo Kovačić and leave Ivan Perišić on the bench. His rationale was that this would make us stronger in the middle, allowing us to retain possession. I told Dalić I thought we were able to control the midfield with three players. England played in a 3-5-2 formation, with two advanced full-backs high. If we had no wingers, their players would attack along the sides and create pressure, and we would have no means to fight back. Their formation exposed their flanks. We needed fast wingers who could take advantage of that fact, especially on the right side where Ashley Young, at 33 years of age, had a hard time keeping up. Perišić and Ante Rebić were key players for our attacks. Dalić accepted my suggestion – he felt that the players were behind Perišić even though his performances had not been at his usual level. Perisic is a beast, sometimes a bit sleepy, but when he wakes up, there's no holding him back. We had to wait for him; we had no alternative. Ivica Olić, Dalić's assistant and once a winger just like Perišić, shared our faith.

Making it into the FIFA World Cup semi-final had us psyched. The English pundits and commentators only made our resolve stronger. They openly underestimated us, and their lack of respect only made us more motivated. The England team and their manager, Gareth Southgate, were respectful and showed true sportsmanship. As we did for them. England's performances in Russia were excellent. With Raheem Sterling, Harry Kane and Marcus Rashford they were a team fast up front, young and energetic. They had a good midfield and defence – but ours, I was convinced, was better. England is a great nation, and a great team. The coach had chosen his team well, creating a homogenous squad – and after a long time, England seemed ready for big things. Time is on their side. But in this match, we were convinced we could beat them.

The bus takes us to Luzhniki Stadium. The anticipation and excitement are palpable. Everyone keeps to themselves: headphones on, music playing. The atmosphere in the dressing room is positive. We are focused; we cheer each other on. Croatian music blares from the speakers. During the warm-up, I search for my family and friends in the stands, as do other players. We know where their seats are, and we make them out in the distance. We wave at each other; they're all here, which gives us an extra boost of energy. There are a lot of people from Croatia, which gives us strength. We forget all the troubles, injuries, fevers, tiredness. This is a battle for the final.

The match starts badly – for us. In the fifth minute, I try to stop Dele Alli, who tries to break through. The referee awards a free-kick in the dangerous zone. Kieran Trippier steps up and curls the ball above the wall and into the top right corner, just where the post and the bar meet. England celebrate; they are off to a fantastic start. We are shaken, but we keep going forward. Still, they have another chance – Kane gets one-on-one against Danijel Subašić. If he scores, they'll have a 2–0 lead. Fortunately, he misses. Once again, fate won't let us have this easily. Had we fallen two goals behind, it would've been almost impossible to come back into the match. As time moves on, our game gets better. It's vital we keep possession – our passing is better, we spend less energy. In the second half, our dominance grows, we feel the goal is in the air. And then, in the 68th minute, Šime Vrsaljko crosses the ball deep, Perišić spreads his wings, goes behind Trippier, masterfully pokes his leg out, and the ball is in the net! The goal not only levels the score, it rattles England. The tide has turned. We dictate the pace; no one can say we're feeling the effects of having played so much more time than the England players. Our extra work in the training camp, during preparations and even before at our clubs, now comes into play. We are ready. Adrenaline does the rest and, among other things, eases the pain of our injured players. The match goes to extra time – our third match in a row. By now, we have played the equivalent of one match more than anyone else at the World Cup. We're taking the game to them. We assert our dominance in the first half of extra time and, in the 109th minute, the ball somehow reaches Mario Mandžukić, who makes no mistake and rifles in a left-footed shot! We're beside ourselves with happiness. A bundle of players topples over on a Mexican photographer just behind the goal. Our players hug and kiss him as they help him up to his feet. He's our good-luck charm!

By the second half of extra time, we're exhausted. Dalić brings Mandžukić off in the 115th minute. I watch him, the tank, leave the pitch; he's so tired he can barely walk. If this man, who can run non-stop for two straight days, has been so battered, I can only imagine what it is like for the rest. England drill their crosses into our box, but time is running out. Dalić brings on Vedran Ćorluka – he's fresh and experienced and gives us added height. In the 119th minute, I'm being replaced too. I'm drained; Milan Badelj comes on. These last tense moments are even harder to watch from the bench. We are two-on-one when Andrej Kramarić storms into the penalty box – two defenders run to block him, and Perišić is completely alone in front of the goal. All he has to do is push it to Perišić, but Kramarić goes for goal, at a terrible angle, and the ball goes wide! Perišić goes completely mad – we're all angry because this could have been the end of it. Now we're on tenterhooks. After the match, it's lucky for him that we're in a good mood, as we tell him, 'If we'd conceded, we would've killed you!'

The referee adds four more minutes. That's too much I complain to the fourth official, who tells us to calm down. How can we calm down? We're one step away from football glory. Who's going to survive those extra four minutes?! And then Marcelo Brozović takes the ball and makes a run toward the England goal, but there's the final whistle! It's over! For the first time, Croatia will play in the World Cup Final!

The Final

After the final whistle I stay on the pitch, taking my time to enjoy the view of the stands. It's taken 12 years of playing in Croatia's shirt to see this. It's the moment I've hoped for since I was 13 years old and watched the generation that came third in the world. This is where my career and my story as a footballer reaches its conclusion. I've won everything with Real. I'm playing with Croatia in the FIFA World Cup Final. No matter how it ends, I feel I have accomplished what I hoped for.

But is this possible? Am I dreaming? Is this real? I clasp my face and watch the joy around me. *The most important football match in the world will be played on Sunday, and we are going to be on the pitch!* I need another moment to make sure this is real.

I congratulate the England players, although I know they're devastated. At such moments, you just want to get away from everyone and lick your wounds alone. Gareth Southgate is a true gentleman – he comes up to me and congratulates me on our victory.

I shake hands with Danny Rose and Kyle Walker, we swap shirts. We always get a set of shirts, and I kept one from all the matches in Russia. I have the shirts of almost all the opposition teams I ever played against in my career. I love such mementos. One day, each of those shirts is going to tell a story and revive the moment in which I received it.

The only set I didn't want to exchange with anyone is the one from the final. It's going to tell a special story. When we're talking about our memorable chequered shirts and kits, I have to say that the lighter red and white combination is exceptional. But I have a liking for the darker kit because, for some reason, it's brought us more success.

Soon, I feel slightly nervous. I look for Vanja and the kids, but I can't find them. This is the greatest moment of my career, I want them by my side. When we get into the dressing room – it's complete madness in there – I make a call to see where they are, and I'm already a little worried because they don't answer. Finally, Vanja calls back. She explains they had to leave before the end of the match because they had a flight for Zagreb and the traffic was terrible. I'm angry and sad, both at the same moment. I'm so sorry they weren't with me down there on the pitch. But Vanja had to take care of our families and friends, and then fly to Moscow and back to Zagreb with two children. She's also sad it turned out this way, but there was nothing else she could do.

The dressing room is full of smiling faces. Everyone comes down to congratulate us. There's Zvonimir Boban, a FIFA official at the time, and we fall into each other's arms. Here we are, 20 years after France: the captain who led the team to the bronze medal, and I, the captain of the team that will come back home with at least a silver around our necks.

A new party at the hotel. What else?! It's crowded; it feels like we're back home in Croatia. Families, girlfriends, friends, delegations. Everyone is singing, dancing – total madness! There's no sleeping tonight anyhow. I try to close my eyes sometime before morning, but I can't. The semi-final match replays itself in my head over and over again and gives me no peace. A sweet distraction, if there ever was one.

The next day is always special. After a couple of hours of restless sleep, realising everything has been real brings true pleasure. Surprisingly, I don't feel tired. My mood is too good to feel any pain in my body. There are three days until the final. The French have played the equivalent of almost one match less than us. And now, as it happens, they also have one day more to rest. That's what happens when everything is going your way. I check my other mobile phone – countless messages. I can't even read them all, let alone reply. I hope people will understand. Our heads are at the Luzhniki Stadium, in the final. I catch myself thinking we're so close to the world title. Honestly, I imagine myself and my teammates lifting the trophy into the air! What a moment that would be – for us, for Croatia, for anyone anywhere in the world supporting our team. There are a lot of people rooting for us; I can feel that most football aficionados are on our side. Celebrities and famous people around the world post messages on social networks and all of them have Croatia in their hearts. We're a small country, and people have a special emotion for underdogs who stand up against the big and the powerful. For a day at least, most of the world is on our side.

Training is there just to warm up the muscles. What is there to practise three days before the final, and 50 days from the beginning of the campaign, after six top-level matches within 25 days? Zlatko Dalić sticks to tradition: it's the young players against the old. Before the first match against Nigeria, the young won. Then we beat Nigeria. That's why we let them win all the matches until the end of the tournament! Why test our luck?! Alright, I'm not superstitious but have to be objective and say the younger teammates were more energetic, they wanted to prove themselves. We did cut them some slack, but not too much. Before the first match, there were some tensions. The training session didn't go as planned; it seemed we were too relaxed. We practised keeping possession. Three-against-three. Ante Rebić entered a tackle lightly and lost the ball. I raised my voice: 'What's up with that?!' His reaction was positive, and he immediately got serious. I'm always like that. When something is not right, I make myself heard. I get angry in Madrid when I see someone is not giving their best in training, and I let them know.

At UEFA Euro 2016, before the first match against Turkey, Milan Badelj and Darijo Srna quarrelled. Badelj was fussing about with the ball in one play, and Srna told him, 'Keep it simple.' Badelj tried to explain himself, but I raised my voice and yelled at him: 'Why are you talking? Do what he told you and that's that!' To an outsider, this may seem like a problem, but such reactions are good before an important match – they're the signs of positive tension and rising adrenaline. There were similar tensions in Russia too. Before the match against Denmark, the young team played against the old and were beating us. This frustrated me, and at one moment I lost it. I tackled Andrej Kramarić, bumping into him so hard that he went up into the air and landed on the ground. That was uncalled for; I immediately apologised. But I also noticed a good thing: Kramarić didn't whine. His reaction was good; he took it and said nothing, wanting to get even on the pitch.

All of these are normal situations in a team. They show that the team is alive, that the adrenaline is flowing. On the eve of the final, the adrenaline was at boiling point anyhow.

I wasn't afraid of the French. I saw them as physically superior to us but when it came to technique, we had the upper hand. Their running was excellent; they showed a lot of strength. Their counter-attacks, with Kylian Mbappé up front, were deadly. Their set-pieces and their effectiveness had me worried – especially since this was our weak point. Despite everything, I felt we could beat them.

Dalić wanted us to be firm in our block, to keep possession, and to focus during set-pieces. More than once he stressed: 'Be careful when we have the ball because that's when they're most dangerous. They're looking for an opportunity to take the ball and develop a super-fast counter-attack in just a couple of passes.'

I slept well the night before the final. I got up early, around 8 a.m. I usually don't sleep much – I need six or seven hours of sleep and I'm fine. This time, I was a little anxious. After breakfast, I wanted to be alone in my room. As a rule, on matchday I don't like to talk to anyone, except Vanja. She called me to say everything was fine, the children were great. I talked to them for a while. It gave me energy. Countless messages kept coming. I didn't have time even to read them, but I did write back to my parents and my uncle Željko.

That Sunday in Moscow time goes by so slowly, even though the match starts at 5 p.m. In previous matches, we played in the evening. Lunch is at 1 p.m. We're all 100 per cent focused. We know everything, there's no need to talk. I can't sleep after lunch, during our mandatory rest. I just can't. I pick up something to read, just to kill time. Half an hour before we gather, I follow my warm-up programme. I use training bands to activate my muscles. We gather in the hall two hours before the match. The ride to the Luzhniki Stadium is extraordinary. Some say you see this once in your lifetime; it seems more likely that most players never see this. That's why I savour every moment. Police motorcycles escort us to the stadium, as if we're the most important people on the planet. You know that half of the world has come to a halt because of the match in which you are playing. It's an exceptional feeling.

The bus taking us to the most important match of our careers echoes with our motivational songs. Everyone prepares for what follows in their own way. The meeting about the line-up and the tactics takes place before noon. We watch video messages from Croatia of people sending their best wishes. Now we're full of energy and motivation. There's no room for anything else. We arrive at the stadium and, following our usual routine, we walk out onto the pitch. There's something special in this ritual, which allows you to feel the atmosphere of the match. The fans are already in the stadium. They're not holding back, their support is everything, you simply feel it. We know this day will go down in the history books. In the centre circle, I talk to Dejan Lovren, Domagoj Vida and Kovačić. They are my friends, my teammates, my comrades. We finally live with the realisation we've done something great for our country, albeit in our line of work. But when you watch the scenes from Croatia, you know it's huge. For everyone in Croatia, it's definitely bigger than football.

Our line-up is expected: Ivan Strinić was doubtful until the last moment but he's going to start. It's the World Cup Final, and that very fact lifts all the pain. Before the start, the doctors give me another shot. Since the matches against Denmark and Russia, my back hurts – it's a pinched nerve in my lower back. In the semi-final against England, they gave me a shot at half time. The shot was miraculous because it removed all the pain. In the dressing room, everything is as always: focus, cheering each other on. The only difference, an enormous difference, is that we're getting ready for the World Cup Final! The big TV screens are on. The camera pans around the stands, soaking in the atmosphere before the match. And then the shot shows my Ema! She's looking somewhere into the distance and eating a sandwich. She's relaxed and carefree as only a child can be. I'm moved when I see her. I can't wait to throw my arms around her, Ivano and Sofia. I can't wait to go back to Vanja and enjoy our time with the most important people in our lives.

Our moment has come. We come out onto the pitch in the World Cup Final! I've never felt such excitement. I almost shiver as I glance around the packed stands. I soak in the incredible atmosphere. I try to remember all the details. One day, when I'm older, I'll recall these moments. Whenever the Croatian anthem is played, I'm overcome by the feeling of incredible pride. Every time our anthem plays is special. This time, I know the whole world is listening and watching. Later, we'll learn 1.3 billion people watched the final live, and the World Cup had a total of 3.5 billion viewers. Literally half of mankind. Unbelievable!

When the anthem finishes, I immediately focus on the game. We open the match well and soon take the initiative. We keep possession, pass well – the balance between the teams is even. France create no chances. And then, out of nothing – a disaster. Néstor Pitana, the match referee, awards France a free-kick, although there was no contact between Marcelo Brozović and Antoine Griezmann. The French player dived, and the referee fell for it. To add insult to injury, Griezmann whips a free-kick into the penalty area and the ball flicks off Mario Mandžukić's head and ends up in the top corner of our goal! What horror in the 18th minute – and once again, just like against Denmark, Russia and England, we have to chase the opponent's lead. I hope we will once again find the strength to turn the tide. Ten minutes later, my hopes come true when the ball floats into the French penalty box, Vida plays it back to Ivan Perišić, who skilfully transfers it to his left foot and drills a powerful shot into the net! We're back, and this time we're outplaying them everywhere.

But only 10 minutes pass and once again we concede out of nothing. Hugo Lloris' long ball seems like an easy one for Vida, but he misjudges and heads the ball out for a corner from 30 yards out. Griezmann takes the corner, and Blaise Matuidi at the near post misses the ball. Perišić is right behind him and the ball strikes his hand. The referee makes no call, which seems logical because Perišić did not handball deliberately – only our players were around, and this wasn't a chance for our opponent. The French players surround the referee and demand a penalty. The referee waits for the VAR check, and it seems to last forever. When, after 30 or 40 seconds, Pitana goes to check the replay, we know he is going to award a penalty. Maybe I'm subjective, but I would never make such a doubtful call in the World Cup Final. We're crushed. To come back into the match for the second time, after everything we've gone through at the World Cup, and against such a tough opponent – that's nearly impossible. The realisation that we have conceded from half-chances is simply devastating.

At half time, we're aware we're facing the toughest challenge possible. It's all or nothing, and France are most dangerous when they have the lead. They have a fantastic counter-attack with Mbappé and Griezmann – as well as Olivier Giroud, who is excellent at holding up play and bringing his teammates into the game. His importance for France is often overlooked. Perhaps that's understandable because the Mbappé–Griezmann tandem attracts all the attention because they're fast, direct – and deadly.

It's understandable that Didier Deschamps opted for this style of play. At the World Cup, they played to win, they didn't care about impressions. Two years before, they'd lost the European Championship Final played on their home turf, and the wound was still sore. Back then, France played a more attractive style of football. In Russia, they were pragmatic: a firm block in front of their defence, using their counter-attack to cynically punish their opponents.

Perhaps we should have had a Plan B. When we levelled, perhaps it would've been better if we had allowed them possession, closed down in a firm block, and waited for counter-attacks. But we kept attacking after Perišić's goal; we thought our domination could bring us success. Of course, when everything is over, it's easy to theorise and think about what could've happened.

We cheer each other on in the dressing room, and Dalić tells us to keep it up because we are playing well. But in the 59th minute, France's third goal crushes our hopes. It's yet another counter-attack – Paul Pogba delivers a fantastic throughball for the oncoming Mbappé. He lays it back into the middle and, in a move similar to our goal, Griezmann finds Pogba, whose first shot is blocked, only for the ball to come back out to him, and he fires a left-footed shot into the net! We haven't even recovered, and it's then 4–1, following a powerful 25-yard effort by the new phenomenon called Mbappé. It's too much of a punishment considering what both teams have shown. But that's football. We're not giving up, we keep attacking, and Mandžukić forces Lloris into a mistake and slots the ball into the net for 4–2. We have no strength for more.

France have been stronger, and they are deservedly crowned the World Champions – for the second time in their history. Our destinies are interconnected: when Croatia won the bronze back in 1998, it was France who stopped us in the semi-final. They won their first title as hosts. Two decades later, we are in the final, and once again they are the team stopping us, one step away from the most beautiful dream.

At the final whistle, we were utterly exhausted. I fell to my knees, as did many of my teammates. We had given it everything we had. We were so disappointed, but as the minutes wore on, we became more and more aware we should be proud and we should celebrate. What we did in Russia was sensational, historic.

CHAPTER TEN

The heavy rain at the Luzhniki Stadium seems to want to wash away our sorrow and make room for joy. As we walk down the tunnel, the reporter from Croatian National Television stops me. I say a couple of words into the camera, and once again there's a lump in my throat. I break down. The reporter realises what state I'm in and lets me go.

In the dressing room, we soon become aware we have accomplished something we should be happy about, not sad. Vladimir Putin comes into the room and shows us great respect. We are taking photos with countless people who are there with us; we pose with our medals; the laughter and the music grow louder.

We go back to the hotel. The members of our families are there and we have dinner together. The euphoria is growing. That great master of parties, the Croatian singer Mladen Grdović, is responsible for the atmosphere. The party goes on until 5 a.m. We are all there. And then, one by one, we retreat to our rooms. I try to close my eyes for a couple of hours before going back to our homeland. Sleep evades me. I watch the scenes from Croatia once again – I see happiness on people's faces; they turned moments of defeat into hours of celebration. This is what lifted our spirits and encouraged us to do the same. It made no sense to be sad at the moment of our greatest triumph. And we *were* happy, perhaps as never before, though first we had to process the defeat quietly.

The atmosphere on the plane that's taking us back to Croatia after 35 days is lively and cheerful. We sing, take or pose for photos, give autographs. Everyone participates – the players, the coaches, the doctors, the physios, the technical staff, and Davor Šuker, the president of the Croatian Football Federation. I manage to fall asleep for another hour or so despite the noise – exhaustion catches up with me. But when we enter Croatian airspace, I wake up. The sight is magnificent: MiGs accompany our plane as a sign of special welcome. Before this, we could only guess what might happen. Soon we become aware that the party will be fit for World Champions. The atmosphere at the airport is impressive, but we can't wait to get to the main square. There, Croatia is waiting for us to appear, in person and in front of TV screens. As we board the open-top bus, we begin to realise something incredible is taking place. Along the way from the airport to the main square, which is about 16 kilometres, there are crowds of people! We're in shock. We expected the main square would be full, but we have never even dreamed the whole route would be full of delighted people. The police officers who accompany our bus tell us there are more than 200,000 people on the roads leading into the city. There are about 250,000 on the streets around the main square, and then another 110,000 in the square itself! That's about as much as it can fit!

We can't believe it, more than a half a million, in the scorching heat, patiently waiting to greet us. Tears keep coming to my eyes as I watch the old and the young, grandmas and grandpas, children and their parents waving at us, shouting in support, greeting us. It takes a surreal five-and-a-half hours from when the plane touches the runway until we climb the stage at Jelačić Square! The bus inches a way through roads and streets packed with people. We're all in a trance.

At the stage, we thank everyone in the square, as well as all of those who waited along the route. It's an incredible welcome. People have spent the whole day out in the sun waiting for this moment – they want to show how much joy we have brought them. I wonder if there's a greater happiness than what your own people can give you. No, there isn't! The manager and the players, we all say a couple of words and thank the fans. And it seems so little, far from enough to express our happiness and to describe the shivers that are running through us from so much positive energy. It's a welcome that goes beyond our wildest dreams. Croatia celebrates us as if we are the World Champions.

We sing songs we always sing in the national team, just as we did in Russia. These are the songs – such as *Lijepa li si, Moja domovina, Nije u šoldima sve (How Beautiful Are You, My Homeland, Riches Cannot Fill Your Heart)* – that inspired and motivated us, and that's why we invite Marko Perković Thompson, Mladen Grdović and the Croatian Navy Choir up to the stage. More than 100,000 fans sing along – they represent the whole of Croatia singing with us.

It was so emotional and unforgettable that even today, almost two years later, I get goosebumps. The crowd of people just in front of the stage waved at me and shouted, and I remember my young friend Petar, a boy with Down's syndrome, who waited for hours in the sun. He was a big fan of mine and he wanted to say hello. I invited him to join us on the stage and we sang together. He transferred his happiness and love to me, and I'm forever grateful. I know how much children love our team and that's why, whenever we can, we try to give back to them and thank them for the warmth and faith they have in us. During that fantastic welcome, meeting Petar was one of many gifts that the proud Croatian people offered to me.

After everything, sometime after midnight, we gathered at a restaurant. We had dinner and relaxed with a band until two or three in the morning. When I arrived home, I fell into a deep sleep.

The next day, Vanja, the children and I drove down to Zadar. Our hometown threw another amazing welcome for their silver medal winners: Danijel Subašić, Dominik Livaković, Šime Vrsaljko and I. It was spectacular. The boat took us along the town quay, where the whole of Zadar had gathered. I can't remember if there ever was such a party. All four of us were truly moved by this gesture. When the people from your hometown give you such a welcome, your heart brims with happiness. Proving yourself among your own is the toughest thing in the world, but when they accept you, you can be truly proud.

Three days later, I went to Istria for Vedran Ćorluka's wedding, so we had another reason to celebrate. And then, after a week with the family, we went on a cruise along the Adriatic. This finally allowed me to calm down and relax. But it was too short – I had to report back to Real Madrid early in August 2018. A couple of training sessions and four or five days later, I was about to play again, this time in Estonia for the European Super Cup final against local rivals Atlético Madrid.

Starting on the bench, I was brought on in the 57th minute, and the game finished 2–2 after 90 minutes, with Karim Benzema and Sergio Ramos scoring for us. That meant another extra time, where we lost 4–2. And so started my eighth season at Real, which turned out to be as turbulent as this match, with defeats and the atmosphere they generate.

I was mentally exhausted, physically drained and the strains of the fantastic World Cup had taken their toll. But it was worth it. It was so worth going through all of it.

From day one, Florentino Pérez was nothing but fair to me. The club kept their word and fulfilled every part of our agreement, and Pérez showed great respect for me, so I can say our relationship is great. I think he's an excellent president. With everything he does, in terms of the team's talent and quality, the club's marketing, building an impressive training camp and, most recently, initiating a spectacular reconstruction of Santiago Bernabéu, he constantly raises the club's standards. The trophies won under Pérez speak clearly about the team's success. And so, during that summer after the 2018 World Cup, when the story broke that I might be leaving Real, the president was brief and clear: 'Your place is at Real. And that's where you'll stay.'

Still under the influence of everything that had happened in Russia, and after long deliberation, I made another crucial decision. My great friends Danijel Subašić, Vedran Ćorluka and Mario Mandžukić announced that they would be taking off Croatia's shirt. They decided it was the right moment and they deserved to be seen off as heroes. I decided otherwise. Many people told me it was best to say goodbye at the moment of my biggest success. But my heart told me to stay. Playing for your national team is one of the most fulfilling experiences; I still want to feel it. I feel fit and motivated. It's true that in terms of my career wearing Croatia's shirt, retiring after the silver medal in Russia would have left the biggest impression – but I don't care much about impressions. Nothing, ever, can change the fact that we won the silver medal, just as nothing can erase everything that happened along the way. That's why I decided to stay at the team's disposal for as long as the manager thinks he needs me. Or until I realise I am no longer good enough to wear the shirt.

I'm convinced I can help younger players mature and gradually take on key roles. Having qualified for UEFA Euro 2020, I want to try and win it, and then conclude my career in the Croatia national team. No matter how it ends, as winners or not, it is going to be the most difficult moment of my entire career.

And the Awards Go To . . .

After the FIFA World Cup in Russia, a completely different football life began for me. Nothing was the same. The years of celebrations and success at Real were surpassed by Croatia's historic achievement in reaching the World Cup Final. Just before my 33rd birthday, I felt at peace – like a man who could say he had fulfilled his dreams. Actually, a man who had fulfilled all of his wildest football dreams. My 2018 achievement with Croatia was the crowning moment of my footballing career.

But as happens in life, after one great success, others sometimes follow. And so I had to find a place on my living-room shelf in Madrid for the Golden Ball award. This individual prize is given to the best player at the World Cup. Understandably, as the pinnacle individual award at the pinnacle football tournament, it has a special place in my heart.

In all honesty, I wasn't hungry for any more prizes. That was enough for me and I certainly wasn't preoccupied with all the other honours that were yet to follow. I had won the 2018 UEFA Champions League with Real and come second in the world with Croatia. I was voted the Best Player of the World Cup. What else did I need?

I travelled to Monaco, where the award ceremony for UEFA Player of the Year took place, in the company of Keylor Navas and Sergio Ramos. Keylor was voted the Best Goalkeeper of the season, Sergio the Best Defender, and I won the award for the Best Midfielder. I was also nominated for the Best Men's Player. It was a nice feeling to come to the award ceremony and take a stroll on the red carpet. I ran into David Beckham and his wife Victoria. We shared a few laughs. He always seemed like a cool guy, open and simple. In the hall, I saw Liverpool's Mo Salah, we were seated close to one another, but I also saw that Cristiano Ronaldo wasn't there. Along with Salah and I, he had been nominated for the Best Player, but he was also supposed to be here because he had won the Best Forward award. When the UEFA president, Aleksander Čeferin, read my name in the category of the Best Men's Player, I felt more excited than I expected. I had relaxed a bit, but this recognition made me shiver once again. Literally, as I climbed to the stage, my knees buckled. It was my first award of this kind and I wasn't used to this main role. It meant I had to deliver a speech. In all fairness, speeches have never been my thing, let alone in front of all the football celebrities who had gathered in Monaco. Among them was the Real delegation, led by the president and club legends Emilio Butragueño and Roberto Carlos.

On occasions such as this, Real never fail to show how much they care about their players. Ronaldo didn't come, which provoked criticism in the media. It didn't bother me he wasn't there, even though I think he should've come to receive the award for the Best Forward. The next day, he sent me a message and congratulated me on the award. Right after the ceremony, we took the club plane back to Madrid because we had a La Liga match in two days.

Right away, the media started talking about me being a contender for the Ballon d'Or – football's most prestigious prize. I hadn't thought much about it and, to be perfectly honest, I thought the trophy awarded by France Football would go to someone from France, considering that they had won the World Cup. But I did think I could perhaps win the Best FIFA Men's Player Award. *You never know,* I told myself while the media heated up the story of whether, after a decade of domination, the rule of Cristiano Ronaldo and Lionel Messi would come to an end. But I didn't pay much attention to such stories; it's not my thing. I play football because I love it and I consider myself a part of the team. If what I bring to the team is recognised as something special, fine. If not, that's fine too. What matters to me is that my teams are successful.

FIFA people soon informed me that I was among the three players nominated for the Best Award. They also told me that FIFPro and FIFA had selected me for the World 11 of the year, and this made me look forward to the trip to London. I took Vanja and the kids with me. London is our city and we have some wonderful memories of it. It was a pleasure to meet so many famous faces from the past and present of world football. I ran into Zinédine Zidane for the first time since he had left Real. I was glad we could talk for a bit. It's nice when you feel that this legend – which Zidane undoubtedly is – is happy you accomplished so much at the World Cup.

When I went to find my seat, I noticed that the chair reserved for Ronaldo was empty. He hadn't come. Neither had Messi. Both of them were supposed to receive the awards as members of the World 11. Before the ceremony there had been a lot of talk about whether they were going to show up or not. To be perfectly honest, I was so thrilled to be announced the Best Player of 2018 that I didn't bother asking why they hadn't come. I climbed onto the stage and with great pride received the trophy from the hands of Gianni Infantino, FIFA president. I had prepared a couple of sentences to say in case I won. But, when I got on the stage, something else entirely came out of me and I think this was what made it one of my better speeches. I even managed to make Zvonimir Boban cry! The excitement was at its peak, and I think I found the best answer to the question of which language to use to thank everyone for this great honour. I wanted to send a universal message – *Thank you all!* – in English, Spanish and Croatian. I was truly honoured by personal compliments from football legends including El Fenómeno, one of my all-time favourites – Ronaldinho, and Didier Drogba. Some of the highest Real Madrid officials, led by Florentino Pérez, were by my side, which made me immensely proud. I felt like one of the greats and I understood, finally, how Messi and Ronaldo had felt in the past 10 years sharing this honour. When all is said and done, I was sorry they weren't part of that unforgettable evening when I received the great privilege of putting an end to a decade of their domination. I think it would've been much more elegant if they had showed up, even if they did not win. This would have shown respect for all the people who had voted for them in the past, but also for the footballing movement as a whole – the movement they lead as players. Because the two of them truly are special. They brought their unique talent into the game and made it even more spectacular. I learned later that Messi voted for me – and I saw this as a great player's recognition of my tremendous season.

Just when I thought all the celebrations and fantastic recognitions had come to an end – there came the icing on the cake! People from France Football called me to say I was among the three candidates for the Ballon d'Or! They also told me they would inform me a week before the ceremony, to give me details about protocol in the event of winning. That was the first time I actually thought, 'Could I really win the Ballon d'Or?!' The very idea gave me goosebumps. But, realistically, how could I win against all of the French players, World Champions? And as a midfielder at that? How many fantastic midfield players, such as Andrés Iniesta, Xavi, Andrea Pirlo, Francesco Totti, had failed to win this prestigious award? How many fantastic players in general – Zlatan Ibrahimović, for example – never had the honour?

It was Monday, 19 November, 2018, and I had just woken up. After the match against England in the UEFA Nations League, I was staying with Vanja in London. I had a day off. I was still in bed, rolling around, when I remembered that France Football was supposed to call today. Or not. I washed my face, got dressed and I was about to have breakfast. My mobile phone rang. I recognised the number – it was the director of France Football – and I froze instantly. I was beside myself because everything indicated I had won the Ballon d'Or. But maybe he'd dialled the wrong number? Maybe he just wanted to tell me he was sorry, but someone else had won the Ballon d'Or instead? I decided not to pick up. Let the hope last for just another second. I didn't think I would feel such an adrenaline rush, especially after the awards I had received from UEFA and FIFA. But the Ballon d'Or is special, magical. There's a long tradition behind it and it brings to mind all the legends who have won this tremendous trophy.

I looked for Vanja, who was having a shower, and I told her, 'They called. France Football called.'

'And what do they say?' she replied and I recognised the excitement in her eyes.

'I didn't pick up,' I said. It was completely insane, obviously.

'Why?! Go call them back.' Vanja was as composed as always.

'Wait, wait a minute, I need to calm down.'

By this time, I was slowly losing it, but after five or six minutes, I finally dialled the number. Pascal Ferré, the director of France Football, answered and said:

'Luka, congratulations, you won the 2018 Ballon d'Or! I'm happy for you, and I'm happy a player such as yourself has won the Ballon d'Or. Your personality and your performances truly deserve this award!'

I listened and wondered if this was really happening.

'You're first, by a wide margin. No one is even near you. I congratulate you once again and I look forward to meeting you soon.'

I was in heaven. I told Vanja what Pascal had said. Our eyes filled with tears. This was the cherry on top – the Ballon d'Or to make the perfect 2018. We fell into each other's arms: a long, firm embrace. We had reached this moment together. It was our miracle. I had to call my parents, even though Pascal told me not to tell anyone. I wanted to share this perfect moment with my dad, especially with him. And it was as if he knew.

'You earned it, son, you earned it. And it would've been unfair if they'd given it to someone else!' That's all he managed to say before he started crying.

Florentino Pérez called and said, 'Congratulations, Luka, you deserve it!'

Vanja and I were in London with Mateo Kovačić and his wife Izabel. We often spend time together. I love Mateo like my kid brother. We grew close during our three-and-half years together at Real. He's a great guy and a fantastic player. Despite our close friendship, I succeeded in the toughest mission of the day – hiding my euphoria. Not being allowed to reveal the fantastic news of winning the Ballon d 'Or to anyone was tough. I didn't know where I was from all the excitement.

The award ceremony in Paris, at the splendid Grand Palais Hall, was magnificent. David Ginola, the host and once a Tottenham legend, was very kind and warm: 'Congratulations, Luka, I'm happy for you! You earned it!'

Didier Deschamps, an excellent coach and a true gentleman, came up to me and congratulated me. His words were honest and kind. Many gave me their compliments, and I savoured every moment. My family and closest friends were in the audience. Naturally, all of the Real officials were there. After the official party, we had dinner together.

In the morning, we took a plane back to Madrid. The players were in training, but Santiago Solari moved the practice so that I could arrive on time.

I arrived at Valdebebas, Real's training complex, with the Ballon d'Or trophy. As I walked into the dressing room, about a dozen players were receiving treatment from the physios. But when they saw me, they went crazy, and gave me a standing ovation. They applauded for more than a minute. It was impressive and touching at the same time. To be honest, I didn't expect it and I was a bit embarrassed. I think I even blushed. The guys showed me how sincerely happy they were for me. Is there a bigger recognition than that? Then we all took photos together with my newest trophy. Had it not been for my teammates from Real Madrid and my teammates from Croatia, I would never have experienced my perfect 2018. The year finished with yet another FIFA Club World Cup trophy with Real, which meant that the golden circle begun at the same tournament a year before had now closed. It's incredible what happened in those 365 days. The crowning moments of my career.

In this book, I've tried to describe how all of this happened. I don't know if I've succeeded. Perhaps most important is the fact that despite all the obstacles before me, I had enough persistence and confidence to overcome all of them. Every one of us has their own path. Every story is as different as we are as players and people. But the foundation of every success is the belief in yourself, even when someone tells you, 'There's no point.' There's always a point, trust me. I have already been told that, after reaching my zenith at 33 years of age and after becoming the best player in the world, playing for the best club and for the national team that came second in the world, I would not be able to play at the same level. This has only given me the motivation to show this up as a prejudice – one of the many that have followed me in my life and my career. But my biggest motive, the one that led me from the first training session until today, is my unconditional love for football. This love is the reason I'm going to play for as long as my feet can carry me and the ball will listen to me. And I'll continue to give it everything I've got.

I know it won't be simple. I know my career has always taken the more difficult road, but, in the end, I reached the top. Staying on it is difficult, but I know from experience – the best things in life never come easy.

. . . ONE MORE THING

At the end of anything, there's always one more thing to say. Maybe that's because every end also marks the beginning of something new.

It's been, well, two years since I concluded the story told in this book. In other contexts, I'd say 'just' two years, but in the life of an athlete and a footballer this is a long time. Especially when you reach my age, and I'm close to 35, the passing of time carries a lot of weight.

Two years ago, thinking of what could happen next, several scenarios seemed possible. I had long wished to bring my career to an end at Real Madrid, at least the part of it colloquially called 'top-level football'. By signing the contract that would keep me at Real until 2021, which the club had offered after the FIFA World Cup, I made the most important step towards fulfilling that goal. I knew from previous years and players that it was a rarity for veteran players of my age (back then I was 33) to extend their contract for more than one year. So, when the club offered to renew my existing deal, due to expire in 2020, for another season, I saw it as a sign of recognition and respect. Not because the new contract included clauses that fitted the status of the world's best player, the title I claimed after winning the Ballon d'Or in 2018, but precisely because this had not been the custom at Real for the past several decades. It was an indication of how highly they thought of me. Even though, in the footballing world, it is unwise to make predictions a year in advance, let alone longer, I was convinced that I would bring my top-level footballing years to an end wearing Real's shirt. No one, including me, can tell what will happen in the summer of 2021. I don't have a crystal ball to predict what direction my professional or personal life is going to take. Will something change at Real after the summer of 2021? I really don't know. But what I'm certain about is that I'm going to stay here until my contract expires. Then we'll go on from there.

The last two years have confirmed what I learned a long time ago: in football, nothing is certain. When at the end of May 2018 we lifted our third consecutive UEFA Champions League trophy, I couldn't have imagined that our great team would undergo such huge changes. Zinédine Zidane suddenly left. Cristiano Ronaldo left too. Without them, that great generation was not the same. However, I was convinced that the quality of Real's team with its exceptional accumulation of talent would follow a similar path of success under the helm of the new coach, Julen Lopetegui.

Unfortunately, it wasn't to be. The team ran into a rough patch and, as often happens, the coach was the one who paid for it. I always feel sorry for the coaches when they get replaced; it's human to put yourself in their shoes. Coaching Real Madrid is a dream, and just when you realise it has become your reality, the burden of the club's constant ambition and search for the very top begins to weigh you down. If the results are not there, it simply eats you alive. Lopetegui was doing a solid job, but in October when we recorded three defeats in a row, the third of which came in *El Clásico* where we lost 5-1, it was clear he wouldn't survive the pressure. He was replaced by Santiago Solari, another former Real Madrid player, and things took a better turn. Results improved, and seemed promising for the club's ambitions. Unfortunately, however, by March 2019 we had dropped out of the race for trophies on all fronts. In La Liga, we were in third place, far behind top-of-the-table Barcelona. Our great rival eliminated us from the Copa del Rey too, while our ambition to save the season through the Champions League was shattered by Ajax in the Round of 16.

I realised then that we were in for a long and depressing finish to the season. There's nothing worse for Real than not being able to fight for a trophy. However, a new shock was in store: less than a year since his departure, Zidane returned to the dugout. Everyone on the team was caught by surprise and I think his return lifted our spirits. In terms of results, we responded well, but as time went by, our form once again dropped, and it seemed that the end of the 2018/2019 campaign would be just as bleak as its beginning. The most successful year in my career had been followed by a season of disappointments. I was having a hard time dealing with it, although realistically that's how it goes – in football and in life. After a calm comes a storm, and then a calm again, and then …

The summer of 2019 finally brought a real, long vacation. I needed it badly; I felt exhausted from all the excitements of 2018. I was feeling the toll of all the strain, stress, elation after the unique success of winning the third consecutive European title, after the fantastic World Cup with Croatia, after all the recognition and awards and the pressure to prove my worth at the highest levels.

I received several transfer offers during that summer. But for me, from day one Real Madrid was the first and only option. There was a lot of media speculation about the arrival of new players and my status in the team on account of my age. They said I was among the players whose position was in jeopardy. I never feared competition – on the contrary, it motivated me to be even better than before. What mattered most was to be healthy and ready when the coach offered me a chance. I knew I would prove my worth. When I was on vacation, I talked to Zidane on the phone. He told me I was an essential part of his plans; he couldn't have been clearer when he said this, and for me that was it. We started a new season in which we had some brilliant performances and runs, but also some rough patches. By March, despite being knocked out of the Copa del Rey, Real were still in the race for the European and Spanish championship titles. No one could have imagined what happened next – not only when it came to football, but life in general. A nightmare.

We knew a new virus epidemic had broken out in China, but to be perfectly honest, we didn't pay much attention. It wasn't the first time that the world had learned about a new virus, and it always seemed that those epidemics posed no real threat for Europe. When we went to Saudi Arabia to compete in the Spanish Super Cup, there was word that some players wouldn't be allowed to go because they had flu-like symptoms, and that's when I learned more about the coronavirus. But we were far from worried at that time – we weren't aware of what it was, nor did we know what it could, and unfortunately would, bring. In the two matches we played in Jeddah, we beat Valencia and Atlético Madrid to win the Spanish Super Cup. It was my 16th trophy with Real. I was really happy because we'd put in some wonderful performances, and I had scored my 100th career goal – to secure a 3-1 win against Valencia. It was one of the most beautiful goals I have scored in my career: receiving the ball just inside the area, I performed a stepover before using the outside of my right foot to curl the ball into the bottom corner. The perfect finish to a great game and victory.

Two months later – what a shock it was – we learned that all football activities were to be suspended! COVID-19 brutally attacked Europe and changed our lives completely. Everything we had been used to, our everyday lives, which we thought nothing could ever change, suddenly came to a halt. I remember when they told us we had to stay indoors and were not allowed to leave our homes. It seemed surreal. Stay in, avoid other people, and no football – is this possible or am I having a bad dream? Unfortunately, unfortunately (how many times will I repeat this word?), it was real. It seemed as if someone had suddenly pushed a button and turned our lives upside down. Living to see football stop in the middle of the season, around the world, is simply surreal. No matches, no practice, no hanging out with your teammates; you need to lock yourself within your four walls and wait for better days.

Leaving aside the bizarre situation football found itself in, reality soon became immensely more brutal than the first experience of concern, fear for your family, the uncertainty of where this pandemic would lead.

Coronavirus spread everywhere, but after Italy, it was Spain that became Europe's virus hotspot. The consequences were devastating.

The way I've experienced this pandemic and, as much as I can tell from the press, the way many other people have too, is as the decisive moment of our era. Not only because the world literally came to a standstill, but also because the virus caused immeasurable damage, made our lives more difficult and our future more complicated. This is a historic moment in which it seems some omnipotent power decided we had to stop. All of us. It forced us to re-examine our behaviour – we have to become aware of all the damage we are inflicting upon nature and ourselves, we have to change the way we treat each other and the way we understand life. Each and every one of us, within our families and communities, in our respective lines of work, is creating a system of values according to which we live.

If the coronavirus pandemic hadn't happened, would we have ever had a chance to reset? Who would have managed, and how, to put aside time for this opportunity, when life at the beginning of the third millennium was moving at the speed of a Formula One race?

I don't think I have ever before had to spend two months within the confines of my own home. This was a first. I spent those two months with Vanja and our children, and I feel we made the most of it. In the beginning I'd thought the quarantine would be long and monotonous, but to my surprise, time passed quickly. In the mornings, we helped Ivano and Ema with their online school, and later worked with them on their homework. Sofia, our youngest, demanded the regime of fun and constant care typical of a two-and-a-half-year-old. We spent a lot of time together, cooking, talking to each other, playing all kinds of games. I can boast that I learned to make pancakes and the kids really enjoyed them. I made frequent video calls to my family and friends back in Croatia. Unfortunately, on top of the pandemic, Croatia, or specifically our capital city Zagreb, was hit by a devastating earthquake! But our people back home responded with courage and promptly got to grips with the new situation. At the moment when it was vital to stay at home and protect themselves from the virus, many Zagreb families lost the roof over their heads.

My homeland, as always in times of trouble, responded in a way that made us all proud. Great unity was shown. Institutions took care of those who had lost their homes. People jumped to help each other. Even while Zagreb was still shaking, they organised themselves, they helped at hospitals and wherever it was needed, just as was the case when the pandemic broke out. Athletes initiated humanitarian actions and made donations to help fight coronavirus and to help Zagreb. Solidarity is one of the biggest qualities of the Croatian people. In this difficult period, our people showed great responsibility and strictly followed the instructions prescribed by the National Civil Protection Directorate. Together with our doctors, epidemiologists, nurses and all the other services standing at the frontline of the battle against the virus, who selflessly and despite great risk of infection worked day and night to help people, this discipline allowed Croatia to emerge as one of the countries that offered the best response to the challenges of the pandemic. I'm immensely proud of my compatriots. And, when I think about it, this story – about solidarity, humanity, unity, order, respect towards institutions and rules – seems to offer a framework for the struggle against the pandemic around the world. As I've said before, it feels that this is a reminder to all of us, a reminder that humanity needs to reorganise; that we need to move forward with more real values in life.

But, let me go back to football. Every day of the quarantine I trained, following the programme the club and my personal trainer had developed for me. I have the privilege of having a house with a big yard, lots of greenery and space to train. I also have a well-equipped fitness room within the house. My work was really intensive and to a schedule. But what surprised me was the level of my motivation, which was at a maximum, despite the constant uncertainty about when our activities would resume. It never crossed my mind to stop and ask: 'What's the point in training this hard if, for example, they decide we won't play until the autumn?' Far from it, my desire to train, to go back to the ball, only grew stronger day by day – I just missed working with the team, playing matches, spending time with my teammates. I've always loved football, but now, on the cusp of my 35th birthday, I love it more than ever. And I'm even more certain I will actively play for as long as I feel this fire, and for as long as my legs will serve me.

On the day I wrote this, the club called. We begin training again, first individually and then in groups. Football is coming back! It's a hopeful sign that life is beginning to normalise. They say we'll have to live with the virus until scientists discover a vaccine. But now we're going to be stronger because we – all of us, I hope – have learned an important lesson: that nature and life will respect us, as long as we respect them.

ACKNOWLEDGEMENTS

2018 brought me the most beautiful and most emotional moments of my career. With my teammates at Real Madrid and the Croatia national team, I made all of my childhood dreams come true. Even more than that. I won the fourth UEFA Champions League with Real, and then, right after that, Croatia won the silver medal at the FIFA World Cup in Russia. These were sensational accomplishments that culminated on a personal level with the most prestigious awards for the Best Player in Europe and the world. All of this left a lasting impression on me and it filled me with pride and happiness. And this is why I felt the need to write a book about everything that came before this magnificent year. Along the way were moments of happiness, hardship, sadness, suffering, joy; there were all kinds of moments, such as everyone has to go through. This made me who I am, as a person and as a football player. Each of us has the right to dream and to hope to make those dreams come true. Now that I have shared my story with you, I will be happy if it helps you always, even at the toughest of moments, to have faith and never give up on your goals. This is the mindset that helped me make my most beautiful dreams come true.

This book is my story, and there are many people who helped me tell it. First and foremost, I wish to thank my wife Vanja and our children. Besides bringing me joy, their support made it easier to write this book because it meant being away from them. Vanja's memories and recollections helped making this book. I wish to thank my parents, who were once again there for me, especially when it came to writing about my childhood and teenage years. I would also like to thank my loving sisters, and close friends and companions in the story of my life.

I am honoured and thankful to Sir Alex Ferguson and Zvonimir Boban for their forewords to this book. I am touched by their kind words.

Special contributions to this book came from Drago Sopta and the Croatian Football Federation, who gave their permission to use their photographs. I am thankful to them, just as I am grateful to Real Madrid, who gave their permission to use photo and video materials. I want to thank Antonio Villalba Calderon for the cover photo, as well as my dear teacher Maja Grbić, who saved my third-grade assignment and school photographs.

Special thanks go to two people who were by my side throughout the year of writing this book. Diana Matulić, my agent and publisher, and her team did a tremendous job and helped the project with their experience and knowledge.

Finally, I want to thank Robert Matteoni, who helped me put on to paper everything I considered important for my story, especially my emotions. They are the essence of every story.

AUTHOR BIOGRAPHIES

Luke Modrić (born Zadar, 1985) is a professional football player who plays as a midfielder for Real Madrid. He is also the captain of the Croatia national football team. Luka's footballing career began in Zadar, his hometown club, while he won his first titles with Dinamo Zagreb. After four years at Tottenham, he signed for Real Madrid, and playing with them he has won more than 15 trophies, culminating with four UEFA Champions League titles. Luka is considered one of the best midfielders of his generation and the greatest Croatian football player of all time. In 2018, he became the first footballer to win four prestigious individual player awards in a single year: Golden Ball for the Best Player of the FIFA World Cup; Best FIFA Men's Player; UEFA Men's Player of the Year; and the Ballon d'Or. Among his awards and trophies, there are also three European Super Cups; four FIFA World Cup Championship titles; UEFA Midfielder of the Season Award for his performances in the Champions League; the Best Midfielder UEFA Club Football Award; the FIFA Club World Cup Golden Ball; and the International Sports Press Association (AIPS) Athlete of the Year. He is married to Vanja (née Bosnić) and has three children. *My Autobiography* is Luka's first book.

Robert Matteoni (born Pula, 1962) is a columnist, writer and editor, and one of the most prominent sports journalists in Croatia. He played for Istra, and subsequently held office at a number of sports institutions. Robert got involved in sports journalism while still a footballer and soon became a professional sports reporter. He has worked with major Croatian newspapers and sports magazines, including *Večernji list* and *Vjesnik,* and for *Sportske novosti*, on whose editorial board he has sat since 2011. As both a reporter and commentator, he has followed the Croatia national football team since 1994, reporting from three FIFA World Cups and three UEFA European Championships. He has also followed Croatia in countless qualifiers and friendlies all around the world. Specialising in Italian football and European club competitions, he is a member of the International Sports Press Association (AIPS) and a member of the international jury for the Best FIFA Football Awards. In 2009, he received the Columnist of the Year Award given by the Croatian Sports Journalists Society, and in 2012 the Sports Association of the City of Pula awarded him special recognition for his outstanding contribution to sports development.

INDEX

INDEX